# CHASED BY PANDAS

# CHASED BY PANDAS

## My life in the mysterious world of cycling

# DAN MARTIN

Written with Pierre Carrey

QUERCUS

First published in Great Britain in 2022 by Quercus.

**QUERCUS**

Quercus Editions Ltd
Carmelite House
50 Victoria Embankment
London EC4Y 0DZ

An Hachette UK company

A CIP catalogue record for this book is available
from the British Library

HB ISBN 978 1 52942 758 5
TPB ISBN 978 1 52942 759 2
Ebook ISBN 978 152942 761 5

10 9 8 7 6 5 4 3 2 1

Typeset by CC Book Production
Printed and bound in Great Britain by Clays Ltd, Elcograf S.p.A.

Papers used by Quercus are from well-managed forests and other responsible sources.

# Contents

# Chapter 1

# Sprint with the Panda

We'll walk rather than ride up the road, but I'll still have the same sensations as that day. Jess, my wife, will be with me, as will Daisy and Ella, our twin daughters. They weren't born when it all happened, so I'll set the scene for them. Their fingers will be covered with sauce from the chips they've been eating when we reach the critical point high above the city, close to where I scored my craziest win in the ninety-ninth edition of Liège–Bastogne–Liège. I won't hesitate for long at the location that's the reason for the visit, just enough time to show them the place, on the right-hand side of the road, almost at the top of the Côte d'Ans, 300 metres before a left-hand bend.

The girls, always curious, will ask me: 'Daddy, is this where you crossed the finish line in first place?'

'No, but we're very close to it. You have to keep going around that bend.'

'So what happened here?'

I'll pause, because this is the best part of the story.

'It was just here that I was chased by a giant panda. Well . . . by a man dressed as a panda.'

'Why was he chasing you?'

'I don't know.'

This stretch of road isn't the most picturesque in cycling's small world, but it's one of the most fascinating. This was the location of the finish of one of the most coveted races, one of the most gruelling to win, this incongruous spot reached after almost seven hours of riding through the hills of the Belgian Ardennes. Liège–Bastogne–Liège, my favourite race. It's a 250-kilometre race that reflected the way my career went. It was all or nothing. Black or white. I never finished it comfortably in the heart of the peloton. I won it once. I abandoned it more than once. I had two heavy falls. I experienced snow and, even worse, cold, penetrating rain. I left blood and joy on the tarmac.

The race ended on this wide road running between terraces of brick houses. The huge white carcass of the railway station, which looks like a dinosaur skeleton, can be seen below. Yet the Côte d'Ans was a 'Ghost climb'. The organisers didn't deem it worthy of categorisation, considering it a mere false flat. However, it was an extraordinary psychological battleground. Your head would explode before your legs . . . On 21 April 2013, it was here that I distanced my last opponent, Spain's Joaquim Rodríguez, before celebrating victory with both hands aloft. And it was here that I encountered the Panda.

On the morning of the race, a thought popped into my head: 'I'm going to win today.' At first I felt embarrassed by the enormity of that possibility. This was nothing less than one of the five biggest Classics on the calendar and one of the most venerable: Liège–Bastogne–Liège, also known as 'La Doyenne', was first run in 1892, eleven years before the inaugural Tour de France. This thought, this vision, wasn't an attempt at self-persuasion on my part, and certainly not a moment of misplaced pride. It was a premonition of what I was going to experience. I accepted this omen that sprang from within me.

The first time I'd had this kind of intuition was when I was racing the Giro Ciclistico della Valle d'Aosta in the French Alps in August 2007, at the very end of my amateur years. And I'd won. The thunder cracked overhead. A deluge came down on the last pass. I did the fastest, riskiest, most acrobatic descent of my career. Nothing could deny me.

I don't know if I won because my head imagined the prospect or if I imagined it because my body was sending out secret signals that it could win. Sometimes it's best to leave the final word to chance. On other occasions, I think it was the fact that my belief in myself was so intense that I forced myself to draw on unanticipated resources, to watch for tiny details along the road, to avoid mistakes or crashing.

On the morning of the Liège–Bastogne–Liège, I sent my parents a text message that summed up this strange and obsessive feeling: 'Today, I'm going to win.' Maria, my mother, has intimate knowledge of the uncertainties and brutality of cycling, even though she didn't have a career in a peloton herself. My father, Neil, was a professional in the 1980s and raced until the early 2000s, purely for the pleasure of the sport. My parents were surprised by my text message but they always believed in me. If I said it, if I felt it, it had to be true . . .

On the way to the start, something strange happened. I had the feeling that my mind had left my body and become a spectator of the day's events. My body itself felt very light. I was driven by the sense that events had been preordained. What must happen will happen ... But don't get me wrong: I never waited with arms folded for fate to open the doors to victory. I always tried to commit with all I had to the task that lay ahead.

I felt serene during the first part of the race, breezing over the climbs of La-Roche-en-Ardenne, the Mur de Saint-Roch, Wanne, Stockeu, Haute Levée, Rosier, Maquisard, Mont Theux and the mythical La Redoute ... Liège–Bastogne–Liège is an authentic 'Mountain' race in Belgium. The Ardennes plateau, which we crossed in its entirety, features the highest points in this 'flat country'. Not far from the course, at the Baraque de Fraiture, which sits 652 metres above sea level, there's even a ski run. It's a rugged region, covered with pine forests. The inhabitants are reputed to be hard-working and tough. They have calloused hands, are sometimes gruff, but have big hearts. These are the same qualities that racing demands of cyclists.

In the last half-hour, I could sense a feeling of fear beginning to grow: palpable, voluminous, unbreathable. Fear has a form, a smell, a colour, a consistency. All around me, riders were starting to become afraid. They were afraid of crashing, of their teammates being too weak or their rivals being too strong, afraid that their legs would give out, or that their mind would. They were afraid of taking too many risks or not enough, afraid of producing the wrong attack or not pushing hard enough. Afraid of losing or of winning. Afraid of being afraid ...

Was I afraid? Yes, a little. Only the unconscious don't feel any fear, but they're the ones who put themselves in situations of terrible danger. I was reminded of something Mark Twain said:

'Courage is resistance to fear, mastery of fear – not absence of fear.'[*]

Fear is a taboo among cyclists, who are reluctant to disappoint the sport's fans. I learned this the hard way when, during my last pro season in 2022, I criticised the decision made by the Giro's organisers to test us out on a downhill section of the *strade bianche*, Tuscany's white unsurfaced roads. The Italians also refer to them as *sterrati* (dirt roads). Gravel, holes in the road – it was almost as if the race had been transformed into a game where you had to guess who would be the first to hit the deck. Some fans supported me, but another section were unhappy. According to them, I no longer had enough hunger for cycling to take risks, and I also had a real nerve complaining when I was paid well to do what I did. These people insisted that I needed to be a superman, but I've never regarded that argument as valid.

It's rare for a racing cyclist to open their heart and share their truths. Well, here's one: this job has at least as much to do with suffering as with fear.

With 5 kilometres to go in La Doyenne, fear turned to panic on the Côte de Saint-Nicolas. The peloton was reduced to a small group. There was movement on all sides. There were always one or two who attacked, but it was important not to respond to them. Any rider who made an effort to close a gap had lost. His last drops of paraffin would be burned up within a minute.

At this point in the race, I was content to follow. My Canadian

---

[*] Mark Twain, 'Pudd'nhead Wilson' in *The Century Magazine* (December 1893).

teammate Ryder Hesjedal, winner of the Giro d'Italia a year earlier, was a handful of seconds clear on his own, which had forced our rivals to chase behind him. Because it was my teammate who had moved, I wasn't tempted to make the fatal mistake of closing the gap. Ryder's acceleration put some important riders out of the picture, including former Tour de France yellow jersey Alberto Contador, and Philippe Gilbert, racing on his home region's roads in the rainbow bands of the world champion.

Two kilometres further on, we reached the Côte d'Ans. The road was too long and too wide at this point. We could see an inflatable arch, the *flamme rouge*, that marked the start of the final kilometre. It felt like it would never end. We climbed it in the larger 53- or 54-tooth ring, in slow motion, in an almost dreamlike state, our bodies starting to slip inexorably out of our control. Our legs were on the verge of paralysis.

The fear was still there, but it was of a different nature to what we'd felt on the Côte de Saint-Nicolas. You're no longer afraid to let a rider attack, but you're afraid of making an attack yourself. Your nerves are on the point of giving out. They could shatter at any moment. To be on the safe side, it would be better to rely on the sprint. You could end up finishing somewhere back in the group but have all the excuses you want. On the other hand, a badly timed attack on the Côte d'Ans will produce an immediate backlash. But there's no way of knowing if your attack is presumptuous until you try it ...

My fear was very contained. I delineated reality by using numbers. Rather than telling myself that there were, at a glance,

500 metres to go before I reached the *flamme rouge* and thinking that this damned climb was endless, I could already see myself passing beneath the inflatable arch and knew that there was that turn to the left; from there, only 200 metres remained. The remaining functionality in my brain gave me a head start. I turned reality to my advantage. I didn't make any calculations about the last and most painful few hundred metres we had left to face; I thought instead of all those kilometres behind us, pushing us like wind in our sails.

In the same way, I turned my opponents into numbers. I didn't think about 'who' they were but 'how many'. I worked out the probability that they would devour each other. I knew that if I was there, alongside them, it was because I'd been spared the race's pitfalls, from crashes to extreme fatigue. I'd earned the right to fight as an equal. I was as strong as them. But was I stronger than them?

There were only five of us left. Spaniards Alejandro Valverde and Joaquim Rodríguez, Italy's Michele Scarponi, all riders at the top of their game, who had won a Grand Tour or held the world number-one ranking. They had the power, the craft and the confidence. Carlos Betancur, a rising star in Colombian cycling, was also in the picture. And then there was a rider who was relatively unknown to the general public, Irish on his mother's side, British on his father's, formed in France (in Marseille), resident in Spain (in Girona), racing for an American team (Garmin–Sharp) – me.

I had cycling history bubbling up inside me. I went to my first race when I was one month old, in a pram. Almost a year after I was born, my uncle, Stephen Roche, my mother's brother, won the Giro d'Italia, the Tour de France and the World Championships in the same 1987 season, a rare feat known to the British as 'the Triple Crown'. I knew the weight that victory at Liège–Bastogne–Liège would have in the balance of history. I knew it, but didn't think about it. My mind remained detached from my body and exclusively focused on the sequence of gestures and reflexes. Thinking about something bigger than yourself is bound to crush you.

Normally, as the finish line looms, a cyclist is afraid of his fate. This is the case in all races, whether big or small. You can feel the enigma unlocking, but sometimes you don't want to know . . . The race is a door and most riders fear the moment when it opens, afraid of the truth that lies behind it, of the fate that will tell them if they have won or lost. But in those final moments, whatever happened to be on the other side of that door, I wasn't scared.

With 1,200 metres to go, Joaquim Rodríguez fired away, making one final effort. Michele Scarponi started to react, then backed off. A critical moment. We were waiting for Alejandro Valverde to chase down the rider ahead. He was the favourite. But he didn't move and Rodríguez extended his lead, victory escaping with him. We were riding on a knife-edge. Then . . . With a thousand metres to go, I attacked. According to my power meter, I was putting out 1,000 watts initially, a big burst of energy at a point so far from the finish line.

I caught Joaquim Rodríguez with 600 metres to go. In these situations, the ideal tactic is to go by your opponent at high speed, taking advantage of the effect of surprise and discouraging them. But I wanted to know for sure. For 300 metres, I sat to his left-hand side. I let him know that I was there. This was the beginning of the duel. The pace slowed down. Our legs were turning smoothly, without pulling or crushing the pedals excessively. For ten seconds or so, we pretended to ignore each other, but we both cast piercing glances backwards through our sunglasses. Our faces became waxen. We concealed our fatigue and our strength within us.

Suddenly, I ended the wait, just as it appeared to have gone on for too long. I stood on the pedals to attack, perfectly balanced on my bike, feeling twice as tall as usual. Joaquim was no longer with me. On the final straight line, beyond the left-hand bend, I turned around to assess the extent of the gap. Ten metres! It was as wide as the sea. It was then that I knew: today I had won.

My mind returned to my body. Emotions came flooding back to me. There were hugs with my teammates, bouquets of flowers, cheers on the podium . . . Twenty minutes after crossing the line, I turned on my phone and saw the first messages of congratulation. Amidst the 'Bravos!', I could see a few saying, 'That was really funny,' or 'We had a good laugh.' I didn't understand. Why had they been laughing? A friend who had watched the race on TV told me: 'Didn't you notice anything? There was a panda with you. While you were watching Rodríguez, he was behind you on the road.' So there were two winners of the 99th edition of Liège–Bastogne–Liège: the Panda and me.

# Chapter 2

# Blood on the Pedals (The Fear of Not Getting Up)

When I felt the rear wheel slide away on the final corner, I had no idea what was happening. Time seemed to slow as the catastrophe unfolded. I registered the microsecond when the tyre lost its grip on the road surface, the bike slipping to the left so quickly that my body had no time to react, so fast that I couldn't put my hand down first, a reflex action that would have softened the impact of the crash. I hit the ground with my two hands still on the bars. I dropped like a stone, taken completely by surprise. But my brain understood everything that was happening and the damage that would ensue. Not physical damage, but it resulted in me losing a second Liège–Bastogne–Liège. As a consequence, it was the most painful crash of my career.

The Garmin-Sharp team had done all it could to get its defending champion ready for the race. We'd made a little video that featured a guy in a panda costume preparing meticulously for the race, having its breakfast and checking over its bike.

What's more, there was once again a panda behind me – literally this time, because it was on the back of my jersey. It was the logo of the environmental protection organisation the World Wildlife Fund, with which the team had forged a partnership. The panda, which was both the emblem of the WWF and my personal mascot, had facilitated the agreement.

History seemed to be repeating itself on the Côte d'Ans. I imagined two films running concurrently on the same screen. 2013 and 2014: a game of spot the difference. A year on from my victory, I once again attacked on the final climb, once again close to the *flamme rouge*, once again with a rider from the Katusha team in my sights – Giampaolo Caruso, filling the role previously played by Joaquim Rodríguez. But there were two significant differences from the year I'd won. The first was that the Panda, My Panda if you like, had disappeared. I noticed this when I moved from the left-hand side of the road, where I'd launched my all-out effort, and switched across to the right into the 'Panda Zone': there was nobody there. The second variation was that on the bend where I flew away in 2013, I crumpled in 2014.

I slipped going into this wide and seemingly harmless turn, just at the moment when I'd gone clear of Domenico Pozzovivo, an Italian rider who'd been with Caruso. I was only a metre behind Caruso. If our speed curves were to be compared, I would have caught my rival coming out of the bend and then sprinted the remaining 200 metres to the line. Instead of which I fell, got back on my feet, having sustained no injury at all, and stood looking bereft in the middle of the crossroads, contemplating the finish and watching the other riders sprint to the line. I was now a spectator. I wanted to do an about-face and start the race again from scratch. I wanted to be sucked into the road, to disappear completely. I shouldn't have been in the position where I finished 39th, my gap behind race-winner Simon Gerrans officially recorded as a minute and thirty-seven seconds. I barely had a mark on me, and I didn't have an explanation either.

A rumour started that a pen had been lying on the road and my wheel had gone over it, but there was no evidence to confirm this, and I don't recall hitting anything at all. Fans on the internet who analysed photos and video footage suggested that my left pedal had touched the ground and caused the accident, but that's an impact that I would have felt, plus we couldn't find any scratches on my pedal.

The most rational hypothesis was that there was an oily residue on the road at that point and the dampness in the air had made it slippery. The irrational hypothesis was that it was down to fate. This explanation was both comforting and unsatisfactory, but I liked it. It was 'written' that I would win in 2013 and lose in 2014.

The mysteries surrounding my crash and the Panda were interlinked. The probability that either would happen was very small. That events like these would occur in exactly the same spot was even more improbable. Luck clearly came into it ... How had I managed to win that year when I had a giant panda on my heels? Why did I crash in such an abrupt and humiliating way on 27 April 2014?

Victory and falling are inextricably interlinked. They are two sides of the same coin.

There's always a moment when you're 'bound to' crash. I realised this in 2008 during my debut appearance in Flèche Wallonne, Liège–Bastogne–Liège's little sister. This Classic takes place in the same week and in the same region as La Doyenne. In what was a baptism of fire, I ended up in a big crash 50 kilometres into the race. I shut my eyes. I was sure I was going to fall. It's an instinctive reaction: you close your eyes to protect them from a piece of plastic or metal. Or perhaps it's just down to the fact that the body refuses to register that split second when it believes that pain is imminent. It saves you from a single second of suffering.

Miraculously, though, when I opened my eyes I saw my front wheel spinning in the air, both hands gripping the bars and a foot on the chest of one of the unfortunate riders who had crashed. I hadn't fallen. I was the only rider to escape this fate in the part of the peloton where I'd been riding. It simply wasn't my time . . . That came a dozen kilometres or so further on, when a rider in front of me somersaulted and I couldn't avoid him. My hip hit the road hard, as did the index finger on my left hand. I thought that I'd broken something.

I was in pain. I was alone. The peloton was disappearing into the distance, the team cars following it. I never wanted to abandon. I reached the Mur de Huy, a climb we tackled three times, several minutes behind them. It's one of cycling's sacred places. One of the bends reaches a record gradient of 26 per cent. Even walking up it, you have to battle against the slope. Fans picnicking in a field beneath a giant screen urged me to hang on. Blood ran down from my knee onto my pedals. I loved that day.

Even though I think I can safely say that I've got a rational mind, I ended up developing an almost mystical rapport with the bike. I accepted that invisible forces were moving against us, with us, around us. As a consequence, I've often found that crashes don't occur completely by chance: you're actually drawn towards them. You know that they're going to happen, but don't do all that you possibly can to avoid them. You accept them. In certain situations, you even hope for them. There are good reasons for this unconscious acceptance.* People talk about 'the wrong place' or 'the wrong time', but I've experienced something even more disturbing: my bike being drawn towards a crash like a magnet with an uncontrollable pull, as if it were absolutely necessary for the crash to happen.

The first time I experienced this phenomenon was at the 2003 World Junior Championships in the Canadian city of Hamilton. At that time, I still had British nationality and was racing in a jersey adorned with a Union Jack. During reconnaissance rides on the race circuit, I'd noticed a particularly perilous section: a wide piece of road, which ran fairly straight and downhill but curved gently to the left . . . As a precaution, I sat behind the peloton to give myself time to brake. The crash happened exactly where I suspected it might, on the very first lap. I had enough time to see thirty-odd riders misjudge the corner and

---

* See Chapter 12.

plough into a safety barrier, only to find my bike was going 3 or 4 metres off the line I'd intended. Instead of swerving around the heap of cyclists on the ground, it went straight into them. I escaped from the incident without injury but shocked that I hadn't been able to avoid it.

Some crashes are the fruit of 'destiny'. Riders are at the mercy of the smallest grain of sand; it might be a rider whose handling is usually exceedingly good but who ends up falling just in front of you; or a dog, a vehicle, a spectator or another moving object in the road . . . We're not always responsible for what happens to us.

Other crashes have a more enigmatic side to them. Are they really down to your bike? I suspect there is a more puzzling possibility: that a part of my subconscious was actually determined to crash . . . I needed it or even wanted it. Every cyclist has this hidden desire to fall from time to time. A rider who (by some remote chance) had never ended up on the ground would be an incomplete rider.

Don't get me wrong, I hated crashing, I hated the pain that came with it because it wasn't a pain that I'd chosen, like the pain that resulted from pushing myself to my limits in training. I'm not one for misplaced masochism. Yet I have to admit that crashes built me up more than they broke me. They taught me about myself, about my profession, about others, about the world.

I didn't have any more frequent crashes than most of my peers, but I can remember each of them in microscopic detail. I could open a Museum of Crashing, perhaps in one of the brick houses on the Côte d'Ans. I would recount the science and art, the philosophy and poetry of this mystery. Nothing is more different from a bike crash than the next bike crash. Each has its own profound identity. There are so many variations, in the speed, the effect of surprise, the aesthetics, the character – funny, tragic – and the feeling you have at the time – guilty or victim, hero or fool. I should underline that when I talk about crashing I don't mean the moment you get back up; I'm talking about those brief seconds when chaos is looming, and then that eternity when you find yourself in between your bike and the road, suspended in mid-air.

My first crash during a race was in August 2002, a few days after my sixteenth birthday, at an event near Birmingham in the UK, where my family and I lived then. I was very proud to be riding in a new jersey and shorts, which I'd received as a gift. But after 5 kilometres, I was one of twenty or so racers who found themselves on the deck. My father, who was in the same team as me in what was an all-categories event, was looking for me. The last thing he wanted was to see me on the ground. Then he noticed me and asked, 'Are you OK?' I told him, 'Yeah.' We set off again, now in desperate pursuit of the peloton. Looking back, I realise that that 'yeah' may have determined the rest of my career. If I'd abandoned, if I'd been reluctant to get back on the bike, if I'd been afraid of crashing again, I would never have become a racing cyclist. I should also add that, after that first incident, I never again wanted to wear a new jersey in a race.

But my very first crash had actually occurred four years

earlier. I'd received a wonderful bike for Christmas. It was flame-coloured and would be my future companion on many epic rides. It had Look clipless pedals, a Campagnolo groupset. Santa had cheated a little bit; he'd reused one of my grandfather's steel frames, had it enamelled in orange, then added the Pinarello logo to it by hand, with all the meticulousness of a forger. On Boxing Day I wanted to try it out. I walked down to the front gate. I climbed onto the saddle. Clack – first pedal engaged. Clack – second pedal engaged. Crash! I fell without having moved a single metre. My father leaned over and picked me up. He asked me: 'Do you really want to do this?'

'No, no, no. Not today,' I responded.

My father then imparted an important piece of advice: 'OK. This is what cycling is all about: you must be ready. We'll put the bike in the garage; it'll be waiting for you.'

# Chapter 3

# There's No Such Thing as a Small Climb (The Fear That the Earth is Flat)

My first Tour de France stage was gruelling, mind-blowing, transcendent. It covered 78 kilometres and included two Pyrenean passes, and then the same route in the opposite direction. Nine hours of cycling. The sun suffocated me, but I didn't burn. My skin stayed ghostly white. I was hungry, thirsty and shivering. Miraculously, I managed to keep my legs turning. I couldn't have been happier in what was the summer of my seventeenth birthday.

In 2003, I was still British and the National Championships were in Scotland. The course suited sprinters and didn't appeal to me. So we went on holiday in south-west France, in Luz-Saint-Sauveur, not far from the sanctuaries in Lourdes. It was a long drive from Birmingham for my parents, my brother Tom and me. We rented a tent at Camping International, with a pool and a looming presence above us. We just had to look up: 'he' was there. He knew that, sooner or later, we wouldn't be able to resist trying to scamper up his flank, out of greed, out of pride, out of recklessness. The Col du Tourmalet was the lord of the valley. But would he be a gentle giant or an ugly monster? I think I could hear him whispering: 'I'm waiting for you.' On 20 July 2003, the Tour de France raced into Loudenvielle, a small village located between the Port de Balès and the Col d'Azet. In order to see the finish, I planned out my own Tour stage with my Dad, starting with the Tourmalet.

I'd read in a book about the pass that his name means 'Bad little detour' in the local patois, because the valley's inhabitants were afraid of his ravines, his storms, his blizzards and even his bears. In 1910, the first time the Tour de France tackled this mountain, a rider called Octave Lapize had yelled, 'You're assassins!' at the race organisers as he passed them. With that in mind, I attacked this giant of road passes with a great deal of respect and humility, riding at an easy pace. At the summit, the signpost told me that I'd reached an altitude of 2,115 metres. I was almost surprised. Was that all it took? The effort didn't seem to take much out of me at all. However, although I didn't know it, the Pyrenean giant had laid the foundations for the suffering that would wrack me on the way back, when I would become well aware of its impact as I battled fatigue and pain. That's the mark of the Tourmalet.

The following pass, the Col d'Aspin, is a gradual climb that didn't test me as much, even though it's still far from being a doddle. The main adversary was the heat. The summer of 2003 was one of what the French describe as *canicule*, which left the country roasting in a heatwave. I searched around cemeteries behind mountain churches to find fountains where I could fill my bottle. We then rode up the valley to the foot of the Col de Peyresourde, where we would stand and wait for the riders to descend, a handful of kilometres from the finish line in Loudenvielle. Initially I saw a small breakaway group that included Gilberto Simoni, who would win the stage, and then a counter-attack that featured Alexandre Vinokourov, who had distanced Lance Armstrong and Jan Ullrich. What stood out, though, was the rush of air as the favourites flashed by just a metre away from me. I read about events on the road in the paper the next morning at the campsite, but knowing what had gone on in the race wasn't my primary focus. The Tour de France was a pretext. I'd gone there for the Pyrenees. To see the passes up close and to discover myself. In fact, my primary concern after the stage had finished was getting back to the campsite before nightfall.

On the way back, I was still looking for water when I could. The temperature wasn't falling much even towards the end of the afternoon. Then came the Tourmalet again, which whispered into my ear: 'Do you understand now? This is what cycling is all about . . .' When we got to the hardest part of the climb at the ski resort of La Mongie, we were stopped by the gendarmes. The Tour de France was due to pass through there the next day and they had orders to block the road to any vehicle, car, camper van or even bike . . . I remember them saying, 'You'll have to turn back.' This would mean going back down and riding around the pass through the valleys, which would mean an extra 65 kilometres. It was getting dark. It was impossible to pedal for another three hours. My father attempted to negotiate. He explained that we were sleeping on the other side of the mountain, at the foot of the descent. But the gendarmes didn't want to know. My father insisted. I watched the summit growing darker and felt the evening wind picking up around the mountain. Finally, we were allowed to continue. It was another 5 kilometres of climbing, then a long descent. I was on the verge of falling asleep on the bike when I arrived back at the campsite. I revived myself by jumping head-first into the swimming pool. Ffffiiiizzzzzz ... I dissolved in the water like an aspirin. To this day I am not sure if my mum was concerned or proud.

## Tamworth Pass (altitude: 65 metres)

I've always felt the need for the mountains to motivate me, to fill me with energy. But I was a long way from them in Birmingham ... I was born there on 20 August 1986, a city whose industrial heritage was partly due to the innovative mind of James Watt, the inventor of the steam engine, a man whose name has gained sacred status among cyclists as our unit of measurement, the unit that records and analyses our every effort. Birmingham doesn't have any mountain passes, and neither does Tamworth, the satellite town of 75,000 where we lived on a housing estate. But I was lucky. Our house stood right next to an empty piece of land with a small, grassy lump in it.

My first Tourmalet was a metre high. The top could be reached on a 'road' 50 metres long. The average gradient was almost 4 per cent. I was five years old. The hardest part was sprinting uphill on little wheels and preventing my bike sliding away downhill. My mother and Joy, my grandmother, were my fan club. My father would wait at the top of the pass with a bottle of fresh water. My grandfather, Vic, a former grass-track racer, would be there too, with a stopwatch. On beautiful English summer days, a tan line would appear just above my socks.

My brother and I built another course, a cobbled sector worthy of Paris–Roubaix, although it was only 2 metres long. The bricks we buried in the garden made our wheels vibrate. Here too, I was keen for someone to use the stopwatch just so that I could see how long it took me to get across the cobbles. Then I'd head for our mountain circuit, where the imaginary finish line was located at the bottom of our little hill. In my head, my rivals were numerous and redoubtable.

I used to watch as many bike races on TV as cartoons. I liked the sprints, and the Flemish Classics too. Above all, though, I felt there was something both grandiose and exciting about the mountain stages, where you watched the riders weaving back and forth on the switchbacks, their heads bobbing as they duelled with mountains far, far taller than they were. I was immersed in cycling. It was and still is my natural element. But I didn't have any posters of riders hanging up in my room. I didn't cut out any pictures from the magazines that were always on the coffee table in the living room. As a child and teenager, I never had a hero in the peloton. Except for my father.

I was my dad's most fervent supporter almost from the moment I was born. I was at the roadside of my first race when I was just a month old. My mother would set up the pram in the shade of a tree, ideally at the top of a hill. She was careful not to hand my father a bottle of milk and give me a can of energy drink. As a result, I watched the end of Neil Martin's career. He had represented Great Britain proudly at two Olympic Games, in 1980 in Moscow and 1984 in Los Angeles, and won the National Road Championship in 1984. Everyone said he had the potential to join a strong team in Europe, but he had to settle for second-rate outfits in the Netherlands and Luxembourg. My father didn't have any luck in that regard.

Martin senior officially retired at the end of 1988, the year I turned two. His UK-based pro team was on the verge of disappearing. He had received an offer to race in the newly emerging discipline of mountain biking that was being imported from the US to England, but the project didn't come to anything. So, at twenty-eight he quit bike racing to, as he says, 'put food on the table' for his family. He went back to being a printer, his trade when he was younger. Consequently, my first memories of him on a bike are of him riding not a racing model but his 'work bike', fully kitted out with mudguards and lights. He got up every morning at six o'clock to go to work. He rode between 60 and 80 kilometres a day. His passion for racing hadn't deserted him; he would pin on a number and ride in amateur events at the weekends and on holidays. In 1994, he went into action for the national team again at the Tour of Belgium. After that, he called a halt to his amateur racing career. He didn't have enough time to prepare himself for the beautiful races that he loved. But he started again in the year 2000, when I started riding, so I raced alongside him. He was my role model. My father taught me all about hard work, honesty and courage.

## Alpe d'Huez (altitude: 1,850 metres)

I set off without warming up. Right from the off, Alpe d'Huez is steep, a tough test, a climb that you have to take seriously, hauling yourself slowly and inexorably upwards. The road extends for 14.4 kilometres, at an average gradient of 7.9 per cent. On each bend, where the slope flattens out considerably, I could pick up my pace. There are twenty-one of them, and as I rounded each one I convinced myself that I was going faster and faster, bouncing from one to the next like a pinball. Bend 10: I passed what would a few years later become the 'Irish Corner', the tarmac and kerbs at the roadside painted green, flags fluttering, the atmosphere noisy, but not quite as agitated as the ambience three corners higher. Turn 7: I went through 'Dutch Corner', which takes on an orange hue when the Tour de France heads for the resort above, an infamous gathering point where boisterous hordes smelling of beer fill all but a narrow corridor of the road. Above it, the numbers on each bend clicked steadily downwards until I reached Alpe d'Huez itself and the climb's finishing line on the Avenue du Rif Nel, overlooked by a ridge of soaring peaks.

It was the summer of 2000. My father had told me the good

news over the winter. 'For our holidays this year, we're going camping on Alpe d'Huez. You can ride up there if you want to.' He'd got a few days off from his employer, Motul. My mother had also been able to take a few days away from her job in a shopping centre. Of course I 'wanted' to try it, but I hadn't really used my bike that much up to that point. My father laid down one condition: he made me prepare for it. We did ten or so training rides on the flat around Tamworth. The eleventh ride was up to Alpe d'Huez.

As was the case in 2003 on that crazy day over the Tourmalet, my father accompanied me, sometimes riding next to me, sometimes following my wheel, letting me find my natural rhythm. I went there determined to give all I had. I wanted to record a respectable time. The climb took me an hour and eight minutes, twice as a long as a pro rider. 'At thirteen and a half, that's great,' my father said encouragingly. He bought a photo from one of the photographers who make a living out of taking pictures of riders on the climb. 'Here's a present for you!' he said. In the photo, my legs and arms look very long. I've rolled up the sleeves of my jersey to increase the extent of my cycling tan. I have my hands on the tops of the handlebars, which helps me to release the tension in my arms. My gaze is fixed straight ahead, rather than peering upwards. My expression is one of intense concentration. There's no indication of the euphoria that I could feel building. I was focused on the next turn, savouring the time I had left before the summit. I felt like I was listening to the music from a James Bond movie, pushing me to go faster, to escape my pursuers. Just as he was my cinematic hero, the mountains had become my favourite action-movie setting.

## Mallory Park Climb (altitude: 121 metres)

My first attack on a climb in a race was on the Mallory Park motor-racing circuit, between Hinckley and Leicester, near Birmingham. I felt proud about the fact that I was making my initial strides as a racer at what was an institution in motorsport. Mallory Park had been built during the Second World War and was first used for horse racing, before becoming a racetrack for brand-new Lotuses and other racing cars. More than twenty thousand spectators used to fill the grandstands. In the 1990s, the record lap speeds were shattered: 204.58km/h by a Formula 1 car and 157.49km/h by a motorbike, on a 2.173-kilometre (1.35-mile) lap. It was around this time that I discovered the circuit. I initially attended rounds of the British Superbike Championship, coming back on my bike, but with the mindset of a motor pilot.

I was counting on Mallory Park's 'Iconic climb', a 200-metre-long ascent that averaged around 4 per cent, to provide a surprise verdict, one that would go against the peloton's routine logic. The first time I raced on the circuit, at the age of fourteen, there wasn't a single attack. We all went through and off, at high speed, two lines of riders, one working their way towards the front to maintain the pace, the other comprising those who were dropping back to the end of the line in order to start their relay again, just as if we were in a breakaway. But this wasn't a breakaway. We were the peloton. Obviously, my rivals, who were used to racing in this way, wanted to set speed records on the flat and then fight it out in a sprint.

Initially, I stayed towards the back of the pack and followed the well-established pattern. Nobody knew me. I kept a low profile until the last four laps. Then, when we came to the climb, I accelerated with all I had. I got clear, but was soon caught by the 'breakaway'. On the next lap, the same scenario, which prompted some riders to talk to me for the first time: 'Why are you attacking? We have to ride together.' Did we really? I recovered for 2 kilometres. Then came the last lap: I made another attack on the climb. I was caught in the final straight and took second place in the sprint.

Two years later, on the day I turned sixteen in the summer of 2002, I stepped up into the junior category and started to take racing more seriously. I won several times at Mallory Park, sometimes drawing on my ability as a 'climber' and at other times as a *finisseur*. One day when my father was competing alongside me, I said to him: 'I want to do the bunch sprint.' So he went to the front on the last lap and raced as if he were leading out the green jersey at the Tour de France. I was on his wheel, ready to launch. We went up the hill so rapidly that nobody could dare to attack. I jumped. My little legs were pushing the restricted junior gear fitted on my bike with all their might. I managed to finish towards the front of a lead group of around ninety riders.

Each race differed significantly in the way that it unfolded, but the route was always the same, as was the ritual that accompanied them. The races took place on Tuesday evenings at 7 p.m. for riders in the youth and junior categories, and on Thursdays for the elites. I'd rush home from school (having done as much homework as I could on the bus), eat my beans on toast as fast as I could and we'd be off in our van to the circuit. We'd meet at a wooden hut to collect laminated numbers – they'd been in use for more than ten years. After the race we'd go back to the race HQ to order tea and cakes and catch up with rivals and teammates. This was the kind of cycling I liked and tried to stick with until the end of my career: a sport where the social aspect was a fundamental part.

## Axe Edge (altitude: 497 metres)

One of my first moments of cycling truth arrived on the climb of Axe Edge. It was one of two on the Junior Tour of the Peaks. It was a pretty straightforward test, extending for around 4 kilometres at about 4 per cent. The battle on its slopes would rage for about a quarter of an hour as the aspiring climbers shook off the peloton's shackles. The sprinters would be dropped for good. The main difficulty was the wind, which was well capable of pinning you to the tarmac because there are no trees protecting the roads in that part of the Peak District National Park. My mates from the CC Giro, a Birmingham-based club where we were all good friends, had assured me that I'd do well: 'You've got a climber's build,' they told me. 'I've also got a climber's mindset,' I replied.

I felt in my element on Axe Edge. Alone on the road, turning my legs at my preferred cadence, with time enough to reflect on the kind of rhythm I wanted. I was counter-attacking behind the breakaway rider, Tim Wallis, who was a good minute ahead. Unfortunately, I made a beginner's mistake on the penultimate lap: I decided that I needed an energy gel to refuel, when I should have downed the contents of my bottle. As a result, I ended up becoming dehydrated and was reeled in by the group chasing behind me on the descent into the finish, where I finished third.

But that counter-attack had attracted the attention of a very particular spectator. Dave Brailsford, British Cycling's performance director, who was responsible for creating a deluge of Olympic medals, had parked his car at the top of Axe Edge. It was the first time I'd seen him and vice versa. He had a stopwatch in one hand, a pad of paper in the other. As we passed by each time, he was evaluating the comparative strength of the talents emerging among the coming generation of racers, marking down the numbers, making a note of the names, shouting encouragement. Although my counter-attack didn't have the result I'd hoped for, it would lead to my selection for the World Junior Championships at the end of the 2003 season.

# The Tumble (altitude: 482 metres)

My first duel with Geraint Thomas took place at the Junior Tour of Wales in August 2004 in the year that we both turned eighteen. I'd finished fourth the year before, when he hadn't been in the field because he was participating in the World Track Championships in Moscow. He had immense endurance and, although it was hard to imagine that he would be capable of winning the Tour de France one day, he impressed with his strength, his class and his tenacity. Many coaches and journalists described us as the two biggest talents of our generation in Britain, but we didn't often get the chance to take each other on.

Geraint was from Cardiff. He was riding in his own backyard and he could count on the support of two regional teams, more than ten riders in all. I was in a team of one, the only rider in CC Giro's colours. On the opening day, I won the uphill time trial on the Tumble, which was also set to be the finale for the road stage on the last day. A Welsh giant, the climb rose like the tail-end of a dragon, fairly gentle to start with, then steep, before easing off as you crested its 'back' towards the summit. The time trial ran between the town of Brynmawr and The Keeper's Pond, so called because the local gamekeeper's hut was in that vicinity. In the 10-kilometre test, I beat Geraint by forty-four seconds.

Three stages later, we went head-to-head again on a stage running through the former coalmining area of Bryn Bach. The old shafts had been submerged beneath a lake and the industrial site had been turned into magnificent parkland, planted with beautiful trees, the air now pure. However, due to some strange phenomenon, on rainy days particles of coal came back to the surface. The closed circuit we were racing on featured two steep climbs and two technical descents, and it was wet. As our duel progressed, we became blacker and blacker, the grime coating our legs to start with, then our kit, and finally our faces. We looked like two miners. Geraint attacked relentlessly. Every assault he made, I retaliated. Finally, he said to me: 'You've got the yellow jersey, let me win the stage.' An agreement was made, although he didn't really need to strike a deal because he was stronger than me in the sprint. At the line, we were almost a lap ahead of the peloton.

Our last duel was on the Tumble. I was convinced that I was the better climber, but I was wary of Geraint, who was very motivated, and clearly wanted to win. The big hill looming ahead of us had an average gradient of 8–9 per cent for 3, 4 or 5 kilometres – there's no clear agreement on where it actually begins. Racing towards it on the Abergavenny road, we went into a tunnel of trees. Then, as we emerged from the woods, moorland stretched ahead, the realm of wind and heather. Two kilometres from the summit, I realised there was a cattle grid just ahead, its metal bars potentially treacherous in the damp conditions. I went to the front approaching it and, as soon as I'd got across the obstacle, I attacked, knowing my rivals were still juddering across the slippery barrier, using surprise to my advantage. The road gets rough and steeper at this point, and I gave it everything that I had.

I reached the summit and the roadside sign that effectively announces the end of your effort and, at the same time, is the gateway to memories of unforgettable deeds. The mountain's name is written in English and Welsh: 'The Tumble' and 'Y Tymbl'. I'd won the Junior Tour of Wales, finishing a minute and fourteen seconds ahead of Geraint Thomas and two minutes clear of the Irish rider Martin Monroe, who won this 'queen' stage from the breakaway that had gone clear in the valley. A Dutch rider, Steven Kruijswijk, finished just off the podium at two minutes and one second. A few years later, he wore the race leader's pink jersey in the Giro d'Italia and finished on the third step of the Tour de France podium.

In those beautiful early years, the mountains were already on my horizon. Not a dream, but a goal. Not an obligation, but a reward. Climbing hills and passes justified my commitment to the road. Unlike many British riders of my age, I refused to commit to track racing. I only tried it once. That was long before my years as a junior, even before I climbed Alpe d'Huez. I was eleven years old when I took part in an introductory track day at Manchester Velodrome, a two-hour drive from my home. I signed up for the keirin, a mini-peloton sprint event that's very tactical and very fast because you sit in behind a motorbike to get up to speed before the racing starts. It didn't start well, as I had trouble keeping my front wheel slotted in right behind the rear wheel of the motorbike. I didn't understand anything about the little world of the track, its rules, its laws, which extended to the laws of physics and gravity. Why did the riders insist on not using brakes? Using a fixed gear was fine. I quickly came to terms with the idea that I would fall if I stopped pedalling. But why race without brakes? What's more, by what miracle did the bikes maintain their equilibrium on 42-degree bends? The only slopes that I wanted to tame were in the mountains.

# Chapter 4

# Twiggy Joins the Armada (The Fear of Becoming a Trackie)

In those days, Great Britain was a minor nation on the cycling scene.* The British junior team, made up of 17–18-year-olds, was not strictly speaking a dream team but it was one where everyone got on and had a good time. Between 2003 and 2004, it featured Mark Cavendish, universally known as 'Cav', who came from the Isle of Man, Welshman Geraint Thomas, who was then known as 'Gerald' rather than 'G', Ben Swift, alias 'Swifty', who hailed from Rotherham in South Yorkshire, and Ian Stannard, also known as 'Yogi' . . . All of them were known more for their exploits on the track than on the road. They were all also future members of Team Sky. And then there was me.

---

* The Tour de France selected London as the location for its Grand Départ in 2007. In 2008, Mark Cavendish began his run of sprint successes, Team Sky appeared in the peloton two years later and Bradley Wiggins became the first British winner of the Tour two years on from that. Similarly, Britain's explosion of success on the track didn't arrive until 2008, when British riders won fourteen medals at the Beijing Olympics.

'We're going to call you Twiggy,' I was informed by another guy on the team, Liverpool-born Matt Brammeier, who would later adopt Irish nationality. It was fair to say that my legs were three times as thin as theirs.

The Great Britain team was sometimes unbeatable, as was the case at the 2004 Junior Tour of Ireland. Ian Stannard won the general classification ahead of Dutch rider Robert Gesink, while I triumphed on the fourth stage after attacking on the final climb. I went clear with 10 kilometres remaining and had a six-second lead at the line as I raised my right arm in a victory salute. By the time the awards ceremony got under way, Ian and I had been waiting for a long time to be called onto the podium – a very long time. Everyone wanted to get back to the hotel. 'Sorry, guys, we're waiting for him to arrive so that we can start the awards ceremony.' But who was this 'him'? And then he arrived, with the easy gait of a villager heading down to the local shop to buy a loaf of bread, dressed in a navy-blue woollen jumper and in trousers stained with soil from his garden. 'Ladies and gentlemen, it is our pleasure and honour to welcome Sean Kelly!' Carrick-on-Suir's most famous son, a living cycling legend, the rival and alter ego of my uncle Stephen Roche during the heyday of Irish cycling in the 1980s, had been the stage's patron. As laconic as ever, he simply said, 'Good ride!' In the souvenir photo, he's standing on the right-hand side with me next to him, clutching a bunch of sunflowers.

I made my national team debut a year earlier, at the 2003 Tour de Lorraine Juniors. Officially we were racing under the name of Team South West. Our line-up featured Brammeier, Cavendish and two other track riders, Bruce Edgar and Ed Perry. This race has disappeared from my list of achievements in the sport's archives because a commissaire confused me with Anthony Martin, a French rider of the time. I finished in the peloton three times on the four road stages. We were dwarfs against the stars of our age category, Slovakian twins Peter and Martin Velits (the former won the overall classification), Luxembourg's Andy Schleck (who was best climber) and Dutch rider Kai Reus (who won the time trial).

We, the core group of the future Team Sky and Team Ineos, hardly had any cash between us when we travelled to races. We were forced to save money everywhere we could. To get to the start of the Tour de Lorraine, we sailed to the port of Le Havre, in Normandy, leaving Portsmouth on the night crossing, sleeping in bunk beds in a cramped cabin with no porthole. Once in France, we headed for Nancy, right on the other side of the country, but avoided taking the motorway. This meant that instead of six hours on the road we spent more than nine, the narrow twisting roads slowing our progress. But we stopped in a quaint village for a boulangerie-bought sandwich and it was magical. It was like that on all of our journeys. We were happy. We felt like we were savouring the hard and even beautiful life of proper racers. One of our favourite events was the race at Sint-Martinusprijs Kontich, a suburb of Antwerp in Belgium: inedible pasta (how can you get spaghetti so wrong?), dinners in a gym (at 11 p.m. after a time trial run in semi-darkness), a night in a monastery (in a cell, without a TV but with bars on the windows). However, if we'd slept in five-star hotels we certainly wouldn't have remembered any of it.

By the time I gained selection for my first World Championships at the end of the 2003 season, I thought I was prepared for all eventualities. We headed for Hamilton in Canada, with its forests that were turning to beautiful autumn colours, and fog covering the Ontario roads. I was sharing a room with Brammeier and Thomas. I slept on a camp bed. When my back started to hurt, I asked for a real bed and was moved into a room further down the corridor with Tom Southam, then the rising star in the British under-23 ranks. The night before his race, we were woken up at three in the morning by the fire alarm and had to evacuate the premises. As we were doing so, we found out that the fire had been started by members of a satanic cult, who had allowed it to get out of hand.

Team GB's juniors didn't produce any brilliant performances at those World Championships. Geraint Thomas finished in the peloton, fourteen seconds behind the winner, Kai Reus, while Matt Brammeier finished outside the time limit and I was forced to retire. That was the day I experienced the strange phenomenon of my bike running straight into a bunch of riders who had crashed, while my head was telling the bike to avoid them. But I didn't give up. I chased alone for almost a hundred kilometres behind the peloton. Initially, the gap stabilised at around one minute. But there's no denying that I was exhausted. One hundred kilometres equals an eternity of pedalling. In the race diary that I kept, recording the date, the name of the race, the distance, the name of the winner, my finishing position and various observations, I noted: 'Crash 1st lap. Did 6½ laps. Pulled out by officials. Not hurt.'

When we weren't racing for the British national team, we were fierce rivals. Ian Stannard was one of those who consistently caused me the most problems. The first time we crossed paths was at my very first race, held on the Birmingham Wheels race circuit, when I was about eleven or twelve. He won and I finished two laps down. I had opted to ride a mountain bike, went down the descents without pedalling, and leaned into the corners as if I was trying to get my knees to kiss the tarmac. My problem was that I thought I was a motorcyclist. I didn't win, but I didn't fall either. That was good enough for me.

As for Mark Cavendish, I only got to know him during the 2003 season. He was said to be fast and agile, like most of his mates who raced on the track, but he was far from being the best sprinter of his generation. That was until I found myself competing against him in the Solihull Road Race, just south-east of Birmingham and not far from my home. It was September and the last round of the National Series. I started the sprint from a long way out, not so much with the aim of winning but in order to score points for the National Series standings. I accelerated with 500 metres remaining, but what I didn't know was that Mr Cavendish was stuck on my wheel. As a result he got a decent lead-out, before jumping past me and winning. It was then I thought, 'Ah, he's actually pretty quick in a sprint.' I only managed to finish 13th. Cav was overjoyed. He jumped on me, holding my head in his hands and hugging me with all of his strength, just as he would later do with Mark Renshaw or

Michael Mørkøv at the Tour de France. The whole world should know: I was Mark Cavendish's first lead-out man.

I rode these races in the jersey of my friends from the CC Giro. It was pink because the club, founded by Bob Grinsell, wanted to pay tribute to the Giro d'Italia. It had about a hundred members, of all ages and levels, but my father and I were the only ones who raced regularly. The club's training ride took place on Wednesday mornings, starting and finishing in Sutton Coldfield, right next to the hospital where I was born. To warm up, we would climb Hopwas Hill, renowned for its free-range pig farm and home-made sausages. Then we'd venture out into the West Midlands countryside, with a mandatory stop for tea and cake. In the winter, we'd have to hurry to get back home before dark. We had three unbreakable rules: 'No one gets left behind'; 'we help and encourage each other'; 'we ride as a group'. On Saturday I trained with another small peloton of local riders, including Andy Birley, Jonny Towers and a few other strong amateurs. The sprints would be very tight between us until the last climb on the route, at Mere Green. I knew that road well as the school bus went along it every day.

I had some very close family links to the CC Giro. One of the stalwarts, John Perks, a racer in the 1950s and former national junior coach, was one of my grandfather's friends. When he opened his cycle shop, John employed my father for a few months as a bike mechanic and provided him with a bike for the season. Then, when I started to race some twenty-plus years later, John was good enough to help the next generation of Martins, generously providing the bike I rode all season. My cycling career is the result of the help that a tiny handful of people like John Perks provided. It's down to them and them alone. These benefactors helped my parents, who were already spending a portion of their savings on buying kit, petrol and race entries. When I won my second Tour de France stage in 2018, Lance Armstrong said on his podcast that I was from cycling's 'aristocracy', because I was related to Stephen Roche. Lance, it's fair to say, hasn't always got things right . . .

The CC Giro community took me under their wing as soon as I joined the club in September 2002 for a cyclosportive in France, the Ronde Picarde. I won the 50km circuit around Abbeville and received a magnificent trophy, a statuette shaped like the Michelin man. The club's members were proud of me because this was the kind of event that corresponded well with their values – a convivial outing on the Channel coast, followed by a great meal and another bike ride the next day. Two years later, the same group of mates were at the roadside cheering me on at the British Junior Nationals. The event was held half an hour away from Birmingham in the town of Henley-in-Arden. I was over-motivated by the challenge, but my fan club managed to help me get through the stress I felt.

The race took place on a 10.3-mile (16.5km) circuit that was covered seven times, making 72.1 miles (115.5km) in all. Given my results at the beginning of the season, I was one of the favourites. Geraint Thomas was absent because he was competing on the track. On the last lap, three of us were clear at the front – Ian Stannard, Andrew Hill and me. To give myself the best chance of taking the title, I wanted to find a way to ride into the finish alone. I was particularly wary of Stannard, so I waited until he had just finished his turn on the front, and as he pulled off to the right of the road I launched my attack on the far left. Not only had I caught my two opponents by surprise, Ian also found himself blocked in and couldn't jump straight on my wheel. I finished a minute and nineteen seconds ahead as I claimed the title. Two days later, I raced in my national champion's jersey at Mallory Park; my dad took victory that day.

At that point, the possibility of me making a career in cycling was, in my head at least, inevitable. When asked by the teachers at St Francis of Assisi College in Walsall, I struggled to even think of any other prospective job. I sometimes raced internationally during the season and my head was often full of images and goals in the sport, but I was very diligent at school. During term time, I limited my weekly training to two one-hour home trainer sessions and a four-hour ride on Saturdays. I made a point of attending every class and finishing every assignment, except in 2003 when I was selected for the World Championships. The head teacher was almost dumbstruck when I asked for a ten-day leave of absence from school: 'What? To go to Canada? Are you cycling at a high level then?'

I found some school subjects particularly enjoyable and they would also prove useful for the career that I was already subconsciously following. French and German, for instance, were both important languages in cycling in the early 2000s. At A level, we had to study *L'Étranger* by Albert Camus and *La Gloire de Mon Père* by Marcel Pagnol. I almost abandoned the second title, which bored me to death – nothing happened to the early-20th-century Provence family at the heart of it – whereas I drew a lot of pleasure from *L'Étranger*'s absurd void. Luckily, it was Camus that I was asked about on the day I sat my French A level.

When the holidays came, we would set off for Ireland, my mum's home country. It was a time devoted to cycling and family. We would go to a race and then spend time with my grandparents in Dublin. The Tour of Ireland took place in August. In 2003, a year before my success on Sean Kelly's home patch, I almost won a stage in the race. I broke away on my own somewhere between Waterford and Thomastown. I felt a surge of relief when I passed the 'Finish 5km' sign. I gave it my all but, six minutes later, I couldn't see a banner looming. A motorcyclist who was providing security on the race came up alongside me and shouted, 'Only five kilometres to go.' Another five? I started to push hard again, keeping it going for another six minutes until the biker returned: 'You've got another five kilometres and that's it!' I went hard again for a further six minutes. And guess who appeared? My friendly motorcyclist: 'You've got–'

'Yeah, it's OK, I know what you're going to say!'

The route markers must have been put out by someone who'd had a drink beforehand. The 5 kilometres extended to 30. The peloton caught me with 150 metres to go and Kai Reus (him again!) won.

At Easter, I lined up in another event, the Gorey Three-Day, which takes place around this small town to the south of Dublin.

I only had one teammate, but he was quite formidable: my dad. We were up against teams that had twenty or more riders in the field. In the 2004 edition, Martin senior, who was forty-four years old, helped Martin junior to victory. I was able to draw on the strength and experience of my high-class *gregario* on the last stage. Racing in rain showers, my father controlled the peloton on his own for a very long time, and at speeds of more than 50km/h. You could see his huge experience behind that fine work. Indeed, in the eighties, he captured two stages at the Tour of Britain, one stage at the Rás, in Ireland, another one at the Tour of Wales, alongside the GP Lincoln, and the overall classification of the Flèche du Sud, when he was racing for a team in Luxembourg. Yet I thought my father was going to go mad when he pulled aside and saw me trailing along in about 100th position. 'Hey, there are often crashes on this part of the course. Get back up there now,' he ordered me. That was undoubtedly one of the final times that he gave me advice, especially up close and in real time, because he felt that I'd already learned a lot from watching him. The rest I had to learn on my own. I was overjoyed to win the Gorey Three-Day riding with my dad, thanks to him and also, to a certain extent, for him. In my race diary, I wrote: '1st non Irish winner in 40 years.'

While riding in Ireland, I used to reconnect with the other half of my family. Before or after each race, we'd spend a few days at my grandparents' house in Dublin. Larry and Bunny Roche were both keen cyclists who met at a cycle touring club in which they were both active members. They had six children, including my mother, the eldest, and two sons who became professional cyclists, Stephen and Laurence. On those Irish holidays, I would sometimes meet up with my cousins, Nicolas and Christel, Stephen's children. Cycling was the lifeblood of our family tree. Nico, who was two years older than me, raced in France, where he'd been born, and Ireland, where he spent some of his teenage years. He won the Junior Tour of Ireland in 2002.

We used to see each other either at our grandparents' house or at the World Championships. My cousin was selected for the under-23 event for the Irish team; I was selected in the junior category for Great Britain. That's how our paths crossed in Canada in 2003 and in Italy in 2004. We could meet up to train, we'd bump into each other at the hotel or airport, but the rest of the time each of us was focused on racing, on chasing our own goals. In 2004, in Verona, I was looking to get the highest result possible and to organise the next stage of my young career. That World Championships accelerated all kinds of things in my life.

The day began in stressful fashion. I almost missed the start because I'd forgotten my shoes, which was quite some oversight. Usually I keep hold of these vital items whenever I leave the hotel, because I know that it's easy to forget them – cycling is full of stories like this. This time, though, I suddenly had the feeling that I'd left something in my room. What was it? My shoes! I'd been holding them in my right hand, then I'd opened the door, put the shoes on the bed and then looked underneath it to see if they were there . . . As I couldn't see them, I concluded that I'd put them in my bag, which was stored in the Team

Great Britain van. I slammed my door closed, leaving the shoes still on the duvet. I realised my mistake once we got to the circuit in Verona, but by then it would have taken more than an hour to go back and recover them. We made an emergency call to someone at the hotel, who agreed to rush them straight to us. With five minutes left before the race began, I was still standing on the start line in my socks. Thankfully, they arrived at that moment. Once on the bike, I gave everything I had and finished 65th, more than nine minutes behind the winner, Czech rider Roman Kreuziger.

My parents came to visit me at the hotel after the race. I was a bit disappointed with my performance, but relieved that a busy and successful era was coming to an end. My dad took the opportunity to request a meeting with British Cycling. We wanted to know what the federation could offer me when I moved up into the under-23 ranks in 2005. We were called to a room packed with sports bags, all neatly arranged in army-like fashion, to sit down with Dave Brailsford, the man who decided everything, and John Herety, the national team's *directeur sportif.* Brailsford spoke first: 'Dan's behaviour has been exemplary. He's very, very polite, he's strong and he's promising.' The conversation had started well, but then he continued: 'What do you have set up for Dan now?' My dad, who had come to ask precisely that question, was stunned: 'Wow ... And you guys? What do you have for him?'

We'd considered several possibilities. At the beginning of the season, the British federation had set up an under-23 academy, comprising a small group of riders who trained and raced together in Manchester and in Tuscany. Alternatively, I could have joined a British or a foreign club, with the guarantee of an international programme in a British national team jersey. British Cycling might have envisaged this kind of formula. In fact, a year later, the federation offered financial incentives to road teams that signed up British track riders. As a consequence, my friend Geraint signed for Team Wiesenhof, a German team in the second division at elite level, with young André Greipel as his teammate. But it quickly became clear that this wouldn't be an option for me.

Dave Brailsford looked at my father, shook his head in an apologetic and resigned way, as if to say that matters were out of his hands. I still remember his words: 'Nothing, we have nothing!' My trips with the national team, my fifth place in the difficult Grand Prix du Général Patton in Luxembourg, my British Championship title, my victory in the Tour of Wales, my stage in the Tour of Ireland ... It all counted for nothing. In actual fact, it was the track that was my undoing. The U23 Academy was only accessible if you went through a 'boot camp' held at the National Velodrome in Manchester, and featured six weeks of intensive training and foreign language lessons between 6 a.m. and 6 p.m. each day. In the same way, as I later realised, the partnerships established between the federation and road teams were reserved for track riders. Whenever British Cycling needed to get its riders back to the velodromes, it could do so with just a click of its fingers. The ultimate goal wasn't to convert the best track riders to road racers, but to get the best road racers onto the track, with the aim of achieving Olympic success. British Cycling's government funding depended on the medals it won. It was simple: I would have to start a career in the individual and team pursuit.

Otherwise it was, 'Nothing, we have nothing.' Naturally, I was going to stay the path I had laid out for myself. I had a growing passion for road cycling and my lack of interest in the track was as clear as ever. I couldn't see myself racing around a velodrome like a hamster in a wheel. I couldn't see myself competing in the sport with a roof over my head. I needed the sky. I wanted to feel the rain and the sun on my skin. I wanted to see the silhouettes of the trees.

My father and I left discouraged. We'd realised two things. Firstly, that I needed to consider adopting Irish nationality as soon as possible; Ireland's Dublin-based federation had been interested in me since I'd first participated in the Gorey Three-Day. I could work with people who were motivated, take advantage of what they had to offer and give them a lot in return. With parents from two different countries, and therefore with two passports, I could easily change my sporting nationality. And it was true to say that I'd always been a fan of Ireland's sports teams, whether football or rugby.

Our second conclusion was that I should move to the continent, preferably to France, as dozens of British, Irish, American and Australian racers had done before me – as, ironically, Dave Brailsford and John Herety had had to do during their own careers, the former to an amateur club in Saint-Etienne (although he didn't manage to turn professional), the latter to the ACBB in Paris (which led him to a pro contract). At the end of our interview, Herety gave us the telephone number of a Frenchman he knew, Frédéric Rostaing, manager of Vélo Club La Pomme Marseille, and said to mention his name.

The cycling world is small: my cousin Nico had joined this team and, while in Marseille, he'd been able to learn the basics of the job and show off his talent. He had signed a professional contract with Cofidis. Like Nico, several other Irishmen spent their final amateur years with this club in the south of France, notably the Junior World Champion Mark Scanlon and the promising climber Philip Deignan. Then, in 2010, Sam Bennett, a future green jersey at the Tour de France, would join the team. So, my dad made a phone call. By chance, Fred Rostaing was in Verona as a spectator. We met him at a point along the Sunday's pro race route. He was looking for a climber who was still a novice but had shown some encouraging signs. My cousin persuaded him. I was heading for the Mediterranean in the 2005 season . . .

## Chapter 5

# Pom! Pom! Pomme! (The Fear of Being No Good)

It was 6.30 a.m. I was fast asleep when I felt a hand grab me by the shoulder and shake me. 'Daniel, what the hell are you doing? We're all waiting for you.' Because of my earplugs, I hadn't even heard a knock on my bedroom door. It felt like some kind of meaningless dream. I saw my sports director, Fred Rostaing, leaning over me. The boss at the Vélo Club La Pomme Marseille was switched on twenty-four hours a day. He saw my bewildered look. 'You're doing the Ronde de l'Isard! I sent you an email yesterday, you're replacing another rider. Hurry up, the truck's waiting outside in the car park.' I was sitting in bed in my underpants. 'What . . .?' I thought. Held in the Pyrenees, the Ronde de l'Isard was the biggest stage race in my age category. I'd forgotten to check my email. Was this worse than forgetting your shoes before the start of a World Championships? I threw some jerseys into my bag, then my helmet, my toothbrush and three pieces of fruit for breakfast.

Maybe it was better that I'd been selected at the last minute.

It didn't give me time to worry. On the second stage, we climbed to the little ski station of Goulier-Neige, which is nestled beneath towering peaks in the Pyrénées Ariégeoises at an altitude of 1,475 metres. It's very similar in gradient to Alpe d'Huez, with tight bends that allow you to push up the pace. I finished in 16th place and with a touch of heatstroke. On the next stage, I gave it a go in the bunch sprint and finished 12th, one place ahead of the American Tyler Farrar, who would become my teammate in the pro ranks. On the final day, I got caught up in a huge crash with twenty riders in the pouring rain, but I felt in my element, happy in the mountains and equally happy to be suffering. I managed to finish ninth in the overall classification, five and a half minutes behind the Spaniard Eduardo Gonzalo, while helping my teammate Thierry Hupond to a top-five finish. I felt like I was entering the big world. However, a few months later my managers almost fired me.

When I arrived in Marseille, in January 2005, I found myself in a stunning world on the road from the airport: the sea was very blue, the sky was very blue, and everywhere there were small rocky hills. The club member who had volunteered to come and pick me up gave me a guided tour by car: 'Marseille is the sea, but also the mountains,' he explained. 'The city is huge. We've been on the autoroute for twenty minutes and we're still in Marseille.' The tour continued. 'We're passing very close to the service-course,' said my guide, pointing towards the location of the team's HQ. 'The club is called La Pomme because that's the name of the neighbourhood.' There was now a mountain looming on our left. 'That's the Garlaban massif. There's no road up there on which you can cycle to the top. Have you heard about Marcel Pagnol? He used to go picnicking with his parents in the Garlaban. The family lived in Aubagne. Pagnol talks about all that in his books.' Perhaps I should have read everything that was on the curriculum for my French A level . . .

We pulled up in a council estate in Aubagne, where my accommodation had all the modern comforts. There were three bedrooms but six riders. Each room had bunk beds. I got the bottom bunk after drawing straws with a Japanese guy called So Tanaka, who was both a pleasant and discreet companion during those first months. When other riders happened to be passing and needed a place to sleep, there could be nine or ten of us. In those situations, we made use of the worn leather sofa in the living room and the fold-up beds that were stored on a balcony.

The kitchen would be busy from six each evening as everyone gathered in there to prepare their own meal using their preferred brand of pasta. The packages were lined up on the shelf of an iron cupboard, trophies that were well earned considering that we had to walk 2 kilometres to a budget supermarket to buy them – we had no car at our disposal, of course. Similarly, the bathroom would be mobbed as soon as we got back from training. The washing machine was running almost night and day, its power cord snaking across the wet tiles to the socket in the nearest room. Luckily, there were never any accidents.

I didn't feel that this rather rudimentary set-up was a problem.

In fact, I thought that it was probably an important part of a rider's life. In February, when the racing season was just starting to get going, my father came to visit me. He rushed out to the shops to buy me a proper mattress and kitchen utensils.

Within the team, everyone kissed each other on the cheeks, as men do in Marseille when they greet each other. Everyone was friendly right from the off. I didn't understand much despite the eight years I'd spent studying French at school. The accent was very strong, the intonations lilting, the local expressions numerous, and everyone spoke loudly, but cheerfully, with most conversations accompanied by extravagant hand gestures. The French, who comprised half of the team roster, didn't speak English, so the group naturally split in two. I stuck with the foreigners, especially my roommates. What's more, the French riders had nicknames for each other, but not for the rest of us. Consequently, Thierry became 'Titi', Julien was 'Ju', while I remained 'Daniel'.

This development team was effectively a professional set-up and had one overriding obsession: victory in the amateur version of the Coupe de France series. The pressure to excel in it was enormous and constant. Fred Rostaing, who was in his forties and had once been a good regional amateur rider, was an excellent leader of men, a formidable tactician, and organised the team according to this supreme objective.* We had to be on our toes all year round. This started with the January training camp, where we were given a ridiculous

_____

* Ironically, I never competed in a single round of the Coupe de France during my amateur career.

programme: thirty-eight hours of riding over seven days, with sprints in the morning and time trials in the afternoon. At every race, we had to be in the leading twenty riders in the peloton from kilometre zero to the finish line. If not, Fred would give you a rocket through your earpiece, a tool that hadn't been banned at that point in amateur races. At the finish, the post-race debrief would last twenty minutes at least. If we'd finished fourth, a crisis unit would be set up to establish why.

The tension that Fred propagated was devastating in the long term, but his recommendations and flashes of insight were instructive. For example: 'You have to attack the foot of a climb hard, otherwise you lose your rhythm because your tempo is too low, and the gradient ends up attacking you.' After one of my first races in the mountains, where I'd only managed to keep up with the best for 2 kilometres, he came to me and said: 'Why did you blow up?'

'Well ... I was dead,' I told him. He shot back: 'Two kilometres on a climb is six minutes of effort. If you manage to hang on for six minutes, you've done the hardest part and you can ride the whole pass like that.' From a physiological point of view, it was wrong, but the idea that the brain controls the legs corresponded to my philosophy. I've always kept this advice in mind.

Thanks to the roads around Marseille and in its backcountry, I was able to improve my pedal stroke on the climbs. Sometimes all I had to do to work on this was to ride on the flat into the teeth of the mistral, one of the strongest winds in France, which comes barrelling down the Rhône Valley from the north, heading for the sea. Sometimes it was so fearsomely powerful that you would drop down onto the little ring and even then be grinding your legs as if you were on a mountain pass. This wasn't just an exercise in resistance, but the only way you could ride in it. Most of the time, I trained on the region's many hills, which had magical names. I loved the Petit-Galibier (which, averaging about 4 per cent for 4 kilometres, had very little in common with its legendary namesake in the Alps), the Route des Crêtes, which ran along a ridge above the Mediterranean between the ports of Cassis and La Ciotat – the first section of it is the steepest, with 3 kilometres at 10 per cent and some short pitches that reach 20 per cent. The Col de l'Espigoulier, topping out at 723 metres, was the highest in the area and I loved its zig-zagging roads as much as the legends associated with this rocky pinnacle. It's said that the Massif de la Sainte-Baume, where the Espigoulier is located, is home to the tomb of Mary Magdalene, who is purported to have left the Middle East and spent the rest of her life in a cave in Provence. Not far from the road to the pass is a sanctuary that's watched over by monks.

Despite all of my hard work and determination, my first seven races were painful – a mixture of hope and devastation. Here, word for word, is what I wrote down in my little notebook, which I continued to fill in scrupulously just as I had done in my early days in Great Britain:

13 February: Circuit de Peymeinade (135km). 27th. La Pomme 1, 2, 3.

18 February: GP Rocheville (135km). Result? Punctured 20 K to go. Was in Top 20.

19 February: GP Vence (142km). 9th. 180 starters. V. cold. Good result.

22 February: Menton-Savona, Italy (124km). Finished in the peloton. 200 starters. Shortened due to snow.

26 February: GP Jean Masse (125km). Result? La Pomme race team! 1, 2, 3. Crashed badly.

5 March: GP La Londe-les-Maures (110km). DNF. Back screwed after crash. Flying.

19 March: La Durtorccha (105km). 37th. Back very bad. Bent crank. 1 lap down. Very hilly.

The problem with a big team is that when you finish ninth, at least two or three teammates have done better than you. As the club always raced with all guns blazing, sometimes 'we' and at other times 'they' filled the podium places. Week after week, my experience was moulded by pain, and never more than on 26 February, when the signs of it were imprinted on my flesh. It was my first big fall in a race and took place on roads close to our flat in Aubagne. When I got back from races, I used to collapse. Most days I was overly optimistic, others totally depressed. Why hide it? I cried a lot. I let all the stress, the fatigue, the feeling of being alone and left to my own devices evaporate in tears.

The club was particularly impatient with its foreign riders. We were paid between 200 and 600 euros a month, compared to 600 to 1,200 euros for the majority of the French racers.* But the situation was very clear. The foreign riders, who were supposed to be the best in their countries of origin, came to Marseille on the understanding that they would work very hard with a view to making the grade very quickly. The French riders regarded us as lawless mercenaries. They'd get annoyed when they had to be *domestiques* for us foreigners, who were often designated as the team's leaders at the start. I could understand my French teammates' point of view: this set-up didn't offer them anything, beyond delaying or even ruining their chances of becoming pros. I didn't hold it against them and actually enjoyed the fact that I did find myself rubbing shoulders with some of them in the pro peloton in the years that followed. In 2005, our road captain, Rémi Pauriol, tried to bind the different clans together, and he relieved some of the collective pressure by winning the French amateur championship. After his professional racing career, Rémi became a wine grower on the lower slopes of Mont Ventoux.

The jealousies and misunderstandings only grew during the 2006 season, when the club thought it had found a sponsor prepared to invest a million euros to set up a third-division professional team. Some riders would be part of it, while others weren't going to be recruited. The latter were devastated.

---

\* The club paid me 200 euros and provided free accommodation. I also received support from the Dave Rayner Fund, a charity that helps young British riders to try their luck in Europe.

Lithuania's Ignatas Konovalovas, winner of the Ronde de l'Isard in 2006, had been offered a place in the new team, as had three Frenchmen, Julien Antomarchi, Maxime Bouet and Thierry Hupond, who would all go on to ride professionally, but for other teams. And the others? On a provisional and 'secret' list that was changed several times a week, the names of recruits appeared and then disappeared. Fred Rostaing was considering making an offer to Jérôme Coppel, who was one of the best young riders in France, and to the Estonian Rein Taaramäe, a future stage winner at the Giro and the Vuelta. He had also approached, without success, foreign talents who had committed themselves elsewhere, including the Australian sprinter Matthew Goss, who went on to win Milan–San Remo in 2011, and a Kenyan who was quite gifted as a time triallist, Christopher Froome.

For my part, I was never that concerned about Vélo Club La Pomme's professional team, and especially not in 2005, when the project was still in its very early stages and my performance level was considered too low. I was too young, foreign and didn't have a win to my name: this meant that I had a triple burden in the eyes of my managers whenever I asked them for something. For instance, when I asked for the set-up of my bike to be changed because of persistent backache, I was told by the *directeurs sportifs* and mechanics: 'It's impossible! It's not the equipment!' Yet it was taking me three or four days to recover after each training session. I begged several times to have my bike checked. In the end, the staff realised that my cranks were bent from the crash in

February – only by a millimetre or two, but it was enough to cause intolerable lower back pain.

I opened up about my problems to my teammate and flatmate Daryl Impey, and he shared his in return. Daryl was two and a bit years older than me. He'd been racing in South Africa for a team sponsored by Microsoft that would later become MTN, the World Tour squad. Daryl also felt that his French teammates and the managerial staff had taken a dislike to him. 'They're driving me crazy,' he told me. This period of shared misery created a permanent bond between us, which was highlighted by him inviting me to his home country for his wedding in 2011. Unfortunately, we didn't spend enough time together because our racing programmes were never the same. We'd only see each other fleetingly – although on one occasion we did manage to get our feet wet when, during an easy ride to Cassis, we took an impromptu dip in the Mediterranean in our cycling kits. I was afraid that Daryl would quit the set-up. His sense of weariness was compounded by homesickness. Within the club, some were saying in hushed tones that he was 'rubbish'; this about a rider who would, in 2013, become the first African to wear the Tour de France's yellow jersey.

Similar rumours were circulating about me: I was 'rubbish'. I was 'too phlegmatic', because I seemed quite laidback – or I tried to give the impression that I was. For many French people, the British are 'phlegmatic'. I didn't have 'the right stuff'. Even though nobody ever said it to me directly, I could tell that I wasn't held in high esteem. As a result, when I was alone in my room, I used to cry. When my parents called, I told them that everything was fine, except for a fall here and a puncture there. But my father could sense that I was becoming quite unhappy. He said to me: 'This sport is really tough, not only because of what you go through on the bike but also because of what you go through away from it. I know this as well as you do, because I realised it long before you did. If you decide to come back, this experience won't have been a failure.' But giving up never entered my mind.

Shortly afterwards, my parents travelled to France. They used their summer holiday to come and watch me race in the Cinq Jours des As, a series of one-day races held in early August in the Marseille area. They sought me out in the car park of a supermarket in Salon-de-Provence, where the start of one of the races was set to take place. They found me wandering around in my tracksuit. My father was surprised: 'Aren't you racing?' I tried to explain: 'No, the club pulled me out at the last moment, I don't know why.'

That got my father's back up. He went to see Fred Rostaing and took him aside, so that the rest of the team couldn't hear what he had to say.

'Fred, what's the story?'

'Well, Dan isn't doing the race today. We have too many riders. Not everyone can ride.'

'Why didn't you say anything to him?'

'It's just that not everyone can . . .'

My father exploded, in his own way. Very calmly, with a smile on his face, he put his index finger on the *directeur sportif*'s shoulder and looked him straight in the eye: 'You have to be a father to him. That's not me now, it's you. Look at your riders. Dan will be the best rider you will ever have. He's the guy that you need to look after, OK?'

This cold anger provided a release for a lot of buried tension within both my father and me. We felt as if we were re-experiencing with Vélo Club La Pomme Marseille the abandonment we'd endured by Dave Brailsford in the Verona hotel room. In addition to that, my father was reliving a part of his own personal history, when he'd been a rider with the best amateur club in France back in 1979, the ACBB, based in Boulogne-Billancourt, near Paris. He was eighteen years old. The internal competition was brutal. The foreign riders, guys like the Scot Robert Millar and the Australian Phil Anderson, who were both on the team that season, were destined to turn pro; but they were isolated, holed up in a flat where they were bored to death. Mickey Wiegant, the manager, used to inspect the place by running his finger along the walls. If he found a speck of dust, it would end in uproar.

This former mentor of Jacques Anquetil used to find riders who were from distant parts and then cast them away. In the autumn of 1979, the club management promised my father that he would still be on the team the following season and that they were also taking on another English-speaking talent, Stephen Roche, his future brother-in-law. The team seemed to be very keen on having the pair of them, but eventually changed their minds. My uncle was taken on and my father was shown the door. A quarter of a century on from that, our stories were starting to feel eerily similar.

I don't know if it was my father's intercession that sowed some doubt in Fred Rostaing's mind, or the increase in the roster's numbers that was decided over the winter. The team expanded to twenty-two riders, at least four and in some cases eight more than the numbers retained by our rivals. If the team had stayed the same size as it had been in 2005, it's very likely that I would have been thrown out. Even then, it took many months for me to earn real respect. In May 2006, Fred hesitated over selecting me for the Ronde de l'Isard, and in the end I was only picked for it when a French team member withdrew due to injury. I finished eighth in that race replete with mountain passes. It would take another three months before the prejudice shown towards me ended. The perception of me started to change when I won the uphill time trial at the Tour du Val d'Aoste, which was held at the foot of Mont Blanc and other giants of the Alps.

## Chapter 6

# Sweets Versus Red Wine (The Fear of Going Too Fast)

There are so many hills and mountains in the Aosta Valley that everything is at altitude: the castles were built there, its vineyards flourish there and its bike races take place there. The Giro Ciclistico della Valle d'Aosta, its route split between three countries – Italy, Switzerland and France – was one of the most mountainous and prestigious events in the 19–26 age group, a category that only existed within Italian racing. Its format was very straightforward: climb, descend, then climb again.

This race took place in late August of 2006, towards the end of my second season with Vélo Club La Pomme, and revealed what I was capable of. I was determined to assert myself and as a result didn't do things by halves. Each evening when we had dinner, I would point to the bottle set aside for the team manager and the mechanic: 'Pass me some red wine, please. I just want a small glass before going to bed.' My teammates were shocked. I don't know whether I earned more respect for my performances in the Giro Valle d'Aosta or for the fact that I insisted on having Valle d'Aosta wine each evening.

The final stage comprised a 10-kilometre hill climb from the village of Landry to the ski station of Vallandry over in France, not far from Bourg-Saint-Maurice. I'd often done well in this discipline during my junior years. When I got to the start I was only half awake, because the alarm on my watch hadn't gone off. I had only been woken by the bedroom door being closed as my room-mate quietly snuck off to breakfast. I didn't have any gloves on. I was in the small chain ring as I waited on the start ramp, because we went straight into the climb from the off. But a race commissaire made me put the chain in the big ring to prevent me skating wildly away from the start.

' . . . Trois . . . Deux . . . Un . . . Zéro . . .' After a dozen metres or so, the course took a left turn and immediately started to climb. A sense of calm returned. My cadence was steady, as if on a track bike. I didn't know how my time compared to previous riders; no race radios here! I just had to push and pull as hard as possible on the pedals, for what was half an hour of pure and quite simple pleasure. As I crossed the line, I almost passed out. Someone from the race organisation told me that I'd won the stage and had a big lead: forty-three seconds on the Italian Alessandro Bisolti and forty-nine seconds on the Belgian Tom Criel. And that I'd finished second in the final classification, a minute and twelve seconds behind Bisolti. In a picture taken on the podium, my teammates bore me aloft like a prize ham. A significant change had happened.

In Val d'Aosta, one of the teams we were racing against was a recently established, aggressive and enthusiastic American outfit called TIAA-CREF, whose sports director was Johnny Weltz, who'd been the last rider to take a Tour de France stage victory on the iconic climb of the Puy de Dôme. He congratulated me warmly on my success. 'Do you know that we're going to go pro next year, in the second division? Jonathan will get in touch with you.' Ten days later, Jonathan Vaughters, TIAA-CREF's manager, sent me an email:

> I really do think you have the correct skills to do well and start moving toward the Pro Tour. Also, we aren't a team you'd get lost in. We are small enough that you would be able to learn at a pace that is right to you. Johnny is a great European director with tons of experience and a love for young riders. I promise you this will be a good move if you choose to make it. Thanks so much and let me know if you are interested . . . JV

I knew Jonathan Vaughters was an outspoken, smart and wise former American pro cyclist, who competed for two years as Lance Armstrong's teammate. He came across as some kind of intellectual hipster with his round glasses and his argyle gilets that secretly contained a pocket watch. I found out later that we shared a common passion for wine – him burgundy and Châteauneuf-du-Pape, me more tannic wines, like Spanish Rioja. About his cycling career, I could remember two highlights. The first one was in 1999 when he held the record of the ascent of Mont Ventoux in a time trial, with an average of 22.7km/h, breaking by 3:19 the old record set by Charly Gaul in 1958. The second achievement that I remembered was the 2001 Tour de France, where he decided to pull out because he didn't want to use cortisone to cure a wasp sting above his eye, knowing this medicine could be interpreted as doping. Now a team manager, he was committed to changing things within cycling. Two months after our phone call, 'JV' gave an inspirational interview to the Cyclingnews website:

> We (me, directors, sponsors, management) have to start treating this as a sport, not just a business. We have to start treating the athletes as humans, not expandable fodder. If you say to an athlete, 'You must win today or else,' the clever cyclist will make sure he wins, but the way it's done may not be that healthy for the sport or his body.'

I was a bit bewildered. A year earlier, my club had been on the verge of kicking me out. What's more, just a month before, despite my results improving, I still had this rather 'phlegmatic' image. Things were moving too quickly. Was I ready to turn professional? Yes. Was I ready to win pro races? I wasn't sure. At that time, the process between turning professional and winning took between two and four years. Teams like La Française des Jeux sent young riders to the Giro 'to learn'. But it seemed that the only thing they were learning was to spend 3,500 gruelling kilometres sitting in the wheels. Did they enjoy it? Did they really have any chance of picking up a victory? The prospect of enduring this almost compulsory period of limbo perplexed me. I could see myself as the equivalent of an office intern, fated to make coffee and photocopies for ever. I was afraid of falling into some kind of rut.

On the other hand, it was difficult to refuse an offer like this. I'd be taking a risk by turning it down. If I remained in the amateur ranks for the 2007 season and had a crash, I wouldn't be able to confirm my promise as a racer, while Jonathan Vaughters would probably forget about me and hire another young rider. But if I turned professional and then broke my collarbone in 2007, I would still have more than a year left on my contract, during which time I could get back on the bike and still prove myself.

A few days later, the American team manager called to tell me a bit more about the project: 'Hi Dan, this is Jonathan Vaughters. You're brave and very promising. I'm going to put together a team of young riders.' He sounded likeable and cheerful, like someone who would certainly be good company, who was intelligent, determined, and, when he told me about himself, perhaps a little sensitive. 'You know that I won the time trial on the Ventoux at the 2001 Dauphiné. I used to like mountain time trials as well. But I didn't have the opportunity to race in the way that I'd have liked to . . . The team I'll build around you will be the kind of team that I would have liked to ride for.'

It took me more than a fortnight to get back to him with my answer: 'Dear Jonathan, thank you very much for your interest. I'm very interested in your proposal and your vision. If you agree, I suggest that we touch base again in six months. I've decided to have another season in the under-23 ranks. There are some things that I still need to learn.'

Training was one of the secrets I wanted to unlock. I used an SRM power meter to help me. It was a useful tool but I wasn't overly dependent on it. I kept training in 'the old-fashioned way', using intuition rather than sticking to programmed and very precise performance zones. In the same way, I didn't get concerned when I was dropped on our group rides, like those on the monstrous January training camp. I worked out an average power level and let my teammates go on without me. I listened to my body. I didn't want to get wrapped up in science or the agenda of others. When I felt the moment was right, I climbed from Cassis to the Route des Crêtes and completely destroyed myself. This not only gave me a lift, but also developed my talent as a hill sprinter – or, as the French call it quite ono-matopoeically, a '*puncheur*'.

Finally, I felt comfortable with every part of my environment – or would have, had it not been that, in the spring, I was struggling with inexplicable variations in form. It was the same every year, but since I had become part of the Marseille club the trouble was more pronounced. Some days my legs would swell up and feel solid, like poles. The problem was made worse by the dry weather; it disappeared almost entirely when it was raining. But all I had to do was travel to another place or wait a few more days and my calves would regain their usual defined shape, with the veins prominent.

I was disappointed. To me these weren't health issues – I was going to cure those sooner or later* – but a lack of strength.

------------------

* See Chapter 9.

So I trained even harder. And I was starting to think that if I was going to sign the contract with Vaughters' team and turn pro, my spring period was always going to be a difficult time. I'd probably end up watching the Ardennes Classics on TV ...

Apart from these unexplained variations in form, I was confident in my ability to build everything I needed to perform. I started to follow my own path when it came to nutrition, a subject that's an absolute obsession for cyclists. Several teammates told me that I was 'fat'. Thinking he was helping me, a few minutes after my victory in the Valle d'Aosta time trial, our road captain told me something that could easily have messed with the head of a young racer: 'Just imagine what you would be capable of if you were two kilos lighter,' he told me. Someone else said that you needed to see your blood vessels standing out across your stomach. I heard scary sayings like, 'Eating is cheating.' Some had sworn themselves off milk, fast-acting carbs like sugars and even pasta. They compensated with mountains of organic live brewer's yeast – a source of B vitamins. In the evenings, after skipping dinner in order to appear to be starving themselves, they would hide away in their hotel rooms and snack on a chocolate bar or bag of sweets. Once they'd eaten these, they would go and throw up. I was horrified. As a consequence of denying themselves so much, they would eventually crack up.

As for me, I used to buy a piece of tart from the bakery when I felt I needed it. My body demanded it, not as a treat but out of necessity. Its demands were honest and reasonable. If I was hungry, I ate. I wasn't that bothered about the neurosis with weight. As far as I was concerned, the most critical thing wasn't the lightness of the tank, but the fuel that was inside it. However, the diet several of my teammates stuck to meant that they didn't have a drop of fuel left when racing. I kept pasta and dairy on the menu, along with chicken and salad, and topped this up with my little glass of red wine each evening during stage races. It almost became a good luck charm. Even Fred Rostaing used to encourage me to do it, joking: 'Don't forget your little glass, Dan!'

I got used to coping with very long journeys, which could drain us of our nervous energy. We used to travel thousands of kilometres in a van, travelling in one go from Marseille to Tuscany, for instance. We'd drive at night to avoid having to pay for a hotel room. Initially, I'd listen to the Red Hot Chili Peppers and Green Day in order to drown out the metallic din of the engine, or I'd sleep. Eventually I got over the motion sickness and managed to read magazines in the car. I was steadily being prepared for the journeys I'd be making in future as a professional racer, by plane, train, bus, car. I was ready for back-breaking seats, lung-depleting air conditioning and flight delays that would do your head in.

I learned about boredom, the daily routine of a cyclist away from the adrenaline rush of competition. Time seemed to drag interminably in our flat, so I didn't go rushing off to train each morning, so that by the time I got back and had showered and refuelled, the afternoon would already have melted away. I'd watch *The Simpsons* or a race on my computer. I would call my parents on Skype and chat on MSN Messenger with Andy Birley, a former training mate in England, who was based in Lichfield and would provide me with reassurance and the strength to keep going. Occasionally, I would ride into Cassis with a few friends who lived around Marseille, and have a coffee down at the port. As Daryl Impey had left in the autumn of 2005, this small community included two La Pomme-trained pro riders, my compatriot Philip Deignan, a future stage winner in the Vuelta, and Fumiyuki (Fumi) Beppu, one of the first two Japanese riders to finish the Tour de France. In 2007, my Australian teammate David Tanner boosted this little group.

I learned how to win, getting used to the many vagaries of racing, steadily becoming more consistent in my level of performance. Each victory validated the previous one and fore-shadowed the next, until winning became an unshakeable idea, an almost permanent objective. I won the Grand Prix de Rayol-Canadel, a preparation race on the French Riviera, in March. It was St Patrick's Day. We got up at four in the morning because the start was at seven. In May, I won the final stage of the Tour des Pays de Savoie at the top of the 1,924-metre Col du Glandon, a success that also enabled me to clinch the overall title. I was always looking ahead to the next race. No matter where I finished, as soon as I crossed the line I would rinse myself down with water, put a jacket on and sit in the team car with a protein drink to help my recovery. I didn't go over the stage again. Instead, I'd study the profile of the next one in the roadbook.

I got used to paying a high price for being a favourite, to the repeated assaults of adversity and coalitions formed with the intention of making me lose, but also with much more serious ruses. The Gara Ciclistica Montappone in Italy's Marche region was a strange case in point. On that day, a team manager who'd been the centre of controversy when he'd been suspended for doping was somehow still able to direct his team and drive in the race. He was also prepared to take me out of the picture by any means necessary. As I was coming back from a puncture, he got closer and closer to me and I had to brake hard, almost ending up on the grass on the roadside. I could feel the warmth radiating from his car's bodywork. Should I abandon or let him kill me? Miraculously, the British national team car saw what was happening and came to my rescue. Rod Ellingworth, Team Ineos' future deputy principal, was driving. He forced his way through, horn blaring, to get right next to me. Thanks to his protection, I managed to rejoin the peloton. The crazy sports director backed off. We knew he was headstrong, liable to punch someone, so we didn't think of confronting him after the finish. We saved our anger up for future victories.

At the end of June, Jonathan Vaughters got back to me: 'All good? Shall we sign that contract?'

'Whenever you want,' I replied.

La Française des Jeux had also shown some interest, but I'd given my word. What's more, Jonathan had offered me the opportunity to join the team in August as a *stagiaire*. 'You'll start at the Tour of Ireland. Your first pro race will be in your home country.' Great! The event hadn't been held for fifteen years. I could already see myself wearing the new jersey, getting to know my future teammates, having fun on the lumps and bumps of a country where, as everyone knows, the sheep have two legs shorter than the other two so that they can stand up on all the hills. Over five stages, we would pass through Kilkenny, Cork, Clonakilty, Killarney, Tralee, Ennis, Galway, Athlone and Dublin. I could already picture myself there. I might even spend a few days on holiday with my grandparents. I'd ride in the Wicklow Mountains. The only hitch was that the Tour of Ireland was being held on the same dates as the Giro Ciclistico della Valle d'Aosta, the moment that I'd been waiting for.

The Alpine race had me in a bit of a bind. If I finished second again, or further down the top ten, it would have been a solid performance but the general perception would be that I'd gone backwards. It was the win or nothing. I was frightened of being a disappointment, of focusing on a very tenuous ambition: the Tour of Ireland would perhaps have offered me a way out of this. But I stuck to my guns. I chose the Valle d'Aosta. In truth, I'd decided to delay my passage into the pro ranks because I wanted to savour this excitement, these doubts, this fear. I was determined to win. On the morning of the second stage, in the French mountains close to the Swiss border, I had this first flashing sense that I would win and was totally convinced that this would be my day. I sent a text message to my parents: 'I'm going to win today'. They looked over the route on the internet. Three climbs: Les Gets, Joux-Plane and the Col de Saxel. The last summit was 30 kilometres from the finish. In theory, this very long descent should have doomed the hopes of the climbers; it was an impossible task. But within me I could hear an inner voice whispering something far more reassuring.

For the first hundred kilometres, my legs felt numb. Then a thunderstorm bore down upon us. It was only 4 p.m. but it started to get dark. The last descent was the descent of my life. I let the road take my bike and me with it. There were three of us in the breakaway: defending champion Alessandro Bisolti, another Alessandro by the name of Colò, and me. The rain poured torrentially down, the deluge so heavy that it was getting into my mouth. But it could have been snowing and I wouldn't have noticed anything. I took my turns setting the pace on the front like a true *rouleur.* I sprinted like a true sprinter. As the final straight in the town of Ville-la-Grand was on a gently rising false flat, I was the first to move, using surprise to gain a decisive length. I'd done it! My Giro Ciclistico della Valle d'Aosta was over. Although I didn't win the Fontina-cheese-sponsored yellow jersey, I had opened up new possibilities. I was shaping up to be a Classics rider. I'd struck on a day when only fate had believed in me.

My teammates were satisfied and exhausted, as they always were at the end of these battles. They were happy and proud of me. Reassured, liberated, I was making jokes in French. After the final stage, we replayed the week's best moments: the difficult passes, the Colombians climbing at unattainable speeds, and the mysterious van that had secretly picked up one of the main protagonists on a pass, overtaken the lead group and then parked under some trees, where the rider had got out again – the UCI commissaires found out about the cheat and offered him a chance to abandon 'for health reasons' rather than causing a scandal.

We laughed a lot. Then I shared out the booty that the race organisation had given us, earned thanks to my placings on the stages and by my fifth position in the overall classification and the points competition. Each team member took an equal share of the cake and, as is usually the case in professional racing, we gave a final share to the staff, the mechanic, the *soigneur* and the *directeur sportif*. Everyone went home with almost a thousand euros. Bringing money into the community definitely builds respect.

That was it: the French adventure was over. As I left Marseille, I saw pride and a touch of sadness in Fred Rostaing's eyes. I surprised myself as well as my teammates when I told him: 'I'm going to miss you.' It's always like that when you part.

# Chapter 7

# Team Garmin Is Clean (The Fear of Doping)

The hardest thing about riding with David Millar was avoiding the snakes. There weren't thousands of them crossing the road in Girona's backcountry, north of Barcelona, my new home, but at least one scared us to death. One day we were riding near Mas Lunes when, in the middle of conversation, David let out a scream. I turned my head and saw him do a bunny-hop, luckily without falling. He was trying to avoid a viper that was coiled up asleep on the tarmac, warming its belly. The serpent was a metre long. When it heard the commotion, it shot off to the right. We laughed: 'Imagine if that had got stuck in the spokes!' After that, we didn't come across any more reptiles, although the rocks, forests and waterholes in the hills between the Mediterranean and the foothills of the Pyrenees were undoubtedly full of them.

David was more than just my new teammate. Being nine years older, he was a sort of big brother on the bike. He had taken me under his wing in 2008, when I started with my first pro team. We were the only two riders in the squad who lived in Girona all year round, so we rode together, went to the gym in the morning, or to the Irish pub where I'd already made friends with all the staff – you always make friends in an Irish pub. When we had a glass of wine or a bottle of cold water, David would say to me: 'You're really lucky to be in this team.' He knew what he was talking about, as it was exactly the kind of team that hadn't been an option for him when he turned professional in 1997, the kind that would have certainly saved him from misdirection and adversity.

David and I had met even before he tried to convince me over the phone to join Team Slipstream. The first time was in 2003 at Manchester airport, from where we were flying out to the World Championships in Canada. At dinner time the night before we were due to fly, he joined me and the other members of the British junior team, Geraint Thomas and Matt Brammeier, and our team manager Simon Lillistone. David was a star. Winner of the Tour de France prologue in 2000. A regular on magazine covers. A playboy, you could say. But meeting him had left me with mixed feelings. He had hardly said a word during the meal and it was clear he didn't want to be there. Yet a few days later he won the world time trial title.

The following year, the French police found vials of EPO in his home. David was suspended for two years. We didn't discuss our first meeting; in fact, I'm not even sure if he remembers it. In 2008, he'd become a different person. Then aged thirty, he wanted to build a new life. And he wanted to save me time at all costs, to help, to explain, to protect me.

Team Slipstream, as it was originally called,* was an ideal team to get a first pro contract or for a second chance. Their philosophy was simple: to be a clean team and a happy team. A team free of worries, which was quite a statement ... We actually pieced together our ideal world at our first gathering in November 2007. We brainstormed keywords in small groups and then shared them with the others.

Winners
Friends
Genuine
Stylish
Clean
Aggressive

We were sitting in the grandly panelled, stained-glass-lit lounges of the venerable Hotel Boulderado, one of the best-known buildings in Boulder, Colorado. I'd never felt such good energy before. Nor had I ever thought that such words could be spoken in a cycling team. It felt like a company seminar and it was clear that the management was letting us confirm their plan rather than drawing it up from nothing. But at least everyone had the opportunity to remember why they'd signed up with this particular team:

---

* Team Slipstream was formed in 2005 and named after a film project that never came to fruition. The team, led by Jonathan Vaughters and funded by businessman Doug Ellis, was initially established in the sport's third division, then climbed into the second division in 2008, the year that I joined and when it also adopted the name of its new sponsor, Garmin, a satellite navigation company.

Pioneers
Transparent
Revolutionary

Our course took place in this sort of red-brick Lego mansion, alternating between wine tastings organised by an oenologist and lectures on anti-doping supervised by Anne Gripper, the scientist who was tracking down cheats for the UCI. It was a very nice internship programme.

Innovative
Tough
Well-spoken

Finally, David Zabriskie came up with a proposition that summed up everyone's excitement and ambition: 'Not-US Postal'. The room erupted in laughter and we went into town to have a few beers.

Team Slipstream was a splinter group of the former US Postal squad and was furiously trying to make a difference. Zabriskie, an elusive character with a dark sense of humour, a former Tour yellow jersey, had ridden for the US Postal team and its intractable boss, Lance Armstrong. Other riders had been through the same stable: Christian Vande Velde, the Chicago-born *rouleur-grimpeur*; Tom Danielson, who, given his talent, had been hailed as the future of USA cycling and who would often be my roommate on the races; the Canadian mountain biker Ryder Hesjedal ... Our *directeur sportif* Johnny Weltz and our doctor Prentice Steffen, head of the emergency department at San Francisco Hospital, had also worked for that team before being sidelined or walking away from it, due to divergent choices. Not to mention our general manager, Jonathan Vaughters. Even David Millar had been considered for a position as a US Postal lieutenant before his suspension enabled him to change the course of his life. They were all looking for a new way of approaching cycling, united as they were by a 'secret' that we all more or less knew about . . .

Our team was an intriguing mix of experienced ex-US Postal racers and hipsters from TIAA-Cref, the forerunner of Slipstream. Those in the latter group had known the early beginnings of this small team, changing into their race kit in a camper van to which a construction tarpaulin was fixed with three ropes to protect them from the rain. Among them were William Frischkorn, who would finish second on a Tour de France stage a few months later; Danny Pate, a former time trial world champion in U23 and a fantastic *domestique*; and Jason Donald, notorious for having driven a refuse truck to finance his passion for cycling. They were the representatives of this new American cycling. I was of course assimilated into the group of young riders, even though I surprised the older riders to begin with because of my deep voice and strong West Midlands accent. It became the butt of jokes. They'd say to me, 'Are you sure you speak English?'

After the gathering in Colorado, the time came to decide on our permanent base in Europe. The team had set up its service course in Girona, Catalonia, a city where Lance Armstrong had lived in the recent past – we'll come back to that ... It was a human-sized city, very pleasant to live in and often considered a dream location by Spanish magazines. Girona offered not only very suitable training terrain, which took us into medium-sized mountains, but also a living environment full of old stone buildings and close to beaches where we could relax on rest days, superb gastronomy (which ranged from a Michelin three-star restaurant to a snack bar renowned for the deliciousness of the modest Spanish dish of bread rubbed with garlic and fresh tomato) and, finally, transport connections for races, as it was a big hub for the airline Ryanair. I felt that this city was tailor-made for racing cyclists. Unlike Monaco, which I'd visited a few times, and which from my point of view oozed profound boredom, Girona exuded a sweetness of life that was infectious.

Most of the older members of the team settled in quiet houses with swimming pools in the hills around the city to enjoy family life. The younger ones, like me, moved into the old town, with its rather noisy but cheerful alleys. We would find an address by word of mouth, by the market, in the old Jewish ghetto, or close to the cathedral – a huge building where scenes from *Game of Thrones* were filmed. Initially I shared with Christophe Laurent, a Frenchman who had been recruited because he was the Super Combatif at the Tour of California, but he was never around, so really I was on my own. The following year I shared an apartment with my compatriot Philip Deignan, who was then racing for the Swiss team Cervélo. Young, old, Americans, Europeans: we all had the same meeting point at the Pont de Pedra, at nine o'clock in the morning. Between February and September, the peloton could number ten or more. In winter, two or three of us would meet at the Café Boira, next to the bridge, with David Millar and another former US Postal rider who was not on our team but was a friend, the Canadian Michael Barry.

David used to live in the city centre with his wife Nicole and their little dog Zorro, before moving to Banyoles, about fifteen kilometres from Girona, on the edge of the mountains. He'd taken the career option of the team's veterans but had the soul of a new pro. He was amazed at how lucky we were to be on this team. He was surprised and moved by the fact that the further into the season we got, the more uncompromising we were, clinging to the key principles we'd laid down in the hotel's lounges back in the winter. And I was surprised and moved by David. If I were to believe the articles I'd read in the press, especially those that told of his rise and fall and the comeback that he was making, there was always a moment in the life of a new pro when you stumbled into the backstage reality, when you pierced the doubletalk. For decades, that wall of reality had hurt thousands of riders.

If it had been a few years earlier and in another team, the bike rides I did with David would have been the ideal chance to offer tips on doping. The 'old pro', trying quite sincerely to help me, would have given me practical information on how to get products and meet facilitators. Obviously nothing is certain, but at another time or in another team, that's the type of thing I would have heard. My mentor would have said to me, in essence, 'You've got no choice, this is the way it is, you've to go through it.' But when I was with David, our sorties couldn't have been any more different. We'd talk about the most beautiful rides around Girona, about the great passes and sacred places of cycling that he'd climbed and that I couldn't wait to discover, about our common passion for food, and about the snakes that napped on the roads.

On the occasions that we talked about doping and anti-doping, David was very enthusiastic: 'Nobody is going as far as we are. We're ahead of the game. If we can show that we can win races without doping, we'll give hope to other teams and riders. We won't eradicate doping 100 per cent, but I think we'll reduce it significantly. Your generation will be one of the first to benefit from this.' We were going through a very bad period. After Lance Armstrong's sulphurous Tours de France (1999–2005), the winner of the 2006 edition, Floyd Landis, was disqualified following a positive test for testosterone. In 2007, the yellow jersey apparent, Michael Rasmussen, was exiled a few days before his predictable victory for having lied about his whereabouts to the anti-doping authorities while preparing for that race, which might well have allowed him to avoid undergoing doping tests at home. There was a deluge of scandals. When he returned from suspension during the 2006 Tour de France, David had ridden with an Italian climber, Riccardo Riccò, nicknamed 'the Cobra', who was arrested by the police in the middle of the 2008 Tour de France. Many might have despaired of the situation.

But, as David said, we were lucky. Our contracts with Team

Slipstream, now known as Team Garmin-Chipotle (a tech company that was bringing GPS technology into cycling, and a Mexican restaurant chain), included a stipulation to adhere to a very strict anti-doping programme. We weren't allowed to consume any dietary products other than those recommended by the team; we weren't allowed to consult doctors who weren't attached to the team. We weren't allowed to inject any substance into our bodies, including saline, vitamins and minerals and glucose, or authorised products known as 'recovery products'. The team believed that once you got into the habit of sticking a needle into your arm, you could easily resort to banned substances. Subsequently, the UCI extended our initiative in 2011 so that it covered the whole peloton under a rule known as the 'No Needle Policy'. Finally, we had to undergo unannounced doping tests at home that were carried out by an independent laboratory hired by the team. Some months I would give blood and urine three or four times under separate testing procedures carried out by the UCI, by Irish Cycling and as part of this internal programme. The controller would ring the doorbell before the crack of dawn, usually waking me up. It was heavy going, but worth it.

In general, I found the atmosphere within the team very reassuring. At mealtimes, no restrictions were placed on us. Allen Lim, our performance manager, had a human approach to food. He recommended that we ate our fill. 'You need calories, because the body burns a lot of them in your job,' he would remind us. If you suddenly gained a kilo or two during the season, Dr Lim would put things into perspective: 'It may be due to your level of fitness. The body vascularises – you have more blood and, therefore, more water in your body. An increase in your mass is not necessarily a bad thing.' The discourse differed dramatically from the punitive approach that I'd seen in Marseille, which often led to a well-documented spiral: deficiencies, a drop-off in performance, depression and, possibly, doping. Yet, I was on a team whose performance director had fun inventing gourmet sports recipes in his spare time, such as home-made cereal bars or a snack that would soon be copied by our rivals, a rice cake with bacon and scrambled eggs (with maple syrup and sometimes a touch of Parmesan).

I was on the right team, one that shared my vision of sport and life. I was also perhaps racing in the right era. Despite the huge scandals that kept occurring, part of the peloton was in a process of self-cleaning. Even though I was clean, I'd been able to get results in races that had not long before been considered as being out of the range of riders who didn't dope. The Giro della Valle d'Aosta that I loved so much had been abandoned by some teams at the beginning of the 2000s because they believed they couldn't compete with teams brimful with EPO. But I managed to win two stages there, boosted by the whey protein recovery drink I'd down immediately after stage finishes. It was encouraging. I was told the names of riders who were potentially suspect and I managed to beat them. I felt reassured, encouraged, even transcended by these results. I was going to start my pro career in the same way that I'd finished my apprenticeship in the U23s: by taking victories fuelled by those milkshakes.

I wasn't surprised when, in 2012, the former US Postal guys confessed to what they'd done before joining Team Garmin. I never blamed them. I could see that they had suffered in what had been a very dark world and that they'd fought to change and help their sport do so as well. When details of the US Anti-Doping Agency (USADA) investigation started to leak to the press, I was at the Tour de France, sharing a room with Christian Vande Velde. It was the day of the individual time trial in Besançon. The media surrounded our team bus. Our road captain wouldn't make a statement that day and waited until the end of the season to confirm his past deeds and express his regrets, but he turned to me and asked: 'Did you see the news on TV? If you've got any questions, I'm listening.' I told him that I thought I understood.

My character and my approach to life also played a role at those critical moments when doubt can overcome you and tip you over to the wrong side. I wasn't in any way susceptible to doping. I wasn't going to be tempted by it, no matter what the situation. I remembered those races we'd watched as a family on TV during the EPO decade and my father sometimes rolling his eyes. That message was enough. I knew something was wrong with our sport. I loved cycling but I wasn't stupid.

Right from my first professional season, in 2008, I decided not to be swayed from the course I was adamant I would follow. Some said everyone was doped, but I could see that wasn't the case from looking around the members of my own team. What's more, the widespread cheating that was taking place offered me a familiar refuge, given my history and my independence.

I'd got myself to where I was almost alone, helped only by my family and a handful of friends. I didn't belong to any clan and I wasn't trying to please or be like everyone else. By telling me that you couldn't win without doping, it just spurred me on to prove people wrong.

When a rider thinks about the doping taking place around them, they have four possible options:

A. Practise the sport in a despondent and defeatist state of mind.
B. Quit the sport.
C. Turn to doping.
D. Avoid thinking about it.

I chose option D.

I knew that doping was taking place, but I didn't let that knowledge taint my way of thinking. What's more, throughout my entire career I never witnessed an act of cheating. No one offered or advised me about a banned product, nor even showed me one, let alone consumed one in front of me. It's true that I signed for teams where some of the riders and staff members had been questioned for doping, or were going to be in the near future. But none of these people initiated a conversation with me on this issue. In short, I was never offered anything. I was respected everywhere I went. Everyone did their own thing.

I was perhaps also blessed with a good dose of natural physical vigour. Jonathan Vaughters acknowledged that I was far stronger physiologically than average and offered a scientific explanation for this. The Team Garmin manager insisted that, according to the laws of nature, I had inherited all of my mother's DNA; and, as Stephen Roche was her brother, it had to be assumed that I shared some of the qualities of the 1987 Triple Crown winner. This notion amused my mother, who claimed full responsibility for my sporting prowess. My father also laughed about it, saying: 'So I had nothing to do with it?'

Besides, I'd never made a habit of visiting a doctor and my medicine cabinet was almost empty. That's why I was annoyed when I realised that the variations in my form that happened every year in spring must be a problem of allergies. Some friends finally gave that explanation, which was supposed to encourage me: I was not in poor shape, just facing health issues that I could easily cure. Yet I wasn't too happy about the prospect. I'd heard riders recounting their tales of shuttling from one doctor's surgery to another to find the most suitable allergy treatment, and how time-consuming it was. I was worried that the products would be ineffective or have side effects. And I was still reluctant to take medication, even though it was clearly necessary in my case.

I was even reluctant to take a sleeping pill, because I wanted my body to heal itself, finding naturally induced sleep to be much more effective; and by limiting my caffeine intake to just 50mg, taken in a gel, I managed to sleep like a baby each night. This was the synthetic equivalent of an espresso but far, far less than the maximum tolerated dose until 2004, when the International Olympic Committee started to consider an excess of caffeine to be doping. You definitely feel an effect in an event's last hour and, for one-day races when recovery afterwards was not important, I would push my limits to 100mg even though it meant I often couldn't get to sleep until three in the morning.

Pain and cycling go hand in hand but rather than seek to block it, I more often than not chose to embrace the sensation. From time to time, I would take a paracetamol to help mask the fatigue and dull ache that three weeks of brutal racing inflicts on your body, but I then found out it was more of a placebo. I preferred to be in touch with my body's messaging, to feel where my limit was, so that I could more accurately balance on the tightrope that is the upper regions of performance. Often, the difference between blowing up and sustaining the speed to the finish is a matter of a few watts.

In truth, I was able to forgo painkillers because I had a much higher tolerance of physical suffering than the average rider. I'd known this since I was thirteen, when I dislocated my thumb trying to prevent a goal being scored during a football match at St Francis College. I'd refused to leave the game. When my parents picked me up from the hospital later, I proudly told them, 'Well, they didn't score.' The stakes were so high that I was determined to block out the pain. I had the same attitude afterwards on the bike, when I got injured or when I was focused on trying to win and could feel my body burning.

# Chapter 8

# Bluffing Sean Kelly (The Fear of Losing)

Marseille, Mediterranean, Mistral: my first race as a professional rider had an air of déjà vu about it. I started the 2008 season with the Grand Prix La Marseillaise, the opening race in Europe, on the roads where I used to train. Every element of the scenery was just how I remembered it. The appearance of the sun was deceptive, as the wind blowing from the north, the mistral, had forced the temperature down to around ten degrees. We stayed in a hotel two kilometres away from Vélo Club La Pomme's service course. The finish was in front of the Vieux Port, the heart of the city, amid tourists, fishermen and souvenir sellers. I finished in the peloton. I was well and truly on my way.

Tourmalet, Terrible, Tempo: my first objective of the year, in mid-June, was to climb the pass that was so significant during my adolescent years. The Route du Sud stage race took place between the Critérium du Dauphiné and the Tour de France. It was likely to be decided in the Pyrenees, where the heat was blazing and the air dry, the wind offering hardly any cooling relief. My Uncle Stephen won the race in 1985. Fourteen years later our general manager, Jonathan Vaughters, won it. In 2008, the third stage started at the foot of the Tourmalet, just like my teenage holiday adventure had. I took strength from the location, with all its telluric faults. After passing through the small village of Barèges, I could see the road twisting through the green pasture in anarchic curves, like a piece of spaghetti through pesto. Those last 2 kilometres to the summit were the hardest. The Tourmalet whispered in my ear: 'This is your day! You know that I bring you luck. Drink, eat, breathe, spin your legs. And enjoy it!'

The team were setting the pace for me like a yellow jersey in the Tour de France, the guys lined up one by one with me at the end, protected from the wind, because I was lying second in the general classification and they believed in me. We went over the Col d'Azet and the Col de Peyresourde. We dropped from the latter into Bagnères-de-Luchon and climbed again to the ski resort of Superbagnères above it. Christophe Moreau, the former Festina rider, was on my wheel, ready to ambush me. He was my most dangerous opponent. He was upright in his riding style, his goatee well-trimmed, pushing a *rouleur*'s big gear, looking proud in his French champion's jersey. But with 5 kilometres to go, we accelerated a touch, by barely a kilometre an hour, and that finished him off. That was when my last remaining teammate, Australian Trent Lowe, pulled aside to let me finish the job. I maintained this slight acceleration and dropped Moreau without making an attack. I finished fifty-eight seconds ahead of him. The stage victory went to Polish climber Przemysław Niemiec. I took the orange leader's jersey. It was a beautiful moment but, out of superstition, I told the journalists: 'I don't want to say today that I'm happy.' However, I managed to hold on to my leader's jersey on the final stage. At twenty-one, I became the youngest winner in the Route du Sud's history.

When I got back to Girona I could tell that my teammates were very excited, particularly the young guys, because they'd realised that there were opportunities for them in races. If they felt they had the legs to win, the team wouldn't hold them back. They weren't simply going to be condemned to roles as water-carriers for the older members in the team, like office interns making coffee. Everyone had a chance. A few months later, when racing the Tour of Great Britain, I even got support from our 'friendly giant', the Swedish Magnus Bäckstedt, the winner of the 2004 Paris–Roubaix. Magnus was one of the last riders from an era where a cyclist's weight had a range of 50kg to nearly 100kg – he was at the top end, with 94kg that he managed to pull up the hardest Alpine or Pyrenean passes. At that race, although I ultimately missed victory, my teammate really considered himself a proper teammate. There was no pecking order according to the *palmarès* or the age of the riders: it was one for all and all for one.

My win at the Route du Sud was a fantastic way to launch my first year as a professional rider but I was still troubled by the feeling that the race had been easy, that I hadn't suffered enough. I hadn't expected my first pro victory to be like that, and to win so soon. I replayed the scenario that unfolded over the four stages. On the opening one, I got into a breakaway with about thirty riders. On the second, a 17-kilometre uphill time trial to the spa town of Cauterets, I limited the time I lost to forty-four seconds. Ultimately, I only had to beat Christophe Moreau. 'It's part of the game, a victory is built stage by stage. You were the smartest and the most consistent,' some veteran teammates said to encourage me. 'The others needed to start the race by getting into that breakaway on the first day!'

Then I spoke to David Millar, who also enjoyed success during the first half of that season as part of Slipstream's team at the Giro that won the team time trial in Sicily at the beginning of May. He was delighted with our respective victories: 'These wins give us good reason to hope for more success looking ahead. Before, you had to make a choice. Either you won but had to dope to ensure this, or you refused to dope but it was almost impossible to win.'

The Irish National Championships were held a week after the Route du Sud, and I turned my focus to the Midleton circuit in County Cork, which seemed to suit *rouleurs*, sprinters and aggressive riders equally well. Given my form, I was hoping for a podium finish, assuming that I could get rid of Team An Post. I was a team of one, my father acting as team manager in a rented team car, and up against a battalion of 'Irish postmen', whose team director was Sean Kelly. I had to play it smart . . . Initially, I wanted to get in a break. I attacked after 10 kilometres in order to avoid getting stuck in a peloton, where everyone is watching everyone else and, as a result, ends up neutralising the attacks of their rivals rather than chancing their arm. One of the most experienced riders, Ciarán Power, was tracking me in the break. We were reeled in about 50 kilometres later, but I slipped into another breakaway. Each time, Sean Kelly ordered one of his men to stick with me. Paídi O'Brien was one of them. A native of County Cork, he was renowned for his speed in a sprint, so you had to watch out for him. I knew that he might join forces with one of the other breakaway riders, such as Brian Kenneally or David O'Loughlin, depending on the circumstances. For them, I was the man to beat and their plan would succeed if they took it in turns to attack me.

I started to roll my shoulders and wince in pain. Sean saw me doing this and told his rider to go hard, hoping that he would break me. I hung on in the wheels. None of the other riders asked me to do a share of the work at the front of the breakaway, because they were expecting me to explode at any moment. With 25 kilometres to go, that's exactly what happened, but I exploded away off the front rather than going backwards. I launched my attack on Saleen Hill and nobody could follow me. There was no sign of anyone on the back of a motorbike holding out a blackboard with the time gaps between the different groups marked on it, and in fact I never saw one in any break I was ever in. So, to be on the safe side, I just kept riding as hard as I could. With 5 kilometres to go, my dad came alongside me in the hire car to tell me that my lead was slightly more than three minutes. I pressed on and won the race, ahead of Paídi O'Brien and Brian Kenneally. My cousin Nico finished fourth. Near the podium, I bumped into Sean Kelly, who asked me: 'I saw you were in trouble. What happened to you?'

'Sean,' I told him, 'I never felt bad. It was all an act.' I'd managed to trick that master tactician.

We celebrated the shamrock jersey as a family, because the trip to Ireland was a great opportunity to spend a few days with my grandparents in Dublin. We spent an afternoon on the beach at Seapoint, where my grandfather and mother once used to swim almost every day, despite the cold and the currents. A few years earlier, too, I used to collect mussels at low tide, together with my brother Tom, Nico and his sister Christel. That house in Dublin was filled with memories of my cousins. Every time I saw the staircase in the living room, I thought of the little cars that Nico and I used to race between each stair. Neither of us wanted to lose; heaven forbid I reveal the name of the winner. I'd also think back to the day, when I was eleven, that we tried to ride a tandem, with Nico at the front and me as the stoker. I was horrified at not being able to control my direction of travel. Since that day, I've never been on one again.

I was looking forward to racing the Tour of Ireland at the end of August in the national champion's jersey. The race had five stages, starting in Dublin and finishing in Cork, with stopovers in Waterford, Thurles, Loughrea, Ballinrobe, Galway, Limerick, Dingle and Killarney. I set out my plans in Girona, in the Irish pub of course, with Alyssa Morahan, our team's head *soigneur* who had become a confidante and friend. She'd seen the set-up grow from being a junior programme in 2003. Part of her family was Irish, so she naturally took a liking to the 'Irish kid' on the team. 'It's going to be great! You're going to love it,' she said to encourage me. The Tour of Ireland was the penultimate event in a series of stage races that the team wanted to test me in, to toughen me up. I'd done the Tour of Denmark and the Tour of Portugal, while the Tour of Britain lay ahead. It meant I'd be racing thirty stages, in four different countries, over a month and a half. It was my first 'Grand Tour', tailor-made by my team managers. The experience was so vital to my development that I gave up the chance of my first Olympic Games, in Beijing, for which I'd been selected that summer. Unfortunately, due to a nasty stomach bug, my Tour of Ireland lasted only two days. More unfortunately still, I never returned to my national tour. In 2009, I opted to make my debut in the Tour of Spain and, sadly, after that the Irish race was cancelled.

On the Vuelta, which was the first Grand Tour of my career, I discovered some of the secrets that lead to victory:

1. Victory is caught like a fish. You put out the bait, you wait for it to bite, you believe you'll land it. You might have to wait a long time for it. You have to persuade yourself that you're going to catch it, not in a vague 'sooner or later' kind of way, but within a determined time frame, short enough that you can hook the fish at the right moment. A victory may come as a surprise, but it will have been desired, the thought of it nurtured deep within you.
2. Victory is cumulative. The more you win . . . the more you win. The opposite is even more true: if you forget how

to win and, one day, need to have the right reflexes to do so because victory finally beckons, you end up losing your chance.

I didn't win on the 2009 Tour of Spain, but I saw my teammates do so and I learned from them how to get better acquainted with victory.

Tyler Farrar won stage eleven in a sprint. Ryder Hesjedal won the summit finish on the next stage. David Millar won the time trial the day before the final processional stage into Madrid. Each of them had shone very brightly in their own personal domain, but each of these victories was also linked to the others. It's said that you boost your appetite by eating. I believe that each victory made the next one happen. It's not really the result of a desire within a group for emulation, of everyone wanting to be as good as or better than their peers. It's simply down to the fact that victory produces a strong and healthy energy, and we fed on this.

The other winner at that Vuelta, even though he didn't stand on the podium during the race, was Svein Tuft, the man who always rode on the front. For a long time, this Canadian rider had worked in a series of small jobs in order to be able to afford astonishing trips on his own – or with his dog, to be precise. He went to Alaska by sled and to Mexico by bike. Thousands of miles of seeing the world and sleeping under the stars. But he didn't give the impression that he was bored by being in the peloton. For him, the experience was just another of his adventures. He gave his all, often for the benefit of others.

Svein was an inspiration for his strength of character and self-sacrifice. He reminded us that the winner of a bike race is the equivalent of the footballer who puts the ball in the net. But who provided the decisive pass? How did the ball get to him? Tyler's victory, Ryder's victory, and even David's time trial victory belonged to everyone on Team Garmin, including the coaching staff. To the eternal question, 'Is cycling an individual or a team sport?', we gave a clear and unambiguous answer.

I finished that first Vuelta in 53rd place, an hour and twenty-six minutes behind Alejandro Valverde, and it was a great performance. A result is different from a performance, even if we tend to confuse the two. There are a thousand ways to achieve a result. Some places can be won on the cheap; conversely, you can make extraordinary efforts without being rewarded with a good result. I remained faithful to the principles of humility that my elders had taught me: do your best and then we'll see; if you're beaten by someone stronger than you, don't have any regrets.

I got my first stage win in a Grand Tour two years later. It was again at the Vuelta, on 28 August 2011. As time passed, I'd learned to approach victory by drawing on all kinds of strategic insight. That day, I imagined myself as a sprinter. I planned to race like them because they are the cyclists who are best drilled in focusing on a target, in making the best calculations – they've got no room for error, their playing field is barely 300 metres long. The finish was at the summit of La Covatilla, above the town of Béjar. Halfway up the climb, with 6 kilometres to go, Vincenzo Nibali made an attack, but he was reeled back in.

Just after that, I told myself that I had to try. I attacked on the left-hand side of the road. I could see a rider doing the same thing as me over on the right. I turned my head: it was Nico. We pressed on. The aim was to get a bit of a lead on the big favourites. I rode very hard, but at my own pace. It was speed rather than power that now counted.

With 3 kilometres to go, the stage almost became like a Flemish Classic. I was caught. A fearsome crosswind buffeted us. I found shelter next to the barriers, trying to protect myself as best I could. The group of climbers was stretching out, on the verge of breaking apart. We took turns sheltering from the gusts. Echelons were starting to form on this mountain stage. The two Team Sky riders, Bradley Wiggins and Chris Froome, were pushing hard on the pedals. Bauke Mollema's long legs were powering him along, energised by the fact that the Dutchman was set to take the red leader's jersey from Joaquim Rodríguez, who'd been dropped. All I could think about was the arch signalling the final kilometre. That would be my finish line. After that, whatever happened ... That's another trick I learned from the sprinters. The *flamme rouge* marked the start of the victory zone. I controlled my breathing. You had to attack before the last 200 metres, because they were downhill. The first one to make a move would win, unless his legs had turned to cardboard, of course. I attacked. At that very moment, I knew that I'd won my stage on the Vuelta.

I thought about my first Tour of Spain. The victories taken by my friends on the team. That race was one of the ones that gave me the most food for thought. Especially when, with four days to go to Madrid, my teammate Christian Meier was forced to leave the race. Christian was a calm and well-balanced rider who, like Svein Tuft, hailed from Canada, where he'd spent a lot of time on his grandparents' farm. After his career ended, he cultivated his passion for very good coffee by setting up a roastery and a shop with his wife Amber that would become a reference point in Girona. I could sense he was closing up. After the stages, he had an absent look in his eyes in the evenings. For some time, he wouldn't tell me what was bothering him. Then, one day, he explained. His older brother had been having headaches and when he'd gone for tests he'd discovered that he had a brain tumour. He was operated on two days later. His and his family's lives had changed in an instant. In September 2009, his brother had a relapse. His cancer was spreading. He died during the Vuelta. Everything else then became meaningless. Our escapes, our falls, our victories. Christian had a message tattooed on his right forearm in memory of his late brother: 'Last chance'. To remind us that we had to live our lives, that destiny could change from one moment to the next . . .

# Chapter 9

# The Birth of the Panda

I had three parts of my body to fix so I could be a proud member of the Liège–Bastogne–Liège club: my legs, my brain and my nasal septum. The last was definitely the most sensitive challenge to succeed in; I spent several months in consultations with eminent medical professors, from one clinic to another.

I'd finally figured out that my struggles in the spring and especially at the Ardennes races were due to a specific pollen and, after scans, I had discovered that the problem was made worse by a malformation of the septum, the bone and cartilage that separates the nostrils. Due to allergies, these tissues inside my nasal passage increased in size by 150% and slowed my breathing. Initially, I learned to control my breathing through my mouth, but then I was forced to resort to medical intervention. My road to Liège in September 2010 went through London, where I took the opportunity presented by competing in the Tour of Britain to have an MRI scan to assess the gravity of the issue. A few days later, the clinic left messages on my answering machine while I was at the race: 'Mr Martin, you need to come back as soon as possible for a follow-up scan.'

I sighed. I didn't understand why they wanted me to return but, because it might have led to me being able to get rid of these bloody allergies, race like everyone else and finally focus completely on the Classics I loved so much, I called the clinic and went back to London.

The surgery on my septum took place in Girona in November 2010. The operation went well – or at least it did until I sneezed during the night. Around 3 a.m. I began having intense stomach cramps, and relief only came when I started vomiting. This was how I found out that a blood vessel had ruptured in my nose and my body was rejecting the blood that I had unknowingly been 'drinking'. As the sun rose, I was transferred to the operating theatre to stop the bleeding. The procedure proved beneficial; by the following spring I could finally breathe through my nose as well as through my mouth.

In order to be chased by the Panda in 2013 I also had to gain experience. It wasn't a case of love at first sight with La Doyenne, more a relationship that needed time to build. My first appearances in it weren't particularly promising. The initial one was on 1 May 2005 during my first year with the Vélo Club La Pomme Marseille, when I was racing in the under-23 category. As was often the case that season, I was called up as a last-minute replacement. This is what I wrote in my racing diary that day: '40th. Told was riding day before. Outside 5 minutes time limit.' This Espoirs version of La Doyenne extended to 178 kilometres and was more suitable for *rouleurs* and even sprinters who could cope with hills, because the route continued beyond the Côte d'Ans on a long false flat to the finish in a concrete velodrome. My Moldovan teammate Ruslan Sambris managed to take third place. The winning breakaway went clear soon after the start, with around thirty riders in it. I reached the velodrome, but the commissaires didn't classify me because I was outside the time limit.

The race started in Bastogne, which lies at the halfway point in the professional edition. We slept there the night before the start. The pasta served for breakfast was so inedible that I slathered it with apricot jam. I did at least get my fill of sugar . . . Before signing in at the start podium, in Bastogne's main square I came across a bizarre US tank painted with a big white star. I read somewhere that the machine was a relic from the Second World War. Stuck in a swamp, it had been shelled by German artillery during the Battle of the Bulge in the winter of 1944–45. Its five occupants were captured. When the war ended, the tank was set to be sold to scrap dealers, but the farmer who owned the field where it had been abandoned objected, fearing that dismantling the wreck would cause oil leaks and pollute the soil. As a consequence, this war memorial was transferred to the town centre, to become what is effectively a museum piece. I've seen no end of riders climbing onto the front of it to pose for a photo.

I returned to La Doyenne three years later. This time I was racing the full 261-kilometre route, in the professional peloton, the race part of the Pro Tour calendar. There wasn't a panda, but Alejandro Valverde was already there. He pulverised Davide Rebellin and Fränk Schleck, his two breakaway companions, in the sprint. As for me, I felt the after-effects of my crash at the

Flèche Wallonne four days earlier. My left index finger hurt. Each time I hit a hole in the road, the vibrations increased the pain. I opted to stop. That performance is another that's disappeared from some internet archives, but I can confirm that I was at the start of that edition of Liège–Bastogne–Liège and that I didn't make it to the finish. I abandoned the race at the top of the Côte de la Haute-Levée, 60 kilometres from home.

I did manage to cross the finish line in my next two appearances, in 2009 and 2010. On the first occasion, I came in 98th, eleven minutes and five seconds behind winner Andy Schleck, and on the second I was 56th, seven minutes and five seconds down on Alexandre Vinokourov. It may not really appear like it, but I was making progress. Every minute you avoid losing contact with the peloton, every kilometre gained, is a small victory. I was getting to know the traps that needed to be sidestepped. Liège is full of them. I've read lots of magazines that dwell on the charms and challenges of Paris–Roubaix and the Tour of Flanders, but nothing of the same ilk on Liège–Bastogne–Liège. However, a race doesn't need cobbles to be epic. Liège is an art form.

For example, in Bastogne you either give up or move up. At this point, there are 150 kilometres to go. My secret was to skip the 'feed'. Grabbing a musette handed to me by one of our *soigneurs* was useless because I wouldn't eat at least half of the food in it. I rode with six energy bars in my pockets, one for each hour of racing. The 'feed' is a dangerous zone. Riders who are grasping for musettes can end up crashing. I took advantage of this to move up the peloton. This was a useful manoeuvre before reaching the 'wall' at Saint-Roch, where the

Luxembourg fans always give us quite a fanfare. The climb is short and very steep, and you're brought almost to a standstill. If you're at the back of the pack, you're forced to put a foot down and wait for the first riders to reach the top. As a result, I preferred to be among the frontrunners, as it also gave me the opportunity for one last pee stop just over the top when the peleton was in one long line.

You have to be aware of absolutely everything during La Doyenne. A descent or a flat section in the valleys can cause more problems than a climb. On the ascent of the Côte de Wanne, I stayed in the first eight places in order to be in the best position to negotiate the descent that follows. It's a fearsome downhill, one where there are often crashes and the air is heavy with the scent of stress. You're often in the same position on the next climb, the Côte de Stockeu, as you were cresting and coming down the Côte de Wanne. There's a memorial paying tribute to Eddy Merckx at the Stockeu's summit. Beyond it, there's not as much pressure on the next climbs, although you can't allow your concentration to wander. You cross off the Haute-Levée, Col du Rosier, Côte du Maquisard, Côte de Theux, before attacking the mythical La Redoute . . .

My first memories of cycling were definitely forged on this ribbon of tarmac that runs up a grassy hillside. The road, 1.7 kilometres long, offers no respite in its gradient, even on the bends. The Côte de La Redoute, a vertical monster, follows a brutally straight line. Sitting in front of my TV in Birmingham in 1999, I watched Michele Bartoli sprint up it, as Frank Vandenbroucke challenged him to a duel, his hands down on the drops.

VDB pushed an incredible gear up that hill where the gradient reaches 14 per cent, using a colossal 53-tooth big ring. I always rode a much more modest gear of 39x28.

As a rider, I discovered that the very fast descent towards La Redoute was as crucial as the climb. It's tackled at 80km/h and it's essential to be towards the front of the peloton. Getting the balance right is difficult: if you're too close to the front of the peloton, you're in the wind too much and end up expending too much energy; if you're just a little bit too far back, you'll never be able to move up and will get caught behind gaps that are impossible to bridge across when you're climbing La Redoute. You're only ever five places away from defeat.

You have to have suffered over the 260 kilometres to understand them. You have to have climbed in slow motion, wobbling, reeling, in distress, in order to get the chance to analyse every bit of tarmac. The road engraves itself into the human body. I have the map of Liège–Bastogne–Liège tattooed on me from head to toe.

After abandoning in 2011, following a crash in Flèche Wallonne – history has a slight tendency to repeat itself – I discovered the key to Liège–Bastogne–Liège in 2012. On my fifth appearance, I took fifth place. Rain soaked the roads after Bastogne. Our legs felt like lead. It took us half an hour longer to reach the finish compared to the previous edition. I kept arm-warmers on to ward off the chill. Nobody seemed able to make a telling acceleration. On La Roche-aux-Faucons, the climb that follows La Redoute, Vincenzo Nibali edged rather than romped away, followed by Maxim Iglinskiy. Then Joaquim Rodríguez went on the counter-attack. With 5 kilometres to go, I made a move on the Côte de Saint-Nicolas. I bridged across to Rodríguez. But Iglinskiy was still in front of us, and he would go on to catch and drop Nibali shortly before the kilometre-to-go banner. That left us and a few others fighting for the third step on the podium.

At that point I had more than six hours of racing in the legs, but I could still cope with this very unusual effort's size, thanks to my dedicated training. I had sought to develop my *puncheur*'s skills; although I had a better sprint than other riders of the same build as me, these skills are anything but natural. I had a last big rehearsal two weeks ahead of the Ardennes Classics, with one session generating more than 5,000 kilojoules, equivalent to the energy expenditure on a long day like the Doyenne. The plan was to ride four hours at steady yet hard tempo, at the same kind of pace as the peloton chasing a breakaway, then to increase my power for an hour and a half, as though I was fighting in the final part of the race, between La Redoute and the Côte d'Ans. I was riding in the slipstream of a motorbike driven by my dad on a short circuit I had designed close to Girona with multiple short climbs. My goal: to defeat the motorbike. We continued to lap until I couldn't pedal any more, and then added in one final hill sprint. This was true mind over matter, mental preparation to ignore your muscles' requests for mercy, to prepare for the race-winning efforts required in the hardest of all one-day races . . .

*

This special day was the very last layer of varnish on a long-term programme that I followed on and off the bike, including in winter, visiting the gym three times a week. My coach, Adrie van Diemen, a Dutch sports scientist who had worked with three-times Tour de France winner Greg LeMond two decades prior, designed this special '*Puncheur* Program' that requires you to do squats (30 repetitions in 35 seconds, 30 seconds' break, to repeat 12 times) and leg-press the same – on each leg. It was a huge amount of work that left me almost unable to walk home, but it trained my body to tolerate high amounts of lactic acid and to recover from effort quickly. Even if my body was full of toxins, it could just keep repeating high-power efforts. I don't think the gym's other customers appreciated David Millar and me hogging the workout stations for so long; sessions often took longer than an hour. Our post-gym ride would be at a snail's pace. But I understood the process, and I was feeling more and more ready for Liège.

Finally, here it was: the Côte d'Ans. We were on what would become the most crucial section of road for my career. I negotiated the last part of the climb, the bit that would become the 'Panda Zone' the following year, without any worries. A sign indicated that 400 metres remained. I tried to control my shoulders, which had a tendency to move as fast as my legs. I concentrated on Liège–Bastogne–Liège's final trap, a point on the course that I've always been wary of, despite its innocent looks: the bend with 200 metres to go. I wanted to go into it in first position because I knew that the sprint would be between riders who were on their knees. Due to fatigue, the group of ten or so would all sprint at the same speed. Leading into the bend would give you an advantage. Ultimately, though, I was passed by Enrico Gasparotto and Thomas Voeckler. Third in the sprint, I finished fifth on the day, thirty-six seconds behind the winner.

I had learned that I was capable of winning this race. I would be more than ready for the 2013 edition. I would win – and meet the Panda.

# Chapter 10

# The Bells, the Bells (The Fear of Being Late)

The Giro di Lombardia's route runs along the languid, deep lakes of northern Italy. It is held at the beginning of October in the slightly damp autumn atmosphere and under the pale, bronze autumn light, and at first I believed it was the gentle 'Race of the Falling Leaves' its nickname suggests, an end-of-the-year Classic. That was until I saw the mattresses hastily placed against the rock faces on the exit of the corners, on the off chance that a rider would make a mistake. A mattress is much softer than a sheer granite cliff face! Seeing the protective measures that the organisation was not obliged to make, yet felt necessary, sent a shiver down my spine; you could get seriously injured on these narrow, twisting mountain roads.

In 2009, my second pro season, I launched an attack at the highest point of the Giro di Lombardia, here on the Ghisallo where the gradient reaches 14 per cent. When the peloton slowed down on the approach to the summit, I accelerated with all I had. The *tifosi* didn't know who I was but that was irrelevant; they went wild. I had drawn a finish line at the top of the climb, the Madonna del Ghisallo, one of the most iconic places in the cycling world. I could see this church getting closer on the left side of the road. The bells were already ringing, the chimes deafening above the roar of the crowd; this is an annual ritual, a celebration of Italian cycling. At that moment I felt part of something bigger than me.

The descent towards Como intimidated me: this was where I had seen the mattresses. But I didn't have time to fall, or even to lose concentration for a moment. I was joined by a group of that era's great riders – Cadel Evans, Ivan Basso, Damiano Cunego, Alexandre Vinokourov, Chris Horner. By the end of their careers, they had won one Tour, three Giros and two Vueltas between them. We were racing for fourth place and finished eight seconds behind the winner, Belgium's Philippe Gilbert, my future teammate. I was eighth. The Giro di Lombardia was my first promising experience at a 'Monument'. This was one of my favourite Classics alongside Liège–Bastogne–Liège and Flèche Wallonne, one of the very few that suits climbers, and a race where I could truly show my potential, years before I achieved anything in Liège.

The year after, in 2010, I was taken out by a crash, not on the descent of Ghisallo, but about 20 kilometres beforehand as we raced into the town of Lecco. According to my speedometer, at the moment it happened I was travelling at 68km/h. I thought I was safe, sitting in around 100th place in the peloton, but then some riders right up front crashed. The rain and a patch of diesel – or maybe it was those fallen leaves – meant all it took was one slight pull on my brakes for me to join them; my wheels lost traction in an instant, throwing me to the ground. I closed my eyes. When I opened them again, time had slowed down. I even had the thought, 'Wow, I've been sliding for a while.' I could see a retaining wall getting closer, closer ... I used my foot to kick off the wall in an attempt not to hit it at full force.

Apparently, I slid for more than a hundred metres. And my bike completed a little sojourn of its own. It took me a couple of minutes to retrieve it from its resting place as cars in the convoy passed by and spectators with umbrellas offered me their help. I should have listened to the rider who had told me at the top of the Colle di Balisio: 'I'm stopping here, I'm not going down to Lecco, the road's too slippery, it's stupid to continue.' But, in the dampness of October, the Giro di Lombardia inevitably exposes us to risk.

The following year I finished second and I tried my luck again at the Ghisallo climb. Climbing the queen ascent of the race, I felt like I was stuck to the road. But my cousin Nico came up and encouraged me. He knew every centimetre of the course, because he lived in the area, near Varese. 'Come on, Dan! You're doing great! You can win today!' Those few words lifted me. They have to be said by someone else for you to believe them. I changed down a gear and got out of the saddle.

The bells were ringing. I didn't attack but I was in a good position in the peloton when I reached the Madonna del Ghisallo. The roadbook said this church – more a chapel in size – was built in the 17th century by a nobleman who wanted to give thanks for being protected from attacks by brigands. Or so says a local legend. What is sure is that it was later consecrated by the Pope as the 'Church of cyclists' after the Second World War. Fausto Coppi and Gino Bartali led a procession to the climb on that occasion. Nowadays, the Ghisallo is one of the most sacred places in cycling, along with the Arenberg Forest in Paris–Roubaix, the Koppenberg in the Tour of Flanders and La Redoute in Liège–Bastogne–Liège.

I would add to my personal list the Ty-Marrec (meaning 'The House of the Marrec Family' in Breton), the 1.6-kilometre hill that rises dead straight at a fairly steady gradient and often proves decisive in the Grand Prix de Plouay, the first Classic I almost won, back in August 2010. Having broken away on its slopes, I was caught on the descent back towards the finish. I'd also include the Kogashi climb, hidden in the Japanese cedars, a forest road that enabled me to win the Japan Cup in 2010. But the Ghisallo climb is undoubtedly the most illustrious because, literally and, thanks to its church, figuratively, it's a genuine place of cycling pilgrimage.

My cousin was almost right: I almost won. At the finish, I beat Ivan Basso and Joaquim Rodríguez in a sprint to the line, but it was for second place. A relatively unknown Swiss rider by the name of Oliver Zaugg had attacked with 10 kilometres to go and we had not managed to catch him. He'd employed the perfect tactic for an outsider. You hide in the group, make everyone forget you, and then . . .

In 2014 I finally found an opening. The mouse-hole. The precise second when I could sneak away. The Ghisallo was far too far from the finish, course changes meaning it was now in the early stages of the race. No one was able to break away as the race came to a conclusion. I hung on to the group of favourites, biding my time, but the closer we got to the finish in Bergamo, the more I started to think about the sprint that was inevitably coming. With 4 kilometres remaining, we went through the Porta Garibaldi, one of the historic entrances into Bergamo, an archway with two wooden gates that lead into the Città Alta, the upper town. A right-angled turn took us onto the last climb, the Boccola, a 600-metre-long alleyway, not super-steep but paved with round cobblestones. The crowds packing it made it even narrower, meaning we were riding in single file. Philippe Gilbert was the only one able to attack, but he couldn't open up a gap.

At the top, the race was still in the balance. There was just a descent to the lower part of the city. The problem? There were still nine of us in the group. I moved to the back to observe my opponents. There was Alejandro Valverde, my regular 'enemy', Joaquim Rodríguez and Philippe Gilbert, both double winners of the race, and the speedy Michael Albasini. The other riders who also had to be watched carefully were Samuel Sánchez, who had finished on the Giro di Lombardia podium three times, Fabio Aru, Rui Costa and Tim Wellens. We all knew that the rider who managed to lead into the final right-hand turn, just 200 metres from the finish line, had a good chance of winning. We all had the same tactic. But it's easier said than done.

Suddenly, with 600 metres to go, Gilbert, who was at the

very front of the group, ceased his effort and the pace slowed as the game of poker began. I was on the back of the group and, as soon as I felt the speed drop, I launched my attack on the right-hand side of the road. Gilbert swung across in front of me, but I saw my gap, the narrowest of corridors between the Belgian and the barriers. He had realised what was happening, but was sporting enough not to block me completely. Coming from the back, I had surprise on my side and my speed carried me away from my rivals. Valverde looked at the others, obviously hoping that they would come after me. The others looked at Valverde. Not a moment of hesitation; I never looked back once. Last corner. I didn't care if they were right behind me; I had achieved my first goal of leading into the final turn! I went through it in slow motion and sprinted out with every ounce of force I had left. They'd lost. The final straight was bathed in blinding light, so white that it stung your eyes and turned the riders into ghosts. I'd won Lombardy.

The 'coming from behind' tactic looked to be a very good one and, after my successful experience in Italy, I tried to race in the same style at the Flèche Wallonne.

The 'Flèche' was definitely the race that demanded the most suffering; the final ascent of the Mur de Huy would set our legs ablaze. It has to do with its exceptional statistics. It's only 1.3km long but has an average gradient of 9.8 per cent and a peak of 26 per cent. We barely find a worse gradient all season, except when the Giro or Vuelta organisers discover some unexplored mule-track and add it to the route. All you have to do on a mountain stage is slow down and the pain goes away; but at the Mur de Huy, the unrelenting incline compelled us to push without the slightest let-up. We knew the ritual, that once a year we would be eaten up by lactic acid, to the point where we couldn't even pedal a metre beyond the line and the only thing that would stop us from falling was a member of the race organisation jumping out to grab us and push us further up the road to the waiting *soigneurs*.

This is another one of my favourite Classics that is held in a holy place; the climb, which on maps is described as the Chemin des Chapelles, is a calvary – a way of the cross – and you can easily count the little white-fronted chapels as you ascend it, in much the same way as how I would count the riders I'd passed and those who were still ahead of me . . .

Here was my typical race in the Mur de Huy: a furious chase on the longest kilometre of the season. I never planned to be 'poorly' positioned, at the foot of the wall, I was simply racing the climb rather than my competitors. I'd made it my strategy to pace my effort to perfection. But now I had to get past the fifteen or so riders in front of me, lined out almost one behind the next, like a tiring reptile struggling to maintain its pace. There was a gap of more than 20 metres between the leading rider and me. That gap had enormous significance on the Mur de Huy. I moved up, and up. Only twelve riders were still ahead of me. A bend to the right, the gradient got even more acute. Only nine riders left.

Just as the feeling of being overtaken is terrifying, the feeling of overtaking other riders fills you with energy, joy, pride and rage. We reached the monstrous 26 per cent bend – if you take it on the inside of the corner. Only five more ahead of me. The false flat that follows it actually does look flat on TV, but it fully lives up to its description: the gradient reaches 10 per cent. This makes it a difficult test for the head and legs; you may go into it thinking you might be able to catch your breath but, on the contrary, you find yourself in a state of apnoea, your breathing suspended for the final sprint as if you're underwater.

I pushed even harder when I heard the cries of 'Go Dan!' and saw some green, white and orange flags hung from barriers. Thanks to the magic of low-cost airlines, a hundred Irish fans flew from Dublin to Charleroi every April to enjoy the beer and cycling. They carried me beyond what they could imagine in that body-burning climb. My final efforts were a way of thanking them.

Only four riders were left. Two hundred metres to the line. We were no longer riding in straight lines. We looked like drunks on bikes. Only two left. Would I do it?

Too late. When I crossed the line there were two riders ahead of me. Not quite good enough.

My 'coming from behind' tactic was not working at the Flèche Wallonne and I could see my Garmin *directeurs sportifs* lost for words. My decision was in opposition to what they used to constantly tell us in our earpieces: 'Move up! Move up!' This is one of the most recurrent phrases a rider hears. There's an old rule that has it that you have to ride towards the very front of the peloton all day, because if there's a crash and the bunch splits, you are in the right half. You won't lose any time. What's more, the riders at the back end of the peloton are tired, lack lucidity and are, therefore, more prone to crashing.

But cycling had changed and now there were lots of crashes at the front of the peloton. Why was this? Because we kept hearing, 'Move up! Move up!' Every rider on every team was encouraged to stay in the leading positions. That meant 150 riders were fighting for twenty places.

I even heard this nagging order at the Tour of Gabon as we rode through rainforests on the equator. That was in January 2006, when I was still wearing the jersey of the Vélo Club La Pomme. In Africa, everything was so different from what we'd experienced on European roads – except for the orders delivered via the earpiece. Our *directeur sportif* was Alain Santy, once a French cycling talent and winner of the Critérium du Dauphiné in 1974. Alain was an 'old-fashioned' guy. He smoked as he drove the team car, said little, but wanted to be obeyed. From his car, he would watch to see if we were moving up. The peloton consisted of a hundred riders at the most, and they rode without ever overdoing things. Unless we were preparing for a sprint, I avoided wasting my physical and nervous energy by trying to hang on in the first twenty places. As a punishment, Alain decided to withhold 1,000 euros of the prize money I was owed thanks to our results; the price that I had to pay for not 'moving up'.

In reality, the moment always comes in a race when you have to 'move up'. At Flèche Wallonne, I was in around 30th place when we entered the final 20 kilometres and was about 20th when we passed beneath the inflatable arch indicating 5 kilometres to go. The peloton was stretched out on the rising false flats that precede the Mur de Huy, on the verge of snapping like a rubber band. I didn't want to be caught out by any splits, behind any gaps left by tired riders, so I started to move up. On the Mur, I kept on advancing. Until the final sprint, when I died going for second or third place behind the winner. That's when I thought: 'Shit! Valverde again!'

Alejandro Valverde was my nemesis during the Classics and even the Volta a Catalunya. He often beat me, but I did manage to turn the tables on him occasionally. The Spaniard, from Murcia, brought with him a lot of experience. He had turned professional in 2002, at a time when I only rode two or three times a year, in the Alps or the Pyrenees during the summer holidays. He won a Tour stage in 2005, my first year with the Vélo Club La Pomme. He was still a fixture in the peloton when I retired.

Alejandro was, of course, implicated in the Operation Puerto doping affair and was suspended as a consequence. He subsequently returned and resumed his career. We talked from time to time, in a mixture of Spanish and English, but often there was no need to talk to him. I would watch him moving around the peloton. He would hide away and then come up at the right moment, not too early, not too late. He didn't fight for position in an aggressive way because a clear path always seemed to open up in front of him. Was this privilege due to his *palmarès* and his age? I wasn't overawed by him when I had to take him on, because I felt I was a match for any of my rivals when at my best, but Valverde was able to cope perfectly with the tempo of the Classics, and it was worthwhile observing him to learn just how he managed it. His team took control of the peloton a long way from the finish. When he attacked, it would be in the final kilometre, or even the last 200 metres. I used to attack after he did, but by then I was already beaten.

Some of my *directeurs sportifs* and teammates, and journalists, would say to me after watching the race on TV: 'If you hadn't been in 12th position at the *flamme rouge*, you would have won.' They'd calculated that I'd climbed the Mur de Huy faster than anyone. But you can't apply mathematics to racing quite so simply. If I'd been in third place at the foot of the Mur, I might have finished fifth at the top, because I would have exploded as I tried to take flight on its steep ramps, weakened by all the efforts accumulated in the shadows, simply to be well positioned. I'd respond by saying jokingly that I'd rather be well placed at the finish line than before.

This choice resulted in me missing out on some victories, but it enabled me to capture others. It was also one of the keys to my peace of mind. And I even replicated this tactic in the one race where everyone has to 'Move up, move up!' – the Tour de France. Between 2015 and 2021, I rode the Tour like a naughty schoolboy sitting at the back of the classroom. I got up only when it was time to go up to the blackboard: when the race was really on.

# Chapter 11

# In the Tour de France Whirlwind (The Fear of Becoming Obsessed)

I wasn't born with the usual all-consuming and overwhelming dreams about the Tour de France. I was certainly helped in this by Stephen. Having an uncle who has won the Tour makes cycling's Holy Grail less of a pull. I've spent a few Christmas dinners sitting opposite the former yellow jersey winner as he's eaten his roast turkey and, as far as I can remember, he seems like an ordinary man. So, I never imagined myself winning the Tour de France, even in my childhood or teenage dreams. But I also never imagined that the mountain was too high to climb. I knew I'd go to the Tour one day, and that was all there was to it.

This respectful but bold view isn't very widespread in the cycling world. In the minds of the public, sponsors and team managers, there are two categories of riders: those who race the Tour and those who don't. Unfair as it is, the second category suffer from a lack of respect. Jonathan Vaughters had recruited me to be part of the first category. Unfortunately, I was afraid that he would change his mind during the spring of 2010, after my first Giro. The results were mixed. On the one hand, I finished 57th in the overall classification, which was won by Ivan Basso. On the other, I was ninth on the Monte Zoncolan stage, a magnificently absurd mountain, where the contest isn't with other riders but is all about trying to avoid falling over – to do which, all you can do is pedal, even when the incline seems to be at right angles. Our *directeur sportif,* Matt White, said to me after the race had finished: 'You're not that good on a Grand Tour, it's a shame.' Thanks for the encouragement! I could have offered lots of explanations and even some excuses, but I didn't try. That could lead to a dangerous problem for a young professional: if a twenty-three-year-old rider falls out of favour, their career can end very quickly.

The funny thing is that I almost lined up in my first Tour de France the year before that Giro d'Italia. The 2009 race started in Monaco, followed the Mediterranean westwards, passed through Girona on its way to Barcelona, climbed into Andorra and effectively ended on the Ventoux, the day before the processional finale on the Champs-Elysées. Just two weeks beforehand, I got a pain in my right knee. Initially, I didn't give it much thought. It felt a little bit warm, as was sometimes the case when I came back from training, but in those cases it would be gone the next day. On this occasion, however, the inflammation was still there. Everything pointed to my having tendinitis for the first time in my career; but I was in denial. The osteopath recommended that I take two or three days off. The next day, the team was going to do a recon of the Tour stage between Barcelona and Arcalis, in Andorra. I really wanted to ride the six hours it would take to see the route, and so I did it, putting more strain on my kneecap than I should have. After that, we did some training for the team time trial in Montpellier. The team managers left the decision in my hands: 'It's up to you whether to ride the Tour or not. You can call a halt at any moment.' I confirmed that I felt ready, especially as the pain was starting to subside.

With three days left before the start, I had to face the facts. After a final training session in the Monaco region, I at last understood that the tendinitis wasn't going to disappear in the short term. I think that, strictly from a medical point of view, a doctor could have given me the green light to start. The pain was easing and I could certainly have dealt with it. Naturally, I would have done so without any medication. Except that I didn't just want to 'do' the Tour: I was really determined to 'do something'. This ambition presupposes that the body is in perfect working order. I was afraid of being disappointed and of disappointing my teammates. I made my decision known to our *directeurs sportifs* and was replaced by one of our cobbled Classics specialists, Dutchman Martijn Maaskant.

Two days later, I pulled on a backpack and attended the Tour prologue on the Formula 1 circuit in Monte Carlo. I stood in the middle of the crowds, just another spectator. But I didn't regret not being on the riders' side of the barriers. I trusted fate. Once again, it was with me, it was helping me. It wasn't keeping me away from the Tour. It was telling me that I wasn't ready, that I still had to gain experience at the Vuelta and Giro before committing to the contest for the yellow jersey.

I waited and waited . . . Three years passed before my baptism of fire. In 2010, I was sent to the Giro. The team's management felt that it was better for me to tackle the *strade bianche* rather than the cobbles that featured on the Tour route. In 2011, I was sent to the Vuelta a España because the Tour route included a team time trial, and I ended up claiming my first Grand Tour stage win on the Spanish roads. Matt White's judgement no longer weighed on me. It was now clear that I would be riding the Tour sooner rather than later. I thought I was on the right track in 2012, but there was one last test beforehand. It had been confirmed that I would be lining up at the Tour, but in the Critérium du Dauphiné in June, that beautiful race that's viewed as perfect preparation for July's big rendezvous, I suffered a violent crash. I went down coming out of a roundabout at 60km/h on the second stage. My head hit the ground and my helmet split in two. I was dazed for a good while but I got back on the bike again and finished sixteen minutes behind the winner, guided in by Sep Vanmarcke. I was sorry that I had caused Simon Gerrans to crash and apologised to him the next day. Worse still, though, I had an intense pain in my shoulder. X-rays at the local hospital had revealed that there was no fracture. The pain was apparently muscular in origin. But what pain it was!

I expected the team to send me home to recuperate. But

Jonathan Vaughters didn't think this was the best course of action. He reckoned that I absolutely had to finish the Dauphiné in order to maintain my physical condition. The order was implacable: no Dauphiné means no Tour. I accepted these orders without suspecting that, three years later, the situation would be repeated and cause real torment. I kept on racing, gritting my teeth. My shoulder was so sore that I could barely grip the handlebars. I had to change gear on my right brake shifter using my left hand. I couldn't eat or drink on the move. I held on for five stages, in the mountains and across the plains, and even in a 53-kilometre individual time trial. One day, I enjoyed the little luxury of a sprint to finish 17th. The team seemed satisfied. When they spoke to me, it felt like they were offering me a nice Christmas present. 'It's OK, in three weeks you'll be at the Tour de France,' they told me.

That year, the Tour route went over the Col du Glandon, the summit where I'd won the Tour de Pays de Savoie in the under-23 category, as well as the Col du Tourmalet, the mountain that had marked my teenage years. The icing on the rice cake: it started in Liège, where, thanks to my own leanings as a racer, I always felt at home. At the start of the prologue in Belgium, my shoulder pain had disappeared, but my legs lacked power. The team had designated Ryder Hesjedal and Christian Vande Velde as leaders, while I had a free role. I was aiming for a stage win and also had an eye on the polka-dot jersey of best climber. Unfortunately, I caught a cold and a cough that developed into bronchitis, and the antibiotics I was taking to fight my bronchial infection diminished my abilities. Despite this, I managed to produce an encouraging performance on a stage in the Alps, joining a breakaway of twenty-odd riders on the slopes of the Madeleine. I was one of the seven survivors from that group on the next pass, the Glandon, which was closely followed by the short climb to the Croix de Fer pass. Although I eventually finished fourteen minutes down that day, it was a promising sign.

Six days later, I would be crossing the Tourmalet and then the Col de l'Aspin, the same duo that I had first encountered that summer when I was sixteen years old and later on, at the Route du Sud in 2008. We also climbed the Aubisque at the beginning of the stage and Peyresourde to finish, before diving into Bagnères-de-Luchon. I was eager for the Tourmalet. This time he whispered to me, so that no one else in the peloton could hear: 'Launch an attack and have fun!!' So, I attacked. My lungs were still affected by the infection and, combined with the altitude, it meant my breathing got steadily more and more laboured. I was revisiting my summer of fire, the torrent tumbling down the middle of the pass, the rocks standing sentinel on either side, the village of Barèges . . .

I was accompanied by two Frenchmen, Brice Feillu and the public's favourite, Thomas Voeckler. I looked up at the summit with 3 kilometres to go, and then apologised to the Col du Tourmalet. 'I can't give any more,' I confessed to him. I tried to delay my inevitable defeat. Each time I took my turn on the front of the breakaway, the speed dropped. Feillu and Voeckler didn't wait for me. I finished seventh that day. The next day, I finished 10th on the Col de Peyresourde, which we climbed a second time, on that occasion from the other side. The Pyrenees had saved my honour on my Tour de France debut. A few breakaways, three top ten stage finishes and a 35th place in the overall classification, an hour and twenty-five minutes behind my former teammate Bradley Wiggins. Team Sky's domination of the quest for the yellow jersey had begun. Journalists were telling the story of how this small cycling nation had become powerful, how this team of pursuiters, who were unbeatable on the track, had managed to conquer the road. According to several articles, Dave Brailsford, Sky's general manager, had 'succeeded in his gamble'.

To be honest, I didn't enjoy my first Tour de France. The only moment of brightness during three weeks of darkness was the stage win clinched by my friend David Millar. David had beaten his breakaway companion the day after the Glandon stage. I was as happy as if I'd won myself. For the rest of the time, I felt like I was just going through the motions, day after day. I wasn't mentally prepared.

That year, the race had begun on the narrow and very fast roads of northern France, and as a result the peloton featured lots of Classics specialists, riders who were perfectly at ease in sprints, echelons, and the team time trial. They had Tour experience and were 20 kilos heavier than me. They could knock me aside with just a nudge from one shoulder. So I had to fight for position incessantly. The French use the word *frotter* to describe this shoulder-to-shoulder contest, literally 'rubbing', and I found it an unwanted moment of intimacy with the riders around me. There's an awful lot of jostling at

60km/h, but, miraculously, you don't often crash. When the rider to the right put his shoulder against mine, I could almost hear his heartbeat. The rider behind me would be so close that he'd plant his brake and gear levers in my buttocks. There's not enough air around you to breathe. The craziest riders try to move up the pack through what are effectively mouse-holes. The lower, narrower part of the bike – the frame, the wheels – can be squeezed through, but up above the handlebars scrape the riders on either side. That's when accidents happen.

According to a count conducted by veteran German rider Jens Voigt, who rode around the buses at the end of the race, between 65 and 70 per cent of the peloton fell at least once in that 2012 edition of the Tour de France. The most spectacular crash occurred on stage six, when around sixty guys hit the tarmac at 70km/h on a slight descent. I was very lucky to be at the back of the race at that moment, picking up water bottles for my teammates. I was about to rejoin the peloton when I heard a terrible noise, a combination of the clash of metal and the cries of stricken riders. I braked so hard that I almost tore the rubber pads off the calipers. By some miracle, I stopped a centimetre short of the crash. I avoided all of the pitfalls over the race's 3,494 kilometres, but I emerged from each stage exhausted, as if I'd spent the day being shaken in a washing machine. My nerves were shattered and I couldn't find any pleasure in that. I was hoping things would change on the 2013 Tour. It started in Corsica and included some pretty big climbs on the second day. I figured that would inevitably take a physical toll on the big *rouleurs* and the number of crashes should drop.

I finally managed to find the opening I'd been looking for at the Tour de France on the ninth stage, between Saint-Girons and Bagnères-de-Bigorre. * On 7 July 2013, I was the first rider to cross the line and was overwhelmed by a frisson of joy; but what's more, that moment of delight was the culmination of a great day of attacks, doubts, exultation and what was to be a wholesale change in status, a day that gripped fans sitting on their sofas in front of the TV. I was back in the Pyrenees, although the Tourmalet didn't feature among the five climbs we tackled over 168 kilometres. On the menu instead were the Col du Portet d'Aspet, Menté, Peyresourde, Col d'Azet and the Hourquette d'Ancizan. Robby Ketchell, our director of sport science and a data specialist, had pulled the route apart using multiple algorithms. He was positive that the breakaway would go to the finish that day and that the candidates for the yellow jersey wouldn't contest the stage win. Robby, who two years later would place his skills at the service of Team Sky, encouraged us to put his theories to the test that day. The science told us it was possible. We could derail the Sky train.

We tried something that was unlikely to work: attacking as a team. But it did work! After 5 kilometres, we heard that Jack Bauer and David Millar were at the front together, with a thirty-second lead. I bridged up to them on the first pass. Ramunas

---

* On 18 June 2013 the Tourmalet was the scene of torrential flooding. The village of Barèges was partially destroyed and the Argelès-Gazost and Lourdes valleys flooded. At the foot of the Col du Menté, the Garonne also overflowed and caused significant damage. We therefore decided to donate all the financial gains made on the Bagnères-de-Bigorre stage to help the rebuilding of the affected areas.

Navardauskas and Andrew Talansky were also with me. Our team outnumbered the others. Staggeringly, Chris Froome, the yellow jersey wasn't there. Ideas were running through my head. I could see myself contributing to a small moment in history, the defeat of Team Sky and the overall classification being played out a long way from the stage finish. I saw myself as part of a wave that was breaking. We could do something incredibly exciting, the likes of which the Tour hadn't seen for many years. At that time in cycling history, the team of the main favourite captured the yellow jersey and never lost it, crushing the race with its powerful lead out on every stage. It was only in 2020, thanks to Tadej Pogačar, that the now common form of open aggressive racing began.

I was the second rider over the top of the Col du Portet d'Aspet and Tom Danielson was third. My American teammate took the lead on the next pass, then Ryder Hesjedal went to the front and got into a breakaway. Chris Froome had managed to get back to the front of the race but our aggressive tactics provoked considerable damage. Our opponents' heads were bobbing with fatigue and they gasped for air, their mouths hanging open. Their eyes widened when they looked at us, as if to say, 'What on earth are you doing?' In truth, the pain in our legs hit us as much as it did everyone else, because of the tempo we'd set for everyone. But I was able to cope with it because I was on fire. My teammates were working brutally hard and I had to reward them by sealing the final verdict. I knew that there would be an opening on the last climb. The favourites were weakened, confused and mostly without their teammates. So, I sneaked into a mouse-hole of my own with 35 kilometres remaining. Chris Froome was watching Nairo Quintana, who had just made a small attack. As they watched each other, their pace dropped. I took the opportunity to go up to the right-hand side of the road, almost in the grass, brushing past the rider next to me as I accelerated. Nobody followed. Then the Dane Jakob Fuglsang joined me. We were 4 kilometres from the summit of the Hourquette d'Ancizan. There were 35 left to the finish. Our fate would be decided on the long descent.

We had a minute in hand as we passed a remote stone hut in a field on the right; it's a legendary location, the forge where in 1913 Eugène Christophe had to carry out his own repairs on his bike after his front fork broke on the Tourmalet. Forty seconds. Thirty seconds. With 10 kilometres to go, we had twenty-five. We were dropping at around 70km/h. The TV bike, which wanted to film us up close, took us into its wake. Our pursuers were helped by the second TV bike and they had the two cars right behind us in their sights, a yellow neutral service vehicle and a red race organisation car. For once, this duel behind the bikes was fair. The proximity of these two motorbikes increased both our speed and the chasers'. The gentle descent passed quickly, the wind whistling around us. We entered Bagnères-de-Bigorre. I took the last bend in the lead, 150 metres from the line. I'd studied the route before the start. This was the kind of turn that decides the winner. Fuglsang had allowed me to go through it in first position. That was it, I'd won. I raised my arms to the sky.

Coming down from the presentation podium, I met David

Millar and Jack Bauer, who had just come across the line in the *gruppetto*. 'Dan, what are you doing here? That means . . .' They jumped into my arms and we hugged each other in delight. They'd almost been eliminated, having put themselves on the line at the beginning of the stage for me.

The memory of my teammates sharing my happiness and sacrificing so much will give me goosebumps for ever. We did it. Our team drove a wedge into what was seemingly the Tour de France's impregnable force. For a few minutes we had threatened to topple Team Sky, who had dominated the event since 2012.

That day, Chris Froome almost lost the yellow jersey. It was a close call. His bodyguard Vasil Kiryienka was so far adrift that he finished outside the time limit. With 120 kilometres to go, Froome was isolated amidst his rivals. Strangely, though, no one joined forces against him. Movistar preferred to position their riders at the front of the peloton instead of sending Quintana out in a breakaway. I'm sure that the Spanish team could have harassed the yellow jersey and even taken it away from him. But they didn't threaten him. Stranger still, they indirectly helped him by controlling the final part of the stage. As for me, I remembered why I never wanted to be part of Team Sky. I loved the attacking style of racing above all else. And, for once, crossing the Pyrenees, the cycling that I loved had triumphed.

# Chapter 12

# A Philosophy for Crashing (The Fear of Falling)

**M**y run of misfortune began at the end of the summer of 2013, after a period of success that included victory in the Tour of Catalonia, Liège–Bastogne–Liège and on a Pyrenean stage of the Tour de France. I can provide precise dates for this series of accidents. It began on 30 August 2013 and continued through to 5 October 2014. In total, I suffered six big crashes. Each of them was unique and unpredictable. I can remember every detail of every crash, like a timestamp, etched into my memory.

Crash number one. I ended up feeling drunk with pain. During the seventh stage of the 2013 Vuelta, I'd been sprinting up the side of the peloton to gain a few places on an uphill section, 11 kilometres from the finish. My front wheel hit a rock at 50km/h. Both my hands came off the handlebars and I fell head-first, as if I had tumbled out of a tree. I was dazed by the impact. I suffered terrible abrasions down my entire right side, from my shoulder down to my thigh. I got up and set off again, escorted by my teammates, towards the finish line in Mairena del Aljarafe on the outskirts of Seville. Our *directeur sportif*, Bingen Fernández, went with me to the hospital. As I lay on the stretcher, it felt like my skin was burning, a fire that refused to die down. My skin was red and black like roasted flesh. Its deeper layers stood out, blood-coloured, while rings of encrusted tar and tiny pieces of grit on my thigh looked like charcoal halos. The medical staff covered half of my body with bandages. X-rays ruled out a pelvic fracture, but I couldn't sleep that night. I would almost have preferred to have had deeper wounds, so that the nerves weren't as irritated and raw.

The next morning, I could hardly stand up. I got out of bed and took one step, then a second . . . then started to stagger. The problem wasn't exhaustion or pain. It was even more worrying. The team doctor suspected concussion and applied our internal protocol. Team Garmin was a pioneer in dealing with what is potentially a very serious problem. 'You're not going home just yet. Stay with us for two or three days. We'll take you on the bus with us, you can go to the hotels with us. We'll take care of you,' the team's staff told me. They were reassuring and considerate. They kept telling me things like: 'Take time to recover,' and, 'If you have to, bring your season to a close. Put your health first.' It was concussion, and it affected my whole body. It was that rather than the pain that prevented me from sleeping; I spent two nights with my eyes wide open, staring at the ceiling, but didn't feel tired in the mornings. The protocol included a stipulation warning you not to watch videos on your mobile phone, but I had to make an exception. I wasn't nauseous, I reasoned.

Two weeks later, I was racing again, at the Tour of Britain. Two weeks after that, I lined up at the start of the World Road Race Championship in Florence, Italy.

Crash number two: 29 September 2013. On the World championships' circuit, heavy rain mixed with dust and the coating of oil and petrol that had seeped into the road over the dry summer months, producing a soapy liquid that cyclists dread. It was a massacre. The entire Irish squad was fated to crash: my cousin Nico, Matt Brammeier and Sam Bennett. As for me, the moment I hit the deck occurred with about 50 kilometres to go, when a rider fell just in front of me on a descent. I escaped with nothing more than a bruise on my arm.

A week later, still in Italy and on another rain-soaked road: crash number three. Giro di Lombardia, 6 October 2013. Poland's Rafał Majka and I were in contention for third place, behind Spaniards Joaquim Rodríguez and Alejandro Valverde. Two hundred metres from the finish line on the shores of Lake Lecco, there was a bend. I started to sprint just before exiting the corner and my rear wheel slipped. I was disappointed, but not hurt. I jumped back on my bike, reattached the chain, which had come unshipped. I was unaware of Enrico Gasparotto closing on me fast, but fortunately managed to cross the line before he flew past me. I had taken fourth in the 'Race of the Falling Leaves'.

The infamous crash in the last corner of Liège–Bastogne–Liège was six months later. It all seemed to happen in slow motion, to the point where I was almost a spectator at my own downfall. It was 27 April 2014. Crash number four. Another incident on a bend. My pride was hurt much more than my body; it was the most embarrassing and inexplicable crash of my career. Before taking refuge in the team bus, closing my eyes and clearing my head – trying to think it through was pointless – I gave my impressions to the waiting journalists: 'I think I had tears in my eyes before I even hit the floor. There aren't really words for it. To race for seven hours and for that to happen on the last corner, it's poetry!'

Crash number five: 9 May 2014, on the first stage of the Giro d'Italia. The race began with a team time trial in Belfast, Northern Ireland. It was raining. I should have spotted the omens: the start ramp was located in front of the *Titanic* museum. At the halfway point, with about 13 kilometres to go, I hit the 'iceberg', in fact probably a very deep manhole cover. My hands lifted off the handlebars and I was thrown off the bike. I took down three teammates, who thankfully managed to get going again, while I ended up sitting in the puddles trying to hold my shoulder. Everything pointed to my having broken my collarbone, which it turned out I had. It was the first time I'd broken a bone during my racing career. But I didn't really feel like celebrating the fact that I'd evaded that fate until then.

The crash in Belfast really dented my morale. I felt guilty about taking out half of my team, especially Koldo Fernández, who also broke his collarbone and was forced to quit the race the next day. I thought about my friend Ryder Hesjedal, the 2012 Giro's champion and still a favourite. He didn't fall but, by provoking so much disruption to the opening day's time trial, I didn't exactly help him start the race in the ideal way. In my haste to get to the hospital for my operation I didnt say goodbye to the guys, something I deeply regret. All kinds of thoughts were running around my head. I would really have liked to finish the race, which paused two days later in the Republic of Ireland's capital, Dublin, the city where my grandparents lived . . . I should have gripped the handlebars tighter . . . I don't understand why this second goal of the season had been snatched away, less than two weeks after Liège–Bastogne–Liège . . . I shouldn't complain . . . I've never done anything like this before, I mustn't start . . .

I returned to racing on 29 June, at the Irish Championships in Multyfarnham, finishing eighth, a minute and thirty-two seconds behind Ryan Mullen. After that I raced the Tour of Austria (15th), the Clásica de San Sebastián (25th) and the Tour de l'Ain (third), and set my sights on the Tour of Spain. I hadn't fallen since the Giro and I thought my luck had changed – but that optimism was misplaced. On 27 August 2014, during the fifteenth stage of the Vuelta, as we were racing through the mountains of Asturias, I fell on the climb of the Puerto del Torno. The rider in front of me swerved and I went over a guard rail and fell into a ravine. I felt the impact of my leg hitting the metal barrier. I flew 4 metres downwards, time enough to wonder what kind of state you're going to end up in when you land . . . This was crash number six.

Luckily, I landed on a bed of ferns and soft vegetation. Nathan Haas, who'd seen what happened, scrambled down into the void to rescue me and helped to bundle me back upwards. I clung to leaves, roots, anything I could get my hands on. The team was waiting for me, hoping that I'd emerge in one piece. They checked me over and decided that I was fine, and I signalled that we should get going again. We started to chase. Because lots of riders had crashed on the descent from the pass, we were able to close the gap. We were even in a position to consider contesting the stage victory. Ryder Hesjedal dragged me back to the front of the race and then gave me some critical support on the legendary final climb to Lagos de Covadonga. I finished seventh, and it was almost as if nothing had happened.

I'd always been afraid of tumbling into a deep ravine, but disaster had been avoided. I was afraid of breaking a leg, but had escaped with a deep cut on my shin. After a long bus transfer, the team doctor, Dr Lorenz Emmert, stitched it up in my hotel room at about one in the morning, after administering a local anaesthetic. As the cuts were down to the bone, there was a high risk of infection and I had to take antibiotics until the end of the race, which immediately impacted on my form. Nevertheless, I finished the Vuelta in seventh place, some ten minutes behind Alberto Contador. More than my spectacular plunge into a ravine, it was this performance that I wanted to remember. And the fact that it marked the end of a series of setbacks – for the moment at least – until perhaps another string of mishaps . . .

Strange as it may sound, I think you have to fall off a bike in order to get used to what is always a traumatic event – the brain detests that split second when it realises that the body is going to be in for a bad time. If you don't crash often enough, you forget the effect it has. On the other hand, if you hit the deck as frequently as once or twice every year, you start to downplay the effect it will have, to the point where you don't start to tremble the instant you realise that you're going to go down. When an experienced 'tumbler' sees a pile-up right in front of him, he says to himself: 'I'm going to fall, but it won't be serious . . .'

My six crashes between the 2013 and 2014 Vuelta frightened me in different ways and left me with a variety of injuries, but none of them knocked me off course for too long. On each occasion, I bounced back, and even got some good results between crashes. I took the falls in my stride, treating them as experiences, like a walk through a storm – sooner or later, it stops raining.

My luck changed and my cycling breakthrough took place on 5 October 2014, between Como and Bergamo, during the 108th edition of the Giro di Lombardia that I won, launching my attack from behind the leading group.

The memories of my six crashes ran through my legs like a shiver. Alone in the lead with 200 metres to go, I took the last corner with all the ease of a novice negotiating a turn around a training course bollard. In short, sitting very stiffly and tensed on the brake levers, I almost came to a stop. But I stayed upright and crossed the line first. Several journalists had talked about 'redemption', asking me: 'After all these crashes, is this a kind of deliverance? Is it some sort of revenge?' Yes, without a doubt.

Some theories suggest that there are hidden and unconscious

reasons why a cyclist falls. For example, that you never end up on the ground completely by chance; crashing represents an escape route: the brain decides that it is the best way to get out of a race that cannot be won. Even though it might be putting the body at risk, the brain avoids the traumatic experience of defeat. There may be some truth in this; after what had been a good start to the 2013 season, my run of crashes offered my body and mind the opportunity to rest as fatigue and pressure were starting to mount. They allowed me to forget about the peloton and finish seventh in the Vuelta in 2014 and then win the Giro di Lombardia. What's more, they gave me the chance to experience an unexpected and even perhaps unthinkable moment in the busy life of a cyclist. I'm referring to the start of my relationship with my future wife.

I had met Jess in the spring of 2014, at the Sierra Nevada in Spain, the paths of an Irish cyclist and a British athlete happening to intersect on this summit in the middle of the desert, a peak that's super-heated at the bottom, snowy at the top. We'd both gone there to boost our red blood cell count. Jess was taking part in a university study on the effects of altitude, which encourages the production of blood cells and is a 100 per cent natural method of oxygenating the blood, and over time offers useful albeit limited benefits. I was there to increase my endurance in the mountains in preparation for the Giro. We were staying not far from each other, at the Centro de Alto Rendimiento (High Performance Centre), which is set at 2,320 metres and welcomes athletes from all disciplines. The altitude stimulates natural oxygenation and a degree of mental rest – another benefit ultimately confirmed by the study. The team sent three riders to this miniature training camp – Alex Howes, Phil Gaimon and me – but Phil was called up after a few days to race in the Circuit de la Sarthe in France, so Alex was my only companion in this little adventure. A native of Boulder, Colorado, he had turned pro with Slipstream in 2007, the same year I had opted to do an extra season with Vélo Club La Pomme, and our paths had crossed in 2008: I joined the American team, while he signed for the amateur club in Marseille in order to gain experience before returning to the pro ranks. He was an adventurer who later turned to gravel racing, mountain bike and ultra-trail distances, racing for several hundred kilometres across expanses of wilderness in the US.

Alex also had a passion for the Ardennes Classics. He was an ideal companion for a training camp. We had three members of staff with us: *directeur sportif* Rob Hunter, Juanito the mechanic, and our *soigneur* Ricardo.

On 7 April 2014, we finished our training ride by climbing the Alto de Monachil, one of the routes that connects the Granada plains to the High Performance Centre. We were about a kilometre from the top when we saw a navy-blue car driving in the other direction. There appeared to be five women in it. We continued onwards, cresting the top of the pass and then descending until the terrain levelled out, at which point we signalled to the team vehicle tracking us that they should pick us up in order to avoid the next part of the journey on the main Sierra Nevada road, which was rather long and boring, especially as we'd been climbing it every day for a week.

Just as we were getting off our bikes and putting on jackets, the navy-blue car reappeared, then turned around. Its occupants appeared to be lost. It pulled up next to us. There were indeed five young women inside. One of them opened the door and asked if they could take a picture; she was a cycling fan.

It turned out that they were five British track and field athletes, staying close to the High Performance Centre. The woman who was a fan was Lily Partridge, and one of her friends was Jess Andrews . . .

Our eyes met on that occasion with the car, but it wasn't until two days later that the connection was fully made. Lily, Jess, Alex and I went out to a quiet café. We wanted to get away from the high-performance complex, with its Olympic pool, gyms and cafeteria, where we all tended to end up wandering in circles. We sat outside the café, around a wooden table, and ordered large cups of hot chocolate. In front of us, skiers were lining up for the lifts. I ended up sitting opposite Jess and she told me a few things about herself. She was twenty-one, she'd been born on the Isle of Wight, and she was a middle-distance runner. There was something captivating about her: she was always talking. When she stopped, I would take over, then she'd start again, and on it went. We began a conversation that never ended. I felt like I had known her for ever. Three days after our hot chocolate, I invited her to dinner in town at Tito Luigi's. Just her and me. A plate of Spanish ham and a bottle of wine.

We jumped from one topic to another, focusing less on sport and more on the virtues of Spanish food, especially the Iberian *paleta bellota* we were eating. This is a beautifully cured and prepared black pork shoulder that's one of the best in the world, thanks to the free-range pigs' acorn-based diet.

The next day, we met in the hall at the centre along with about twenty other athletes and watched Paris–Roubaix on the big screen. I had to explain to Jess the intricacies of a sport I'd always thought was fairly simple. Why wasn't I racing Paris–Roubaix? Good question . . .

The next day I had to pack my suitcase and head for the Ardennes. But, by the magic of WhatsApp, the connection continued every day, every hour even.

A week later, messages from Jess rained down like a comforting shower while I was racing Flèche Wallonne, a race she was watching for the very first time. 'Five kilometres to go. This race is crazy.' '500m to go, this climb is never-ending.' 'Can't believe you got 2nd. Are you happy?' Four days later my run of misfortune culminated in my crash at Liège–Bastogne–Liège. In the space of two weeks Jess saw me crash on the final corner of La Doyenne, when poised for victory, and the Giro's opening team time trial. There was no gentle introduction to life with a cyclist and I'm not sure how I would have fared during this rollercoaster of emotions if we had not met, her presence in my life being a guiding light through the toughest moments in my career.

Podium one day, crash the next. The extremities in emotions. Jess knew that it would take me some time to recover after breaking my collarbone. She flew to Girona. I picked her up at the airport, driving one-handed. We spent time at home, doing what we loved most: talking about anything and everything, laughing and enjoying life. We could talk and forget about time passing, as if day and night didn't exist any more. We could share silences. We could read each other.

Sport had nourished us both, built us up, but also made us vulnerable. Jess was incredibly talented and hard-working, but she was already aware of the weariness of chasing places, the quest for a few seconds.

She felt trapped by the track. She missed looking up at the sky and being able to breathe. I suggested that we take a break together. Mine lasted a few weeks, hers a few months. Before going back into battle, I reassured her: 'Jess, don't worry if you see me crashing sometimes on TV. I promise you I won't stay still on the ground. I'll get up as soon as I can. I'll do that for you.'

# Chapter 13

# The Panda Comes Out of the Woodwork

The Panda came after me again. Not in Liège this time, but in China.

Six months after my victory in La Doyenne, I came face to face with no fewer than forty pandas, all deployed on the roadside during the third stage of the Tour of Beijing. Dressed up in costumes, these fans were standing up on their hind legs on Si Haï Mountain climb, one of the favourite climbs among cyclists in that region (14.7 kilometres at 4.3 per cent). They shouted. They sang. They danced. They were there for me and to provide the race with some additional colour. They wanted to award a 'Panda of the Mountains' prize, an unofficial title that would be decided 1 kilometre before the 'King of the Mountains' banner. Using a can of spray paint, they had drawn what wasn't a very straight line across the road. When I saw the first panda on the right-hand side, with the huge belly of a beast that has eaten too much bamboo, I jumped out of the pack. Unfortunately, we had let a breakaway go, so I didn't win the prize, but their objective had been achieved: the spectators were transfixed.

This 'Panda party' had begun on the first day we'd arrived in China. The organisers wanted to kill two birds with one stone: to offer a second life to the unlikely creature that had appeared on TV that spring when it had chased after me in Liège–Bastogne–Liège, while also providing the Tour of Beijing with a mascot, a bit like the Tour de France's stuffed lion. The choice of a panda was for obvious reasons: it's a sacred animal for the Chinese. For centuries, it has represented the duality of yin and yang, because of its two colours, white and black; it embodies values of peace and friendship, as it never attacks its peers – but, if disturbed, it can be as fearsome as a tiger. In 2013, the panda became the emblem of the Tour of Beijing. And because I was the 'Panda rider', a giant mascot chased after me at every start and finish so that we could pose for photos.

To make the celebration at Si Haï Mountain possible, the organisers had chartered a bus. About forty volunteer pandas boarded it. While I was racing, they got involved in a real drama. The bus took a wrong turn and arrived late at the foot of the pass. If they'd arrived five seconds later, the police would have blocked all access, with no possible exceptions. After a long drive, the black-and-white bears were also very hot and bothered. That day the Panda of the Mountains award was won by New Zealander Hayden Roulston. I had to console myself with second place overall, ten seconds behind Beñat Intxausti.

I returned to the Tour of Beijing in 2014. And, naturally, the Panda was back too. It seemed to be becoming something of an obsession. This time, the animal was travelling on my head, in between groves of bamboo, on a white POC Octal helmet that had been specially designed for the event. It was a thing of real beauty that would be auctioned off for the benefit of WWF once the race was over. The team were in good spirits as we travelled from the Tour of Lombardy, which we'd won, via Paris, where we had feasted on burgers and chips in a hotel room. But once we arrived in China, I thought we were going to end up staying at Beijing International Airport for the rest of our lives. We spent an hour and a half sitting in the arrivals terminal. Initially at least, we chatted, laughed and sighed as we watched other passengers picking up their bags, light on their feet, if a little sleepy, happy to be at their destination. Then we were finally told that our bus had arrived. Riders from about half a dozen teams got aboard. False alarm: after half an hour, nothing had happened. We still hadn't gone anywhere. A guide informed us: 'We've got to wait for your bikes to go through customs.'

We got off the bus, but made sure to borrow the detachable foam cushions – much to the driver's displeasure. We used them to make ourselves a sofa fit for a king on the pavement in the car park. Optimum comfort, plenty of room to spread your legs, a real luxury! We waited for two hours, half sleeping, half laughing. It was hot and humid. 'I'm going for a piss,' said Ryder Hesjedal, and went back into the terminal. When he returned, he was carrying a bag full of cold beer. He was like an angel fallen from heaven, standing in front of us, glowing in a halo of light. Thirsty, we opened the cans. At that moment, someone shouted: 'It's all good now, the bus will take you to the hotel!' Finally! The engine started. There was forward motion. We began to applaud. But after an hour's drive and half a dozen turns, we recognised what had become a familiar sight. 'Isn't that the airport?' The shuttle had returned to its start point. We asked the guide why we'd been put on the bus. 'Oh that? That was just to keep you occupied.'

Apparently, the customs officials were still holding on to our bikes. We returned to the car park for another two hours of deadly boredom as the day wore on. As it became obvious that the customs issue would not be resolved that evening, we got on the damned bus again and left the airport, luckily for good this time. We headed to our accommodation, 200 kilometres away in Chongli, the future site of the 2022 Winter Olympics athletes' village. It was one o'clock in the morning when we checked into our rooms. We ordered a snack, which arrived on little trays at two in the morning, then collapsed fully clothed on our beds. It had taken less time to travel from Paris to Beijing than it had to get from the airport to the hotel.

Once our bikes were returned to us, we committed fully to the battle on the road. The Panda of the Mountains prize this year was on a different climb from 2013. Once again, I failed miserably, and the coveted trophy went to Dutchman Karsten Kroon. The team had to settle for two stage wins. The first one came courtesy of Tyler Farrar, who won the sprint in Qianjiadian, located between the mountains and a river and renowned for its cool conditions in summer. The next day, I won at the summit finish. We rode along the edge of the Great Wall, sensing the humid smell of the forests and the serenity of the Buddhist temples, amidst trees taking on autumnal shades

*Above*: Tamworth, UK, 1988. Three generations of the Martins – Vic, Dan and Neil. *(Personal collection)*

*Left*: 1988. My one and only cycling hero: my dad. *(Personal collection)*

Henley-in-Arden. The 2004 UK Junior
National Road Race Championships.
*(© Larry Hickmott)*

Carrick-on-Suir. The 2004 Junior
Tour of Ireland. *(© Peter Purfield)*

Bryn Bach Park. A duel with Geraint Thomas at the 2004 Junior Tour of Wales.
*(© Ron Good/Junior Tour of Wales)*

Alpe d'Huez, 2000. My first Tour de France climb, aged 13. (*Personal collection*)

Col du Glandon, 2007. My first overall victory in a mountainous stage race, the Tour de Savoie. (© *Pierre Carrey*)

Col d'Izoard. Conquering my mythical climb and overcoming two broken vertebrae during the 2017 Tour de France. (© *CorVos*)

Liège, 2009. My year as National Champion, proudly wearing the Shamrocks up La Redoute climb. *(© CorVos)*

Liège, 2013. Humbled to write my name in the history books by winning 'La Doyenne' - the oldest Classic. *(© CorVos)*

Liège, 2014. I had tears in my eyes before I even hit the floor. *(© CorVos)*

*Above*: Bagnères-de-Bigorre, 2013. On my first Tour de France podium after winning a hectic Stage 9. (© *CorVos*)

*Below*: Breaking away on the 'Breton Alpe d'Huez', Mûr de Bretagne. My second Tour de France stage win in 2018. (© *CorVos*)

The madness of the Tour. (© *Lorenzo Verdinelli/Team UAE-Emirates*)

Tour de France, 2018. Morale is high after the cobblestones stage. (*Personal collection*)

*Above*: The power of team spirit with Quick Step, aka 'the Wolf Pack', at Paris-Nice in 2017.
*(© CorVos)*

*Above*: Sprinting to victory atop Laguna Negra on Stage 3 of the Vuelta a España, 2020. *(© CorVos)*

*Left*: Going beyond my limits during Stage 8 of the 2020 Vuelta a España to Alto de Moncalvillo.
*(© Noa Arnon/Team Israel Start Up Nation)*

Olympic Games, 2016. Privileged to share this experience as we check out the stadium the day before Jess' race, at the Maracanã Stadium, Rio. *(Personal collection)*

The best support team I could ever have imagined – Ella, Jess and Daisy. *(© Lorenzo Verdinelli/ Team UAE-Emirates)*

Andorra, 2022. The next generation of Martin discovers the fun of competition at the Wings for Life World Run. *(© Cecilia Belomo)*

*Above*: My panda fan club en route to the 2013 Tour of Beijing. *(© Shannon Bufton)*

*Left*: Here we go – PanDan Martin! *(© A Swiss with a Pulse)*

Dublin, 2014. Charity ride with Cycle4Life. *(© Paul Cook)*

of red and yellow. On that 'queen' stage, Ryder Hesjedal opened the way for us by joining a breakaway. The road climbed Mentougou Miaofeng Mountain, whose name means 'The Peak of Wonder' in Mandarin. There were 12 kilometres of rolling road, made difficult by a headwind. I hit out at the red kite with a kilometre to go. That year I once again finished second in the overall classification, three seconds behind Philippe Gilbert.

We concluded the Tour of Beijing in style thanks to an invitation to Serk, a cycling café and bike shop in downtown Beijing. The owners were the delighted promoters of the Panda of the Mountains prize. Unfortunately for us, though, while other teams joined in with the post-race festivities – in time trial suit, if you please – we had to spend a short night in a hotel; we had an early flight the next morning to the Japan Cup.

My guardian angel was present once again in this second Asian country. Some fans gifted me drawings of a giant panda; the images from Liège–Bastogne–Liège had obviously greatly amused and impressed them. The black-and-white bear isn't native to the Japanese archipelago, and can only be found in a few zoos. However, I think they would have been happy if they'd found themselves in the lush, peaceful Kogashi forest, where the climb that features in the Japan Cup is located. The pass is almost 5 kilometres long and although it averages around 5 per cent, the final 2 kilometres really ramps up, averaging around 9 or 10 per cent. Along the roadside, in place of the fir trees you usually see in Europe, are immense and majestic Japanese cedars. Then we reached a sort of mini-Alpe d'Huez, with hairpin bends, names and messages painted on the road, clusters of very excited spectators ... The race has one of the most passionate audiences I've experienced, perhaps because it is the only one in the Japanese season that allows them to get close to Tour de France riders.

The Japan Cup provided me with a beautiful way to finish the season with victory in a Classic. I broke away with 38 kilometres to go in the city of Utsunomiya, the country's cycling capital. I finished with a fifty-four-second lead over a group of chasers. Two years later, I came second behind former Giro winner Ivan Basso. But I enjoyed my subsequent appearances even more, simply because I did a lot of work for the team. Luckily, this work always contributed to a victory for our group. In 2013, I was happy to ride for Jack Bauer, a rider who was generous with his efforts and had protected me from the wind and other dangers on many occasions. In 2014 I put myself at the service of my friend Nathan Haas, who was always at my side whether I won or crashed. Circumstances meant that I didn't have many opportunities to race in a support role, but the Japan Cup was an exception to the rule, and it allowed me to thank my friends for everything they'd done for me during the season. I tried to be helpful and grateful – just like the Panda.

I was still chasing My Panda, the one and only one, the creature that crossed my path in Liège. This is an important detail in my tricky investigation into the mysterious animal. I've replayed the images dozens of times to analyse the scene and there's no doubt about it: My Panda had accomplices. At least three of them. He led the way, but while he was pursuing me, they were running behind him. Two of them were dressed identically, in suit and ties. The third was wearing a black-and-white check jacket and waving an unidentified black flag, possibly a pirate's skull and crossbones. I'd say they were in their mid-twenties at the most. Their faces were recognisable. These are crucial elements for the investigation. Finding one of the gang members could lead to the unveiling of the alleged leader: the Panda.

## Chapter 14

# A Ship Without a Captain (The Fear of Being a Leader)

The ship cut through the sea like our tyres on a mountain road. The hull shook from its speed through the swell as the roll and pitch increased. All the while, I looked straight ahead, like a good sailor, trying to avoid succumbing to seasickness. Our first stage race of the 2015 season was a sailing tour circumnavigating the island of Tortola in the British Virgin Islands. The team was divided across thirteen boats, each crewed by three team staff assisted by a professional skipper. I was on board with Ryder Hesjedal and our German coach Sebastian Weber. We had to play with the wind just as you would in a Classic, but without the spectators' flags at the roadside to tell us which way it was blowing from and make it easier for us, to enable us to read the sea and its currents, to get ourselves into the slipstream of the others, to glide through the waves with as little friction as possible, to gain speed.

Ryder stood next to the rudder with the quiet, determined air of a fisherman going out to catch tuna. Meanwhile, I was trying to figure out how to hoist and take in the various sails, and, above all, how to avoid getting my feet caught in the ropes.

Each evening the flotilla of thirteen boats anchored in a new port. We ate on the beach together and then went back to our boats to sleep. We ate great local cuisine and enjoyed beer and cocktails on the beach while telling each other about our personal lives and really getting to know each other. In the mornings, we would breakfast on board before heading out into the ocean bound for our next destination, pausing at midday to go swimming in the azure water or take part in flailing tug-of-war contests with our weak cyclists' arms. The atmosphere was nice, but a touch louche, almost as if we were taking part in a reality TV show on a desert island. There actually weren't many cameras or photos, just a handful of images broadcast on the internet. In truth, this sailing race was about bonding a newly formed and slightly disjointed team; it also comprised an urgent search for a leader for the upcoming season.

Team Garmin had just merged with Team Cannondale and would take on the latter's name. We had to mix two different teams and their staff, many of them from different cultures, and some of them bitter about losing some of their former colleagues. The merger had meant sacrificing half of the two teams to create one. On the one hand, there was the old Garmin, the team where I'd started and which had remained fairly faithful to its original ideals and to the great ideas we had floated on that winter's evening in a Boulder hotel; on the other hand, there was the Italian Cannondale team, sponsored by an American bike manufacturer. That meant two clans, two different histories, two languages. To make matters worse, the squad was the youngest in the World Tour. David Millar had retired. A year earlier, we'd lost our marquee riders, Christian Vande Velde and David Zabriskie, as well as experienced racers like Andreas Klier and the South African sprinter Rob Hunter. Cannondale didn't have any heavyweights either. Instead, their ranks featured the peloton's youngest member, Matej Mohorič, the downhill king. The Slovenian, who speaks Italian as well as English, was one of a few who could communicate between the two halves of our new team.

Given the circumstances, I was a candidate for the position of leader. I was ready to update my CV and prepare a covering letter to go with it. I could have said that my teacher at San Gabriel Primary School thought that even then, at the age of seven or eight, I had a strong sense of leadership. She saw me becoming Britain's prime minister. I had missed my calling . . .

I would have said something about my record, even though results alone don't make a leader. I'd always been the type to raise my hand when, during a pre-race briefing, the *directeur sportif* would ask: 'Who thinks he's got the legs to win today?' The question was essentially rhetorical because the directors had usually chosen one or two riders who would be protected, the 'leaders'. I didn't want to succumb to hypocrisy, to sink into false modesty or to refuse a challenge; if I felt capable of achieving a result, I said so. At the very beginning, in 2008, my attitude was perceived as being rather odd. Although the ambience within the team was quite informal, there was an unspoken belief that new pros should keep quiet during discussions and, above all, never assert themselves. I wasn't trying to provoke anyone. I just wanted to say what I thought.

During my very first training camp, I shocked the staff during our individual interviews, because I dared to make a little joke. The team management showed me a draft of my racing programme, which I thought was great, but I said, 'It's a shame, I'm a bit disappointed.'

'Why's that?'

'You haven't put me in the Tour of Flanders or Paris–Roubaix, even though I love those races!'

They looked at each other for a second. Either I was serious and they'd recruited a second madman after David Zabriskie; or I was being funny and I didn't realise my place. Yet I acted as I always had with my previous teams: respectfully, but often offering a word to lighten the mood.

The staff seemed just as embarrassed when, during my second professional race, the Tour Méditerranéen, in February, I said on the team bus, 'We're going up to Mont Faron. I like this climb, I have good legs. I can win.' In the end, I lost time before the foot of the climb that sits above the port of Toulon and several people in the team thought that I should have kept my mouth shut. Two months later, the *directeurs sportifs* were miffed when I decided to abandon the Grand Prix de Rennes, a one-day event that suited pure sprinters, held in horrific conditions with heavy rain and hail. They didn't say a word to me, but I could see from their expressions that they thought I was like a spoilt child who didn't finish their meal. That was how they categorised us: a first-year professional was a child and had to behave like one. In June, when I said, 'I can win,' at the Route du Sud, I won. On that occasion, the team did believe in me. I'll never forget the fact that they trusted me and granted me the status of leader for one race after my breakaway on the first stage.

A year later, I had the same rank at the Tour of Catalonia. After taking third place in a ten-rider sprint won by Alejandro Valverde, the team, and especially our Canadians Christian Meier and Svein Tuft, worked for me on the stage that finished at the summit of Vallnord in Andorra. I had our string of riders in front of me, pulling me along like a fish at the end of the line until, at the right moment, they released me into the deep water. I knew the significance of the situation because I had this train of my teammates ahead of me. It gave me even more strength. I wasn't crushed by the pressure, but lifted by it. Some riders would lose their equilibrium completely when their whole team sacrificed their own chances to help them. They had to be treated as leaders, but without ever mentioning that word, keeping just one or two team members close to them and having the rest close by, ready to intervene, but out of sight.

Christian Vande Velde had given me some tips about the Tour of Catalonia. He wasn't at the race but at his home in Gerona, recovering from a very severe crash at the Giro d'Italia that had left him with a broken pelvis and seven other fractures. I'm not sure he loved being a leader, maybe because he had been prevented from taking on that role for a long time, stuck in the shadow of Lance Armstrong, who was more than just a leader, something of a tyrant. But Christian was a reassuring figure for his teammates, who were bound to his service. He commanded respect and gave off a certain aura of stability, balance and happiness. We wanted to help him. Wasn't that the definition of a leader? Christian always encouraged me and, even when it came from a distance and in bits and pieces, this support really buoyed me. I finished second in the classification, fifteen seconds behind Alejandro Valverde.

And then I discovered that a leader isn't just responsible for carrying his team on the road but also bears much wider responsibilities, up to a point that I couldn't have imagined . . .

At the start of the sixth stage of the 2010 Tour of Poland, I was wearing the yellow jersey of the overall leader following my solo victory the day before. Then the organiser, Olympic medallist Czesław Lang, a Polish sporting hero during the Cold War, asked me to participate in a ceremony. The small town of Oświęcim, from which the race started, is more widely known by its German name: Auschwitz. We stopped in front of the death camp. We had gone from a very colourful and charming town to what was for so many hell on Earth. We arrived in front of the wrought-iron gate with its infamous sign: '*Arbeit macht Frei*'. I was surrounded by riders representing about thirty countries who each laid down a rose. Intense silence fell upon the race as I had the honour of laying a wreath.

A year later, I returned to the Tour of Poland with the conviction that the status of leader wasn't a gift or an honour but a duty, something bigger than yourself, almost a crushing weight. I won another stage, under stormy skies, in the spa town of

Bukowina Tatrzańska, lightning flashing in the hills around us. Spectators without umbrellas ran to take shelter in their cars. I finished alone, white-faced and glistening from the car headlights in the downpour, which turned day into night. My team got ready for the last stage, a tricky circuit through the streets of Krakow. Heinrich Haussler had decided to contest all of the intermediate sprints to prevent my main rival, Peter Sagan, from taking bonus seconds. I was sprinting just behind them, unable to pass them, and I could see the risks Heinrich was taking for me, sprinting right at the limit as is always the case with those guys, harrying Sagan on the bends. Close to me, Tom Boonen was also part of this contest. The emperor of the cobbled Classics had introduced himself the day before when we were staying in the same hotel. He told me, 'I'd prefer for you to win than Sagan. I'll do everything to help you.' Unfortunately, neither Boonen or Haussler could stop him; the Slovakian sprinter stripped the yellow jersey from my shoulders in the final metres, finishing second on the stage and taking six valuable bonus seconds.

I was asserting myself, just as I'd had to do earlier in my career when I'd been riding alone for the CC Giro or I'd been sidelined by the Vélo Club La Pomme, but I didn't want to dominate the others. I didn't raise my voice. It's no good getting angry. You've lost if you're angry. There are a hundred different ways each day you can get angry within the micro-society of a cycling team. But I took it in my stride. I could be uncompromising the evening before a major objective, especially when I was in good form, but I never crossed the line into disrespect.

The night before I won the 2014 Giro di Lombardia, Alyssa, our head *soigneur*, my friend, recognised the presence of the type of attitude that suggested I would win it: I was unpleasant. 'You were just abrasive,' Alyssa told me afterwards. I'd got upset when I saw beef entrecôte on the menu. The night before a race I always ate white meat, which is more easily digestible. For once, I got upset with Alyssa: 'Seriously! I do my job 100 per cent, and I expect the team to do theirs 100 per cent.' I was raging and stormed off to make myself a vegetable protein shake, then went back to my room to drink it.

I made a point of respecting the work that every member of the team's staff did. I appreciated the qualities that underpinned our camaraderie, our 'family' spirit – except the night before a big objective. On those occasions, I would immerse myself in a winning state of mind and expect the team staff and my teammates to be on the same wavelength. And I didn't want to hear any excuses.

Despite this, Team Cannondale wasn't very eager to appoint me as leader for the 2015 season. Sometimes Ryder Hesjedal, Andrew Talansky and I were presented as co-leaders; on other occasions Talansky was listed as 'leader' and I was down as 'road captain'. The difference between the two is subtle. Many team leaders are excellent racers or even great champions, but they lack leadership skills. They don't speak up in discussions, they don't motivate the other riders with little words of encouragement on the bike or at dinner, or even between races with a nice little text message. They don't bring things to everyone's attention or shake things up. The role of 'road captain' was invented to resolve these situations. He's the real leader – the one who inspires, who federates, who speaks out, who makes decisions – even when there's a risk of upsetting people. Contrary to popular belief, the 'captain' isn't the oldest or most experienced rider in the group, but the one who demonstrates all the skills of a leader.

I didn't care about words because I knew that when the time came I could count on the support of the team. In principle . . . But these ambiguities were beginning to annoy us all. Hesjedal felt most comfortable when there were one or two protected riders in addition to him, to allow him a free role. Talansky, on the other hand, craved that title, embracing the pressure that accompanies it. The team was keen to get behind him because he'd won the Critérium du Dauphiné the previous season, an event considered a launch pad for the Tour de France. He didn't climb quite as well as me, but was much faster against the clock, which made him a model of consistency. What's more, he was American, born in New York, and in an American team everyone understood the importance of this symbolic choice. Andrew did eventually rebel, however, during the 2015 Tour de France, on the superheated Pierre-Saint-Martin stage. It was a day of burning heat. The *directeur sportif* kept repeating in the earpiece: 'Dan, you stay with Andrew. Dan, you stay with Andrew.' Until Talansky turned on his radio and said, 'What the hell for? I'm no better than him!' He was right, because that day we both sucked. We respected each other and were honest to each other. We didn't have the same confidence when it came to the team's sports directors. Nor could we rely on the support, let alone presence, of Jonathan Vaughters.

Our general manager appeared to have deserted the racing scene, the training camps and even his phone and internet. We didn't even know where he lived: Girona, Denver, Boulder . . . His presence on the ground had become very limited during recent seasons. During the Tour, he stayed away from the team, in the Relais & Châteaux luxury hotels and restaurants, enjoying fine wines with our sponsors' representatives, which was part of his job. Even though we would have liked clarification from him on the organisation of the sporting side, we let him work behind the scenes to secure the team's future.

The problem was that the team ended up in a worrying position at regular intervals. Through necessity or even desperation JV was constantly considering mergers with other teams, without knowing whether these would provide us with extra resources or help us to avoid bankruptcy. In 2011, for instance, world champion Thor Hushovd, Roger Hammond, Andreas Klier, Daniel Lloyd and a few others became my colleagues when Team Garmin combined with Cervélo TestTeam. More than a merger, it was an amalgamation with a Classics squad that was on the verge of breaking apart. It was like a marriage between a carp and a rabbit. Paris–Roubaix specialists tended to keep to themselves. Four years later, as a result of the union with Cannondale, I shared the jersey with Matej Mohorič, Alberto Bettiol and Davide Formolo, the future winners of Milan–San Remo, the Tour of Flanders and a great hope of Italian cycling, respectively. This kind of merger always had consequences.

Good results were awaited with feverish expectation. Some *directeurs sportifs* believed that it took at least two years for a squad to coalesce. I got a first insight into the downturns these unions would trigger when riding the Tour of Catalonia, my benchmark event in my adopted region, the one where I'd first emerged with second place in 2009. To boost my chances, every season I skipped Milan–San Remo, which took place two days beforehand, even though I was always very tempted to race 'La Classicissima's' 300 kilometres and test myself on its pivotal climb, the Poggio, going elbow-to-elbow with the *puncheurs* and sprinters. At the Tour of Catalonia, I did a bit of everything. I even got involved in a bunch sprint, in 2011, dropped off at the last bend by my teammates – I was overjoyed when I finished fourth out of 155 riders. I battled for the leader's jersey and to win stages. I won the overall classification.

For once, Joaquim Rodríguez and Michele Scarponi ended up below me on the podium. In 2013, my victory was forged at the ski resort of Port Ainé after I'd slipped into a big break-away together with my cousin Nico and my teammate Ryder Hesjedal, who did a colossal amount of work. I attacked from the bottom of the 19km final climb, holding off the peloton and crossing the line thirty-six seconds ahead of Rodríguez. But we had to fight every day, chasing after time bonuses, in what was a very eventful race. Even on the last stage, we were forced to play a dangerous game, one that really tested our nerves. I was in the leader's white and green jersey as we raced through the streets of Barcelona and a breakaway had a lead of more than six minutes. I calculated that with a short

5km finish circuit, if the lead grew any more, we would not be able to enter the lap due to being lapped by the breakaway – meaning I would instantly win. So I did what a leader should do: I asked my teammates to slow down. The other teams had to come to narrow the gap. When we were more than eight minutes back, Rodríguez's team started to ride on the front of the peloton. They had become aware of my plan but I still went on to win the overall.

Disappointingly, Team Cannondale-Garmin missed out completely at the 2015 Tour of Catalonia. I was with teammates I liked, Ryder Hesjedal and Alex Howes, solid men like Andrew Talansky, but we were going backwards. Collectively, we had lost our bearings. We also lacked physical strength at decisive moments. We weren't on top of things at all. Breaks went away in which we didn't have a rider, and we were too slow in chasing them down. We were losing our status, as the following incident underlined.

I thought that I was doing the right thing by suggesting to Etixx-Quick-Step that we ride together to break the peloton on narrow and twisty toads, a few kilometres from the finish of the second stage. But at the agreed moment, my teammates disappeared, letting the Belgian team do the work and taking advantage of the situation. That evening, it became a joke between them. What were we playing at? Our fall from grace became more apparent on the penultimate stage when echelons formed at a decisive moment and we were caught out ridiculously. My teammates had worked hard to set me up for an intermediate sprint to gain three seconds and thus to move up to third overall. We could sense the stress in the peloton. Was there a risk of echelons? Via our earpieces, our *directeurs sportifs* told us there wasn't. As a precaution, and not fully trusting the advice of those in the team car behind us who had significant experience, I started to move up the peloton. Unfortunately, though, I was still too far back when it split. There was no doubt that the road suited echelons. Several teams had prepared their tactics perfectly. I lost more than a minute and a half, dropping from a possible podium position to 10th place in the overall classification. We'd lost our energy, our strength of character, our desire to do things together on that boat in the Virgin Islands. And I was still a long way from having seen it all.

## Chapter 15

# The Race of Broken Bones (The Fear of Destroying Your Body)

711 kilometres of racing in six days

8,187 metres of climbing

0 medical products

2 rib fractures

It hurt every time I caught my breath, thousands of times a day, until the pain became a part of me and of my routine. I put a lid on it but, deep inside me, it pushed and tapped, wanting to come out of its box, and at those moments a silent scream of agony ran through my head. What hurt the most was that I hadn't chosen to be in this situation. I shouldn't have been suffering. Instead of struggling every day, racing with broken ribs on Swiss roads at the Tour de Romandie, I should have been resting at home. But my team denied me that option. It prolonged the torment.

During that spring of 2015, I'd fallen twice in the week before the Tour de Romandie. On the Wednesday, I crashed at Flèche Wallonne, although what were significant concerns about the extent of my injuries weren't reflected in the press release put out by the team that evening: 'Medical staff continue to closely monitor Dan Martin following his crash. Today his known injuries include contusions, abrasions and soreness in his neck. His health is our top priority and we will see how he progresses but remain hopeful that he will be able to start Liège–Bastogne–Liège.' The osteopath did all he could to relieve the discomfort in my neck, but I was concerned that I might have sustained a more serious injury, because my head had hit the road: I was worried that I had concussion. At that time, there were no rules for dealing with this type of accident. The UCI didn't put a concussion protocol in place until 2021: tests that had to be carried out when the rider was still on the ground, a rest period of at least a week ... Our team, which was leading the way on this issue, was less vigilant than usual in this instance. I didn't have a scan at a hospital, and got the green light from the medical staff to race four days later.

The day before Liège–Bastogne–Liège, I felt a bit better. The fact that I was going back to 'my' race seemed to be acting as a cure in itself. But that afternoon, a *directeur sportif* knocked on my bedroom door and delivered some worrying news. 'Dan, you're not going home after Liège. We're taking you to Switzerland for the Tour de Romandie.' What! What on earth were they up to? The *directeur sportif* added: 'You haven't had any results since the beginning of the season, you have to help the team score some UCI points.' I was bewildered. I hadn't prepared for that race. I didn't know anything about the course. I tried to strike a deal. 'If I get a good result in Liège, will you allow me to go home?' The team's messenger didn't want to know. 'We've already booked the plane tickets,' I was told.

As luck would have it, I fell in La Doyenne. There was a pile-up of riders 42 kilometres from the finish. It was my second crash of the week. For a few moments, I felt like I'd been sucked back into the chain of misfortune that had dogged me during 2013 and 2014. As I got up I could feel an intense stinging pain. My handlebars had hit me in the stomach. Nathan Haas, who'd also been injured in the crash, was standing next to me. He rode with me for another 7 kilometres to the top of the Côte de La Redoute, where our team truck was waiting. I said to Nathan: 'I'm sure something's broken.' However, that evening, at the insistence of the team's staff, I had to fly to Geneva. In the end, I said to myself: 'OK, let's see what happens.' Despite the crashes, I was in good form. Perhaps things would fall into place for me in Switzerland?

The next morning I woke up in my Swiss hotel room feeling tired and worried. I'd found it impossible to get any sleep. I asked the doctor if I could be booked in for a chest X-ray. I suspected that I had at least one break and perhaps more. Fabrizio Guidi, one of our *directeurs sportifs*, drove me to the hospital just over the road from the hotel. On the short drive, he reminded me of the team's position: 'Obviously, if you've got a fracture, you won't be riding.' I asked him: 'What if I haven't broken anything but the pain is unbearable?' Guidi tried to play that down: 'The pain will ease as the days go by. Maybe you'll be able to win a stage at the end of the week.' We had to wait several hours for the results, which finally arrived late in the evening. No fracture had been identified. That meant I would be lining up at the start of the team time trial on the Tuesday.

The Tour de Romandie starts two days after Liège–Bastogne–Liège, but you don't often go there after racing the Classics. The event marks the real start of the stage racing campaign for GC riders. When you're there you focus on not getting sick, by covering your chest with newspaper at the top of the passes, for instance, and drinking a cup of hot tea before going to bed – doing things the old-fashioned way. The Tour de Romandie is often more of a winter race than a spring one; the snow is only just starting to melt and icy gusts blast down the valleys, which are thick with cold fog hanging over the lakes. It's not uncommon for the queen stage to be shortened or completely wiped from the race map. But not that year. I was in for the whole shebang.

I thought I might be eliminated in the team time trial, dropped after 600 metres, left adrift on my own and, ultimately, outside the time limit. But I was wrong. I managed to hold on to the wheels of my teammates for the whole 19-kilometre test, which we covered at an average speed of more than 50km/h. That evening I reflected on what my *directeur sportif* had said. 'The pain will ease as the days go by.' Would things actually turn out the way he'd suggested?

That night, it quickly became apparent that they wouldn't. The pain persisted. It felt like a needle was piercing my stomach every time I breathed. I thought I had at least one broken rib, probably two, maybe three. I was really worried about the fact that I was racing rather than resting. I'd heard that some rib fractures develop into pneumopathy and that to prevent this you need to cough regularly or take deep breaths. By spacing out those breaths, I could space out the pain. But as I lay in bed, I felt it getting worse. I almost longed for breathlessness.

I turned to the teammates I was closest to, like my mate Nathan Haas, who was always there for me. They reassured me and promised to help me, even though there wasn't really much they could do for me. I also got some pretty blunt advice from the *directeurs sportifs*, Guidi and Andreas Klier – the latter I knew well; he had been a great roommate on the Vuelta four years earlier. The pair of them urged me to stick at it, accentuating what they believed to be the common interest of both team and rider, and insisting that I needed to hold on to the idea that you should never give up. They pushed me day after day, just as they used to when they were encouraging us on a climb: 'Hang on! Come on! Only three kilometres to go! Only two to go! Grit your teeth, last kilometre!'

The idea of using painkillers was of course an option, but it wouldn't resolve the problem. The pain was actually my body's way of protecting me, of preventing me from pushing myself beyond my limits. Every rider has stories of colleagues who have sacrificed their wellbeing by pushing themselves on a damaged bone, knee or tendon. Over the course of just a handful of days, even a single race sometimes, they ended up ruining their careers and prematurely ageing their bodies. I'd rather suffer than destroy myself.

The team didn't understand my refusal to use painkillers and perhaps, after looking back, neither do I but at that point it was a form of protest as for me I was in open dissent, half following orders, half disobeying them. Racing? Yes. Painkillers? No.

However, I wanted to make my team managers aware of their responsibilities. Every day I would ask: 'Can I go home tomorrow?' And they would answer: 'One more stage and we'll see . . .' After the third stage, I sent an email to our logistics manager asking for an emergency plane ticket to Barcelona. This was refused. I suspected that they weren't solely responsible for this decision, but during this whole period I didn't hear anything from our big boss, Jonathan Vaughters – not before, during, nor even after the Tour de Romandie. But I can only assume that he must have been behind the decision for me to stay in the race.

On the fourth stage, my ordeal became clearly apparent. I was dropped after about 20 kilometres, on an easy climb. The occupants of other team cars stared at me. I wanted to hold up a sign: 'Get me out of here!' I finished in a *gruppetto* that came in twelve minutes behind the winner. On the fifth stage, I lost another twenty-two minutes.

To keep myself going, I thought of riders who'd been even less fortunate than me in their careers, such as Timmy, Blake and Lucas, former teammates from early in my career who'd suffered serious accidents or health problems. Timmy Duggan crashed into riders on the ground on a descent during stage three of the Tour of Georgia on 23 April 2008. He did a somersault and hit his head on a pavement. He suffered a brain haemorrhage. Thanks to the medical care he received, he survived the incident. He managed to resume his cycling career and was crowned US champion in 2012.

Blake Caldwell crashed on a slippery street in Girona between his home and the meeting place where we were waiting for him to go out training on 2 April 2009. He broke his femur. The doctors then diagnosed him with osteoporosis and he was forced to end his racing career.

Lucas Euser was riding a hundred metres behind me on a two-up ride near Girona on 14 May 2009. We had just separated because I had to do some specific exercises on a climb. A car crashed into him. I didn't see or hear anything; when I got home, I couldn't understand why he wasn't responding to my texts. He had been taken to A&E with a shattered kneecap. Despite the obvious after-effects, he managed to resume his career, and raced until his retirement in 2015.

I also thought about the sick children at Temple Street Hospital, Dublin, whom I had met through Cycle4Life. Friends had asked me to work with this charity, which raised funds for the young patients. Our encounters with them brought us face to face with the issue of justice and injustice in life, of true luck and bad luck, and we were inevitably shaken. Compared to riders who'd had to cut short their careers prematurely or suffered serious injury, and even more so to children who were fighting to stay alive, I was lucky. Very lucky.

All I wanted at the Tour de Romandie was for the ordeal inflicted on me by my team to end. I asked for permission to sit out the final stage, a 17-kilometre time trial through the streets of Lausanne. The team insisted that I start. Very well, I'd do it. This was now a contest, their obstinacy fighting mine. I started the TT on a normal road bike because I found it too painful to get into an aerodynamic tuck on my time trial machine. I finished the time trial and with it the Tour de Romandie. I was 104th, one hour and sixteen minutes behind Russia's Ilnur Zakarin. The next day, I decided to take myself off for an X-ray. And what did they find? I did indeed have two broken ribs.

I never found out why my team had treated me so badly. Did they want to ensure that the Tour de Romandie organisers paid up the full costs for their participation in the race? Did they want me to go hunting for UCI points, which we were short of collectively and which we theoretically required to remain at World Tour level the following season? Were they punishing me for a lack of results? That year, I had finished 10th overall in the Tour of Catalunya and 15th in the Amstel Gold Race, before crashing twice in the Ardennes Classics. I'd also been expecting to do better, but that didn't mean that I had to be penalised.

Had the team's management suffered a crisis of confidence, believing that I didn't want to race when in actual fact I simply couldn't? The team had got to know me over more than seven years and were certainly well aware that I never shied away from racing, that I always did everything I possibly could. They also knew which buttons to push in order to make me react: pride, courage, and a hatred of complaining. They'd already provoked me in a very similar situation during the 2012 Critérium du Dauphiné, when they urged me to finish whatever the cost, even though I had a broken shoulder blade (unknown to me at the time) and couldn't hold the bars. Cycling is always about pushing yourself further, but I'd expected that a team would draw the line when it came to wanting an injured and groggy rider to race. I wasn't expecting them to insist on the rider racing if he'd asked to go home. As soon as a rider sustains an injury, they should be taken at their word, and protected.

Was this a case of wanting to put me under pressure because my contract was coming to an end and renegotiations were about to begin?

More than the broken bones, it was the attitude of my team's management that hurt me. How quickly things change! In 2013, the team had been very considerate when I had a concussion at the Vuelta. In 2014, they had paid for me to have surgery on my collarbone after I crashed on the opening day of the Giro. I had first been taken to Belfast Hospital for examination, accompanied by our team doctor Kevin Sprouse directly from the race, but due to the incident occurring in the United Kingdom, the team's insurance company placed the responsibility for payment onto the National Health Service whose normal practice is to not operate on collarbone fractures, despite it being severely displaced. After some phone calls to the friends who I had worked with at the Cycle4Life events, Darragh and Cian Lynch, we managed to organize surgery in a private Dublin hospital not just for myself, but also Koldo Fernández. I was very grateful to Team Garmin for not hesitating in covering the entirety of the medical costs.

I was back with the team for the 2015 Tour de France. Two months after my crashes, with my ribs by then repaired, my morale had just about been replenished too. The start of the race in the Netherlands appeared to be beset with potential traps. The first road stage ended with a section alongside the sea on roads washed by the tides, and then crossed a very windy dike to reach the artificial island of Neeltje Jans. The second stage featured parts of the Flèche Wallonne route, the race where in the spring I'd hit the tarmac. The day before the start, we gathered at our hotel in Utrecht for our ritual pre-Tour meeting. It was a chance for all of us, both the riders and the *directeurs sportifs*, to say some final words.

When it was my turn to speak, I said: 'I usually target stage wins rather than the general classification, but for once I'd like to go for a high overall finish. So, it would be ideal to avoid any stupid time losses in the opening days, in echelons perhaps or if the bunch splits going into a finish. It would be good for the team to help me out a little bit sometimes.' Charly Wegelius, our *directeur sportif*, didn't hold back. In his calm, monotone voice he pointed out that it was a pointless endeavour and that I was not a rider who had any chance of achieving a high finish in the general classification.

Under normal circumstances, a team manager would have mumbled something like, 'OK, that's fine, good idea, we know you've got great legs,' even if they didn't believe it. The internal psychology of a team is based on the idea of making athletes who can't achieve a particular goal believe that they can – not the other way around. I'd been humiliated in front of everyone, even though I'd finished seventh in the Vuelta towards the end of the previous season; the top ten could have been within my reach. Deep down, I felt like I was at the same point as five years earlier, when Matt White had expressed regrets over my performance at my first Giro.* Maybe this was an instructive moment; it appeared the team hadn't taken on board the experience I'd gained and still regarded me as the new pro they'd signed in 2008.

The incident that I'd been afraid might happen occurred on the fourth stage when we were racing across the cobbles in northern France. I fell on a wet road 5 kilometres before the first section of pavé. I wasn't hurt, but I ended up losing five minutes and thirty-seven seconds. Some of my teammates stayed with me and did all they could to help me, notably Jack Bauer, Nathan Haas and Sebastian Langeveld. I was pleased to see that the other riders hadn't lost confidence in me and still wanted to do what they could for me. On the other hand, Charly Wegelius's attitude at the finish once again disappointed me. His evident sarcasm as he offered some words of support highlighted his contempt: 'We thought you'd lose five minutes, and you lost five minutes. That's not so bad, it could have been worse.' On paper, a climber is always going to struggle on the cobbles. But I couldn't take this defeatism any longer. Charly,

---

* See Chapter 11.

the team's head honcho during the Tour, chipped in again a couple of days later.

He had seen me at the back of the peloton coming into the final 10km and questioned my positioning. At this point I was not in the fight for the overall, so for me it was worth the risk of a small time loss to stay out of trouble, as most crashes happened at the front. And I was also saving energy. Charly disagreed, and told me that if I was serious I would always be at the front. His attitude just didn't make sense to me any more. I was actually following his instructions by turning my attention towards stage victories, but he still made a point to deride me.

Jonathan Vaughters, who had not been in contact for several weeks, came out of the woodwork during the Tour de France. Quite unexpectedly, he offered to extend my contract. The discussions around this were like those you might have at the tomato stall on Girona market at the end of the day, when you were trying to pick up five boxes for the price of one. JV began by putting an offer on the table that was worth a quarter of what I was currently earning. He'd spoken to my agent, Martijn Berkhout, who humorously replied: 'Thank you for your offer. It's a very good bonus. Can we talk about his salary now?' Every couple of days my price changed, in informal discussions that were carried out by text message. Vaughters' offer would plummet when I finished in the middle of the pack, then, after my second place finishes at Mûr-de-Bretagne and Cauterets, he would raise it slightly. But still, in the best-case scenario, he wanted to halve my salary. However, it was no longer a question of money. I wouldn't have stayed, not even for 10 million euros. After eight years of great adventures and memorable moments with this team, I needed to regain a bit of dignity.

# Chapter 16

# A Climber in Flanders (The Fear of the Wind)

I never thought I would start a career as a 'Flandrian' in my thirties, amidst riders who love the jarring of cobbled roads, blasting wind, dust in their noses and dirt in their mouths. I was a twig within a group built like lumberjacks. After eight years with the 'Americans' of Garmin, I had opted to join the 'Belgians' at Quick-Step,* a team that reigned supreme at Paris–Roubaix and the Tour of Flanders, rather than at Liège–Bastogne–Liège or the Tour of Lombardy. As part of this 'wolf pack', I was plunged into great storms on the flatlands, discovering new sensations on my bike. I once again became the man and the rider I wanted to be.

As soon as our contracts had been signed, we had to undergo psychological tests, 'to get to know our personalities better'. I filled in the boxes without being convinced it would reveal much, although I did take my time with my answers. Jef Brouwers, a

---

* The team was known as Etixx-Quick-Step in 2016, then Quick-Step Floors in 2017.

sports psychologist, gave us an individual report during one of the winter 2015–16 training camps on the Costa del Sol. In my case, he concluded: 'You need to regain your self-confidence and self-respect.' The test had revealed the affliction that had been eating away at me for months: my confidence had gone through the floor. The shrink used simple words to remind me of the simple things that I'd forgotten: 'It's not a problem if you don't win.' But why would the Quick-Step team, who had hired me to add to their already vast list of achievements, encourage their shrink to say such things? Once I was back in my hotel room, I called Jess: 'I'm me again!'

When I started the season at the Tour of the Valencian Community in February, I got confirmation that I'd made the right choice. Before the second stage, which went to Puerto Fredes, the team's management had announced that I was capable of winning. Then, Niki Terpstra had said to me: 'Today, you stay on my wheel.' The Dutchman had won Paris–Roubaix two years earlier. He can read the road like a novel. He held on for 150 kilometres, always positioning me exactly where I needed to be. He was the boss. He gave it his all until the foot of the final climb, which rose for 12 kilometres at a medium gradient. As he pulled away, he shouted to me: 'Good luck buddy!' I felt something heavy in my chest, not a weight that crushed me but an energy that filled my lungs. I did what I knew I had to do. I climbed the hill flat out and sprinted at the right moment, 500 metres before the line, just before the road began to descend. It was my first victory for over a year.

During the climb, Dario Cataldo, an Italian climber on the

Astana team, surprised me when he yelled out: 'Get out of the way! You don't belong here!' Bad idea: that's the statement I'd been fighting against my whole career. But he persisted and pushed me with his elbow: 'Don't stay at the front of the peloton, you're not in contention for the general classification!' That was true, because I'd lost a little bit more than a minute in the 16km time trial the day before. Cataldo, one of those riders who know the general classification by heart, had decided that I was out of the game. I was stunned. Did I not have a say any more simply because I hadn't had a great season the year before? But even if I'd been a neo pro, should I have got out of the way? I tried to hold a place in the wheels. The next day, Cataldo apologised and congratulated me, but it was clear that you couldn't win races any more without permission or bodyguards.

After the finish, a teammate hugged me as if I had just won a world championship, as happy as he would have been if he'd won himself. It was Tom Boonen. As the days went by, I got to know a man who was not only very friendly to me but got on extremely well with everyone. As soon as Tom walked into a room, the noise in it dropped away. There was a natural, sincere, spontaneous respect. Everyone knew that Quick-Step was 'his' team. He'd been the soul of the team since 2003. He dominated thanks to his physical stature, his *palmarès* and even more so with his attitude: the way he looked everyone in the eye, the way he showed interest in how you were and in your latest news, his concern about our wellbeing, the way in which he tempered the stress he sensed in the younger riders, and the way he would fit our job into what was an almost normal life. Tom stood out all the more because he always did everything he could to avoid appearing to be better than us: I think that's the mark of a true leader.

The team's boss, Patrick Lefevere, showed that same sense of respect, and made everyone feel important. For the first time, I heard mechanics saying: 'The year we won Paris–Roubaix . . .' We were all links in the same chain. Patrick knew every member of the team, which is quite something in a sport where many other managers don't know the first names of half of their staff. Each individual was treated equally, the bus driver in the same way as a racer, the *domestiques* in the same way as the leaders. At training camps, all thirty riders would dine at the same huge table, which consolidated the sense of us all being part of a single group. Patrick, a former rider, car dealer, team manager for more than twenty years and *directeur sportif* for more than thirty years, was still hugely passionate. If he made any derogatory remarks, we never heard about it. When he welcomed me into the team, he told the journalists: 'Dan Martin is a shoo-in for his races. He's a complete rider that any team would like to have.'

We had to race as a family. There was real solidarity between us, a sense of ruthlessness in the face of adversity. The team managers fully agreed with what the psychologist had told me in Spain: 'It doesn't matter if you don't win.' But they added: 'That said, what can we do to win today?' Tom Steels, a former green jersey champion at the Tour de France, used to analyse race pictures, looking for the slightest hole in a garden hedge that might let the wind rush through and help to create an echelon. Brian Holm had the task of saying the last vital words before we raced: 'We know that you, the riders, want to win even more than we do. We trust you. Have fun.' As for Davide Bramati, a former pro who had led the team in all of the Monuments, he provided the final touch with exhortations like those of a fifteen-year-old fan: 'Alleeeeez! We believe it!' At race starts, the bus rocked with uptempo music that made your heartbeat race, like the music you'd usually listen to on your headphones before a time trial.

At my previous team, they used to say: 'This stage is for sprinters and we don't have a sprinter. See you at the finish. Tomorrow will be another day.' But it wasn't like that at all at Etixx. They always looked for some kind of possibility: 'We don't have any sprinters, but we will try to create echelons. Or launch a rider with five kilometres to go, in the style of a *finisseur*. Or let a non-sprinter have a go in the sprint.' If the non-sprinter finished seventh at the finish, he was feted like a hero. There was never a day for doing nothing. We only lost after we'd tried everything.

The team pushed me to ride like a Flandrian, and I was eager to take up the challenge. And why not? I didn't hate echelons as such, or even cobbles. Back in 2004, I'd fared quite well in Acht van Bladel, a junior stage race near Eindhoven in the Netherlands. I'd learned how to move up at the right moment, the right place to position myself on a cobbled road that was roughly comparable to some sectors of the Tour of Flanders. I also learned to ride with gloves; I had forgotten to wear them on the cobbles and the vibrations made my hands bleed. Later, at Garmin, when we raced in crosswinds I got dropped, but not to a ridiculous extent. David Millar even nicknamed me 'Crosswinds'. But I used to lose time more often than I gained it on stormy days, or days that featured cobbles or ended with a sprint. That's why 'Operation Arc de Triomphe' was such a difficult test . . .

It was the summer of 2016 and my reunion with the Tour de France had gone extremely well. I'd escaped the crashes on the opening stages and the team had saved my skin in the echelons going into Montpellier as the race moved from the Pyrenees and towards Mont Ventoux. Without Tony Martin's masterful manoeuvre, protecting me for 5 kilometres into the wind, I would have lost a considerable amount of time. It looked like I was going to finish ninth in the final overall classification, which would have been fine: when the team signed me, the *directeurs sportifs* hadn't counted on that kind of performance, as they felt that my priorities were the Classics and stage victories. Going into the final day, though, just thirteen seconds split the four riders lying between seventh and 10th place, and my directors were very excited. They thought we could turn the tables: 'Dan, you know that the stage on the Champs-Elysées is normally a processional stage, which doesn't change anything in the race? Well, we've got different plans for you. When you're racing up towards the Arc de Triomphe, you'll start the sprint.'

For a while, it looked like I'd be able to slip into Marcel Kittel's lead-out train and be carried along like a real sprinter.

Unfortunately, though, Marcel was knocked out of contention by a broken pedal with 36 kilometres to go and then by a puncture. Iljo Keisse also had a flat tyre. As for Tony Martin, he stopped at the team bus the first time we crossed the finish line because of knee pain, not wanting to jeopardise his chances in the Rio Olympics a fortnight later. As a consequence, when we came to the red kite with a kilometre to go, I only had the Argentinian Max Richeze at my side. But our plan worked: several of my rivals were caught behind splits in the bunch. Coming through the last right turn from the Place de la Concorde into the Champs-Elysées, we were travelling at more than 50km/h. I held on with all I had. My body wasn't happy with this last moment of madness. My lower back was on fire. My legs were screaming at me to stop. But, as we crossed the line, the team exploded with joy. According to race timings, I'd moved up two notches and was now seventh in the final overall classification of the 2016 Tour de France.

We pulled back the curtains at the entrance to the bus and started celebrating. Suddenly, one of our *directeurs sportifs* appeared, looking very serious: 'Sorry, guys,' he told us, 'the commissaires have neutralised the last lap, for safety reasons. The times were taken before the last lap. You're still ninth in the Tour, Dan.' In this instance, 'safety reasons' translated to the yellow jersey being allowed to finish serenely, surrounded by his teammates, for a group photo. He came in more than a minute behind the front of the peloton but was given the same time. Our sense of disappointment evaporated very quickly, though. The team was happy to have worked right until the last second and to have got their climber involved in a bunch sprint. The party restarted. We popped the official team champagne, brought in on pallets by our supplier, Lidl.

A year later, Marcel Kittel and I formed a strong partnership at the Tour. Instead of chasing our own goals, we made common cause. When we reached the passes, Marcel didn't simply think about saving his own skin and finishing inside the time limit, or even conserving his strength: he went all in for me. His green jersey led the way into the foot of the climbs. I was a golf cart sheltered behind a semi-trailer. Even the wind couldn't touch me. None of our rivals had the temerity to try to rub shoulders with me. Marcel was like a doorman at the entrance to a nightclub – which didn't stop him from winning five bunch sprints that year.

The amazing thing was that our partnership worked the other way around too. On flat days, I would take my place in Marcel's lead-out train, and not just anywhere: I used to ride at the head of the team, sitting in behind the line of Team Sky riders who were controlling the peloton to defend the yellow jersey. Behind me, I'd have the whole Quick-Step cavalcade, with Marcel in second-last position – we positioned a teammate behind him to act as 'sweeper', to close the door on other sprinters who might have used his wheel for their own lead-out. When we ate dinner in the evenings, Marcel would laugh about this: 'For a climber, you're a good train driver! What's more, you're always in a good position, you don't take any unnecessary risks.' Perhaps it was the attraction of opposites, or the fact that Jess and his partner Tess got on so well. In any case, when I met Marcel out training on the roads around Girona, time would slip by easily because we would be so absorbed in our conversations.

My guardian angels were riders moulded in the Flemish style, although they came from very different countries. A good example was Czech rider Zdeněk Štybar, three times the world cyclo-cross champion but often overshadowed by another rider on the team who was stronger than him. He seemed to accept this role as a 'deluxe' *domestique*. I soon realised that he was a rider who liked to help others, not only because it was in his contract, but simply because he got real pleasure from it.

In exchange for this unfailing support on the flat, I was given responsibility for passing on my experience in the mountains to the younger riders. Whether it was climbers like Laurens De Plus and Enric Mas, or *rouleurs* such as Rémi Cavagna and Max Schachmann, or the fearsome all-rounder Bob Jungels, I tried to give them as much insight as possible. At the 2016 Tour of Catalonia, most of the team was under twenty-five, but that didn't stop me from winning a stage at the ski resort of La Molina. Rather than being a 'leader', a word that had seemed impossible for me to live up to over any sustained period of time, I felt I was a 'role model'. I let the team's next generation take what they wanted from me.

In the case of Julian Alaphilippe, I was almost like a big brother to him. He was six years younger than me and wasn't yet wearing the yellow jersey or world champion's colours for which he's become renowned. I really liked his enthusiasm, his spontaneity, his craziness and his respect for other riders. Was he a *puncheur*, a climber? At that time, I regarded him as a gifted talent who had learned a lot from racing cyclo-cross, a discipline that had made him very agile and capable of anything. There was never any question of competition between us, even during the 2016 Ardennes campaign when we both finished on the podium at Flèche Wallonne. That year, I was working on my climbing technique in the mountains and not focusing so much on finishes that suited a *puncheur*. Julian, on the other hand, was this free electron, as much a sprinter, if the feeling took him, as he was a *baroudeur*, one of those riders capable of crazy breakaways. Lots of people tried to rein him in, but I encouraged him: 'Keep on being crazy. That's what cycling is to me!'

Young or old, pure Flandrian or mountain specialist, we had to race as what we liked to call a wolf pack. And there was nowhere better to illustrate the pack mentality than in an echelon at Paris–Nice, which takes place in landscapes still under the influence of winter. Run between the French capital and the Côte d'Azur, the 'race to the sun' doesn't always live up to its name when it crosses the snow-covered Massif Central or the frozen vineyards between Burgundy and Mont Ventoux. During the 2017 edition, the team had planned to blow the peloton apart on the first day by using the wind to create echelons. We rode through the woods in the Chevreuse Valley, where the wind set leafless trees swaying, and swept across wide stretches of denuded farmland, where there was no wheat, no corn, no hedgerows separating the fields.

With 80 kilometres to go, we got the order in our earpieces: 'Get into position! In one kilometre, we'll be in the open, there'll be enough wind to force an echelon! Let's go!' Some of our rivals suspected the manoeuvre being planned. They did everything they could to get closer to the front and avoid being caught out. The peloton was splitting into several pieces. Luckily, I was in the first part of the peloton, towards the very end of the line. All of a sudden, the Norwegian Alexander Kristoff came by and pushed me out of his way. I almost hit a low wall. In the confusion, I lost contact with the group and found myself 5 metres behind them. Instinctively, I started to sprint in order to get back on. The road turned right and the wind started to come from behind. It was OK. I'd got back on. I even managed to work my way back up the group to join my teammates, who were right at the front. Once I was back with them, they increased the pace. Now they set about undermining the hopes of our rivals.

The team encouraged me and enabled me to find my place in the increasingly rapid-fire rotation of riders at the front of the group. It was mechanical, implacable. Julian Alaphilippe, Jack Bauer, Philippe Gilbert, Marcel Kittel, Yves Lampaert and me: six members of the pack in a peloton reduced to just twenty-nine riders. I tried to catch my breath for a few seconds each time we found ourselves going into a headwind or with a tailwind pushing us along. Meanwhile, the team's *rouleurs* continued to crush the pedals. We heard that Alberto Contador, Richie Porte and Simon Yates were more than forty seconds behind: 'Come on!' Shortly before the *flamme rouge* announcing the final kilometre, Julian attacked on the finishing climb, followed by French champion Arnaud Démare, who beat him to the line. I had enough strength to sprint as well. Sixth place. It was one of the proudest moments of my career. Thanks to this echelon, or more precisely to the sprint that had enabled me to stay in touch with the front group as the peloton was splitting, I ended up finishing third overall in Paris–Nice.

In these unknown lands, in hostile terrain for a climber, I'd been guided by unshakeable trust, towards my teammates and towards myself, and helped by a secret weapon: my jersey. The blue Quick-Step jersey was enough to inspire respect. Any opponent who saw a 'wolf' from our pack coming tended to move aside, unwilling to cross swords with a 'Flandrian', a broad-shouldered man towards whom you wouldn't dare aim a punch or an elbow. By simply pulling on this jersey, it was as if I had become a *rouleur* myself. You have to prove your legitimacy all the time in the peloton, a fact that was under-lined to me at the Tour of Valencia by Dario Cataldo's words. Evidently, only members of a strong team, who were well placed in the overall classification and were on their preferred terrain, had the right to exist. A 'good' rider in a 'poor' team wouldn't be respected, whereas a 'poor' rider in a 'good' team would be given a free ride.

I was able to gauge the difference in attitude towards Etixx-Quick-Step, a long-standing set-up that was used to winning lots of big races, especially on the flat, and my previous team. I was also aware of the difference between Quick-Step and Team UAE Emirates. Having lost my 'Flandrian' skin in 2018, I sometimes found myself being insulted by second-division riders: 'Hey, you, Emirates guy! Get lost, you don't belong at the front of the peloton!' You have to have changed teams several times during your career to learn this lesson in humility: a piece of material may be more important than the rider in it.

# Chapter 17

# A Panda in the Snow

Pandas love cold weather. They don't need to hibernate and can continue their normal life through extreme temperatures of around minus ten degrees. Yet, My Panda had obviously decided to stay home the day of the 2016 Liège-Bastogne-Liège. Snow was falling. You have to be crazy or a cyclist – which amounts to the same thing – to spend your day outdoors on a day like that.

Four days earlier, we'd almost got sunburned at Flèche Wallonne, but then the temperature plummeted. When we opened the curtains in the early morning, we realised that we were just going to have to deal with it: my favourite Classic could have been raced on skis.

So this would be a 'Neige–Bastogne–Neige', as the French would call it, punning on their word for snow. I was in a vengeful mood. After the crash on the final bend in 2014 and the crash on a flat road in 2015, which was the preamble to the disastrous Tour de Romandie,* I had to break the curse. I coated myself in whole buckets of warming embrocation, covering my body from head to toe, except for the one part that is best avoided. My agent Martijn had given me some excellent

---

* See Chapter 15.

gloves. I changed them halfway through the race because my fingers were getting wet – the worst thing on a bike is not the cold, but dampness.

That year my bike was the jewel in the crown. I was riding a brand-new model, designed especially for me by our supplier Specialized. The name of this work of art was the 'Emerald Panda'. The fork and chainstay were decorated with Irish shamrocks, while the head tube featured a panda stretched out as if it were racing a time trial. Thanks to the combination of the lucky shamrocks and the two-coloured bear, I was surely guaranteed to have some memorable adventures during the 248-kilometre race.

I was like an excited kid in the snow. Steam billowed from my mouth. The light beneath the fir trees in the Ardennes was magnificent. We followed a thread of road that was sometimes whitened by a thin film of snow, but it fell gently in flakes shaped like cotton-wool balls rather than drifting. We weren't going to damage our health on this epic journey. I had at the back of my mind the legend of France's Bernard Hinault, the winner of the 1980 edition, who lost the use of a finger because of the extreme cold. For my part I really wanted to go home with ten fully functioning digits.

My teammates did an admirable job, imposing control on the Côte de La Redoute and the Roche aux Faucons. Then, my legs gave out approaching the Côte de Saint-Nicolas. I warned them via my earpiece: 'You did a great job but it won't be my day. Sorry, guys.' The cold wasn't the cause. Fatigue was, to an extent. So too was the armour that I'd donned for this battle against my rivals and the elements; as I undressed, I realised the problem. I was peeling off layer after layer of fabric, like onion skins. I couldn't believe how many I had on.

What's more, the water had made the fabric swell. I had been dragging around a total of 5 extra kilos! My body was almost 10 per cent heavier. The teams that had been most successful that day had had the good sense to travel light. I learned my lesson, and used that knowledge to good effect on the second stage of Paris–Nice in 2017, on the day after we'd had a great day in the crosswinds and echelons. On this occasion, I was badly positioned, in the fifth or sixth group. The wind was icy and the rain torrential. Around me I could see riders almost at a standstill, their rain jackets ballooning like big parachutes. I took mine off, figuring it would be better to shiver with cold for a few minutes, and suddenly the same speed felt easy and I started to move up again. Fourth group, third, second . . . Luckily, the members of the first peloton slowed down and we all came back together, except for some riders who were too far back and lost almost a quarter of an hour.

Liège–Bastogne–Liège was always a rite of passage. Whether I won or came up short, this race taught me the finer points of the profession. As time went by, I felt that I had less chance of influencing the race. My accelerations on the climbs were less incisive. My explosive abilities were beginning to wane. This was normal. From 2016, the work I was doing in the mountains was opening up new horizons to me. From being a *puncheur*, and very comfortable on 3–5-kilometre climbs, I gradually became an endurance climber, a rider who was solid on Grand Tour stages.

Given that situation, I was very happy to finish second at La Doyenne in 2017. As in my best years, I made an attack at the bottom of the Côte d'Ans. I felt like I was back in 2013 or 2014. But the tactical game left me no choice. I was the sole leader left on the Quick-Step Floors team. Julian Alaphilippe and Philippe Gilbert had both failed to start, the former due to a knee injury, the latter as a result of a slight tear in his kidney. My attack was very predictable but super-intense. I had dropped back to 12th place in a reduced lead group, behind Alejandro Valverde, who was still the favourite. My mission: to try to surprise him. As soon as I saw that he was a little bit blocked in, I seized the initiative, with 900 metres to go. First I had to pass the riders in front of me one by one, then I had to open the gap. But Valverde himself commenced the pursuit behind. He bridged up to me, got onto my wheel, let me take the last bend in the lead and started the sprint immediately. There was nothing I could do: I finished second in the climbers' Classic, one length behind.

The irony of that Liège–Bastogne–Liège was that Alejandro got back up to me after my attack 400 metres from the line. Yes, in the Panda Zone. After my attack, I had positioned myself on the left-hand side of the road, but when I passed the place where the creature had appeared, I had instinctively switched across to the right. It was as if I were attracted by the magnetic force of the place.

I was continuing my research into the Panda. A friend advised me to investigate football fans. The hypothesis seemed to have some potential: five friends, including My Panda, may have been watching a match on the Saturday, having a good time, maybe even a little bit too much of a good time. They decided to have a bet: they had to dress up and get themselves into the final of the bike race the next day without being caught by a security guard. Sitting in a football stadium, the idea would sound like good fun. Besides, the city of Liège is home to one of Belgium's leading clubs, Standard, whose stadium is located right next to the route of La Doyenne, in the final kilometres just before the Côte de Saint-Nicolas. I checked out the possibility.

On Saturday 20 April 2013, the day before the Panda commando appeared, Standard de Liège were playing two hours away by car, against Lokeren (losing 4-1). However, did the fans really support Standard or another club? Did they watch the games live or on TV, in a bar or in one of their homes? And how could we find them? Nobody bragged about it on a fan forum. We had to keep on looking.

# Chapter 18

# Mountain Secrets (The Fear of Climbing)

**M**y renaissance as a racer took place on La Collada de Beixalis, a climb that began as my neighbour became my friend, and bore witness to me both at the peak of my form and at my lowest ebb. It got to know me inside out.

The Beixalis lies in the Pyrenees, in the Principality of Andorra. Topping out at 1,795 metres, it's not a long pass, not a climb where you can spin the pedals almost without thinking about it, or where a *rouleur* in great form can hold the tempo in the wheels. Rising steeply from the lush greenery of the tobacco fields in Andorra's central valley, it takes a significant physical toll on you, requiring an explosive effort, one guaranteed to disturb the serenity and silence of the place.

One day I hadn't eaten enough and got a hunger flat with about an hour to go in a six-hour training ride. It's a terrible feeling, as you become light-headed and have no energy to push the pedals. A voice within me said: 'Pick up the phone, call Jess and ask her to come and pick you up in the car.

This happens to everyone!' Another voice responded: 'What? Are you kidding?' I rushed into a petrol station and bought everything that came to hand – doughnuts, sweets . . . I filled my back pockets with ammunition and went back into battle, my objective to climb the eastern flank of the steepest pass, its average gradient 8.7 per cent for 6.4 kilometres.

My vision started to go fuzzy. Unable to continue, I stopped and sat down on a low wall. I dipped my hand into the bag of sweets and chomped them down. I got back in the saddle and continued for a kilometre, which carried me to Beixalis's notorious 18 per cent section. I knew I couldn't stop here, because I'd never be able to get going again. I ground my way up until the gradient eased off a bit. Then another stop. More sweets. Two more kilometres. Then a third stop. I was actually buoyed by the fact that I was nibbling away at the incline, metre by metre. I began to believe that I was accomplishing an extraordinary feat. Finally, at the crest, I felt like kissing the tarmac.

That bit of mountain made me a climber. The seed of that passion for the summits had been germinating since my crash in Liège–Bastogne–Liège, in April 2014. I felt that I ought to explore other paths within racing. Until that point, I could compete with the world's best riders when climbing for between five and twenty minutes. Once I got beyond that mark, I felt like I was hitting my ceiling; I wasn't anywhere near as comfortable. But after seven years as a pro, I wanted to push through that ceiling, to extend my range from the Classics to the Grand Tours, to switch from being a *puncheur* to being a climber with real endurance.

At that time, I was still living in Girona, where the surrounding climbs demanded a five-to-twenty-minute effort. The renowned Rocacorba mountain climb, for instance, fitted into this category. There wasn't anything longer. Training on hills that suited a *puncheur* had helped to turn me into a *puncheur*. I needed to train on the same kind of climbs as the true climbers. I discussed this with Geraint and a few other riders, and they all confirmed: 'To be strong on long climbs, you've got to ride them a lot. You should come and do some training camps in Tenerife.' They all lived in Monaco, but spent a lot of their time on this island off the coast of Morocco, climbing the Teide volcano (which hasn't erupted since 1909, but you never know . . .). The need to train in the high mountains meant these riders were constantly away from home, but I didn't like the idea of training in isolation from normal life. I decided to move, to find a place where my living and training requirements overlapped. The decision had been a long time coming; I was starting to get a little bit tired of the city. Friends had warned me: 'You'll see, one day you'll feel the need to leave.' There were too many cafés, restaurants, tourists, riders, stairs to climb from the supermarket to our apartment. Too many good things, too many distractions. Too many people staring at me as I walked around the city. I thought about Andorra, where I had done some training camps and reconnaissance rides. Why not?

A few other riders had already established a base within this Pyrenean state, which is perched between France and Spain, halfway between Barcelona and Toulouse. One of the first was Joaquim Rodríguez, who'd been my victim when I'd attacked in the Panda Zone at Liège–Bastogne–Liège. Another Andorran resident was Australian Simon Gerrans, who had won the same Classic the year I crashed on the final bend.

I went to Andorra with Jess for a first round of visits in November 2014. It was a land of shepherds, skiers and athletes, with Pyrenean peaks on all sides. The lowest point is 870 metres above sea level and sixty-two of its mountains are more than 2,000 metres high. We settled on a house at 1,350 metres in La Massana, a small village 6 kilometres from the capital, Andorra la Vella. The high mountains was an alien environment for a young couple from the UK, but before too long we started to relish the outdoor life in the Principality and Jess loved to train in the tracks through the hills and meet the new friends she was making at the cafes of Andorrà la Vella. We lived in a state of osmosis, with each other and, at the same time, with nature. The mountains loomed beyond the living room and kitchen windows. To the left you could see the Col d'Ordino, and to the right Beixalis. Sitting in the living room with a cup of tea in hand, we could watch the 2018 Vuelta peloton speeding down our neighbouring pass.

I had to wait until I was twenty-eight or twenty-nine years old to develop the body and the mind that I'd always wanted, that would enable me to become the climber I knew I could be. Up to that point, I'd always felt comfortable in the mountains and had picked up good results when my races sought out the heights. Yet, appearances can often be deceptive and not all of the riders who distinguish themselves in this kind of terrain are actually authentic climbers. They might be *puncheurs*, forcing themselves beyond their favourite distance of 3–5 kilometres of ascent, or *rouleurs* who've turned a mountain pass into a time trial course, or riders who can't easily be pigeonholed into any specific category but, on a day of grace, have simply managed to follow the pace of the kings of the mountains.

I'd always found it difficult to pin any particular label on myself. In the junior and U23 ranks, I was considered a climber thanks to my spindly legs, but I could just as easily win in a sprint or a breakaway. In my first pro season, Garmin coach Allen Lim told me that I undoubtedly had an abundance of fast-twitch fibres, which confirmed the racing qualities that I felt I had both in sprints and in the mountains – a climber's muscles include a good mix of the fast-twitch fibres of a sprinter and the slow-twitch of a *rouleur*. As a consequence, I became a *puncheur* or hill sprinter.

To be a fully fledged climber, to be able to tame and charm the mountains' twists and coils, I knew that I had to climb at least one pass a day. In May, I rode for six hours over pass after pass at a steady pace, avoiding intense efforts, keeping my power output to around 4.5 watts per kilo. My vertical gain record for one week was somewhere around 28,000 metres. I didn't find out the figures until I got home.

Beixalis became my PPO, *le point de passage obligé*, to use the term commonly used in race roadbooks to describe the mandatory access point to a stage start, featuring on every training ride. These sorties became meditations, because I was fully focused on what I was doing, cherishing the terrain, enjoying the moment. I was no longer competing against time. I climbed, descended and climbed again, and gradually I became a climber, a rider ascending for hours and hours, hurting myself for hours and hours. This suffering diminishes you and replenishes you at the same time.

I started to reap the fruits of these long climbs in September 2015, during the Vuelta. I was cruising up passes like a swimmer glides through water. Gradient became an increasingly relative obstacle. As a consequence, I was highly motivated for the stage that was set to take place on the roads of Andorra. The day's route had been designed by Rodríguez. Six passes, 5,300 metres of climb – thanks, Joaquim! Sadly, though, I never made it that far, having abandoned three days earlier. But the 2016 Tour de France offered me another chance to race in my new backyard. The stage to Arcalis even went over Beixalis.

The Etixx-Quick-Step team were doing all they could to keep my morale high on the Tour. After the race began, in Normandy, I'd dodged crashes and bad luck for more than a week. This meant I felt a serene excitement when we started the ninth stage in the resort town of Vielha, in the Spanish Pyrenees, and began to head towards the ski station of Arcalis in Andorra. Hostilities were unleashed by Alberto Contador on the very first slopes, the Bonaigua pass. The former Tour winner set the peloton on full alert, only to abandon the race with 100km to the finish. Up to that point, we'd all been asking ourselves: 'What on earth is he doing?'

It was an extraordinary day in every other way too. I started it in fourth overall, seventeen seconds behind yellow jersey Chris Froome and a handful of seconds down on Adam Yates and, almost inevitably, Joaquim Rodríguez. Our sprinter Marcel Kittel was always there to help me on the approach to the climbs.

Finally, we reached Beixalis. We passed through the village of Encamp, coming at the pass via its most testing flank, the one on which doughnuts and sweets had got me home previously. At the foot of the descent, we were one kilometre from home as the crow flies. Despite the speed and mass of spectators, I managed to pick out Jess, who was sat with my parents and her mum and dad, Paul and Mary, on the short climb up to the village of Ordino. Seeing them boosted my strength tenfold for the final ascent to Arcalis.

I loved this road, rising to an altitude of 2,240 metres, its landscape so relaxing to the eye. When I was looking for a gentler workout than I got on the Beixalis, I would ride up to this ski resort. It was 20 kilometres from my doorstep to the summit – one hour there, half an hour back. The last part of the climb runs through a series of hairpin bends at a gentle gradient of 5 or 6 per cent. Jess also enjoyed the road to Arcalis. It was the first climb she tackled, riding up on a mountain bike. In the race, though, it's a very different kind of test.

As the *rouleurs-grimpeurs* had a clear advantage on that terrain, I knew that I had to limit the number of attacks and make them at the right moments, especially as it's wise to stay in the wheels on this climb, because the wind often blows head-on and discourages attempts to go clear. But I wanted to take the yellow jersey. There were just seventeen seconds between me and that prize. I attacked, I was caught, I attacked again, I was reeled back ... It was the first time that my legs had caused so much damage on a Tour de France stage. Bit by bit, I became intoxicated by events unfolding around me. Romain Bardet and Vincenzo Nibali had long since been dropped. Only six of us remained in the group of favourites – Chris Froome, Simon Yates, Richie Porte, Nairo Quintana, Jesús Herrada and me. So I tried to slim the group down even more. My goal had changed. I was now preparing the ground for a top ten finish in the overall classification rather than trying to get the yellow jersey for a few days. Then the inevitable happened: I began to fade in the final kilometre of the climb. Although I lost a handful of seconds to Froome, I moved up to third place in the standings. As for the hail and darkness that had fallen on us, I was so focused on the task in hand that I hadn't noticed the change in conditions at all.

That evening, the team was staying just 600 metres from my home. I could almost see whether there was any mail in the postbox. I was sorely tempted to ask Jess to visit me in the hotel lounge either before or after dinner. However, she wasn't feeling well and, concerned that she might be coming down with something, we decided to postpone seeing each other. It was a moment, a decision, that underlined the total sacrifice that's required for the Tour. But, of course, it's never easy to seal yourself off from viruses even when you're mostly shut away inside the Tour's bubble. The proof of that came two days later when I ended up getting a cold, which I hadn't managed to shake off as we set off to attack Mont Ventoux on stage twelve.

\*

The 'Giant of Provence' has never smiled on me. Rising from the midst of a plain that's a patchwork of vineyards and olive groves, with no other mountain in the vicinity for company, the Ventoux cultivates a certain menace. Only a very few riders ever come away thinking they've conquered its flanks. The most testing of these comes at the mountain from the south via the village of Bédoin, the road gravelly and grippy. The final stretch to the summit seems endless, while the weather on the mountain can be schizophrenic, balmy and summer-like at the bottom, raging and wintry at the top.

That year, 100km/h winds raked the highest part of the route, forcing the organisers to shorten the stage by moving the finish line down to Chalet Reynard, the tiny ski station and restaurant that sits right on the boundary between the Ventoux's forested lower slopes and the lunar landscape on its heights, all white rocks and what you could easily mistake for a scattering of meteorites. If we'd climbed 6 kilometres higher, to the wind-whipped telecommunications tower, it would have been a debacle. But for once fortune was with me on the Ventoux. If it hadn't been for the storm, which was flipping over motorhomes like they were tiddlywinks and made our team bus rock dangerously on the edge of the ravine as we headed to our hotel after the finish, I would certainly have lost fifteen minutes instead of a just a minute and a half.

At the line, I slipped from third to ninth place. But it could have been far worse. As I'd climbed I'd focused on not thinking about how sore my throat was, about the fact that my nasal passages were so blocked I was struggling to breathe. In fact,

I don't remember anything about that day at all except, like everyone else, the images of Froome running up the mountain having abandoned his broken bike. Then, that same evening came the tragic attack on the Bastille Day celebrations in Nice and the Tour instantly lost its sense of gaiety, which during that edition never returned.

I'd overcome the Ventoux. I'd loved the Pyrenees and then the Alps towards the end of the race. My new team had helped me on the flat, including in the famous sprint on the Champs-Elysées. My new home in Andorra had helped me in the mountains. I was a new man. I started to look ahead to the next edition. I believed that the 2017 Tour de France could offer me the perfect canvas as a climber, the moment when I'd produce my best work. I was capable of it. Even today, looking back, I feel like I could have danced my way up the mountain passes – if only I hadn't crashed at 70km/h on one of the very first descents.

# Chapter 19

# A Black Cat Crosses My Path (The Fear of Descending)

When you read about descending in a bike race, the language tends to be beautiful, epic, dramatic. But I've never been taken in by that. Descending is essentially an accident waiting to happen: there are all kinds of hazards. You think you're in control, but . . .

I set my record speed on 11 July 2014, on stage six of the Tour of Austria – I've never worked out why Austrian descents produce such crazy top speeds. We were racing down the Radstädter Tauernpass, which tops out at 1,738 metres. My speedometer recorded 101km/h for 30 seconds, 103km/h for 20 seconds, 109 for 12 seconds, 110 for 6. And the peak, over 5 seconds: 112km/h. I should add that the road was wet. I don't know what's more frightening: the fact that I wasn't aware of the speed I was doing at the time; the fact that a rider passed me going like a rocket; or that there were at least a hundred of us descending at this speed, our wheels tightly grouped together as a peloton because the road was wide and straight. Being a descender is all about having trust: trusting the others not to make a mistake and, ultimately, trusting your own abilities.

My most spectacular crash on a descent took place on the ninth stage of the 2017 Tour de France, when I was taken out by Richie Porte as we were flying down the Mont du Chat into the finish at Chambéry. We'd had a taste of this narrow and winding road that lies in the Jura massif, just on the north-western edge of the Alps, during the Dauphiné. We knew that we had to be careful, especially as it had been raining, which meant it would take some time for the road surface under the cover of the fir trees to dry out. I was in the small group of seven riders who were the first to crest the pass. On the narrow, twisting descent, Chris Froome was at the front, followed by Jakob Fuglsang, Fabio Aru, Richie Porte and me. The two best descenders, Romain Bardet and Rigoberto Urán, were behind me.

One moment I was thinking: 'You're on the right wheel, Richie is one of the riders who takes the fewest risks in the peloton,' then, sweeping through a right-hand bend, I could see his rear wheel skidding. Richie was going to crash within a couple of seconds. I had one second to react. Would he go down on the right or the left? Which way should I go? If I went left, I would certainly collide with him. If I went right, I'd hit the cliff face. I didn't want to brake too hard, otherwise I'd veer left. My speed kept my natural trajectory to the right. So far, so good . . . But then Richie flicked off the verge on the left and shot straight across the road. He was flung from his bike by the force of the impact. It went to the left, while his body went hurtling like a falling rock towards the right-hand side of the road. My front wheel hit him. It was a freak crash, the kind of scenario that happens once in a thousand times. I just had time to think: 'Aah shit . . .'

I went down hard, but because I didn't feel at the time that I'd sustained any kind of serious injury, my overriding feeling was one of anger. When you're injured in an incident like that, it usually somehow makes it easier to come to terms with the circumstances; you accept what fate has dealt you and are entirely focused on the pain and on healing up again. Not on this occasion, though. When I got up, I felt annoyed at the thought that the race was slipping away from me. I was more concerned with the seconds I was losing than with my wounds. And to think that Richie and I had agreed a mutual non-aggression pact at the beginning of the Tour, both of us conscious of the fact that we were team leaders who couldn't count on having teammates designated to help us in the high mountains! I could see him lying on the road. He was conscious, but there was no doubt that his Tour was over.

My front wheel had buckled in the crash. My next thought was, 'Where's my team car?' A neutral service motorbike appeared. A new wheel was fitted. I got going again. Twenty-one kilometres remained to the finish. I was raging, full of adrenaline, my mood venomous because of the crash. But then something else interceded; as I approached a tight hairpin bend at high speed, I hit the brakes. Nothing happened. I had no front brake. I pulled the rear brake as hard as I could, locking up and skidding the back wheel. I was almost out of control – lurching, sliding, wobbling. I wanted to slow myself down using my feet but it was impossible. I was absolutely convinced that I was going to fall again.

I was carrying far too much speed to make the turn, but spotted an escape route up and over the grass verge between two trees. I avoided the trunks but went off through the woods for about 50 metres, ending up in a small meadow and continuing until my front wheel hit a hole and I was catapulted off my bike. This time, though, I was lucky enough to fall on grass and didn't sustain any more injuries. I got up, picked my bike up and made a beeline back to the road. The episode only lasted fifteen seconds or so, just slightly longer than I was delayed by my first fall.

I got back to the roadside, my jersey torn open. I was hoping that my team car wouldn't pass too quickly and that it would be able to see me. I arrived there just as the car reached that spot. Three seconds later and I would have missed it. I don't know whether it was Brian Holm, who was driving, or Tom Steels, who was sitting in the passenger seat and helping him with directions, who glimpsed me emerging from the forest, but what mattered was that the car skidded to a very controlled halt, its tyres smoking on the road surface. I was handed a new bike and got going once again. My focus was completely on the race. Adrenaline was not only masking my pain, but also stimulating my mental processes. I soon caught up with Nairo Quintana, who'd passed me when I went down the first time. I picked up speed, going faster and faster. I hurtled through the finish line like a rock that had fallen off the mountain.

That day, I hit the deck twice but also went close to crashing on two further occasions. The first collision took place about 30 kilometres after the stage start in the picturesque lakeside town of Nantua, in the Ain region. I hit a spectator's arm with my head and, as a result of the force of the impact, almost lost my grip on my handlebars. I managed to grab them with my right hand at the last second. Seventy kilometres later, on the Col de la Biche, Geraint Thomas fell just in front of me, breaking his collarbone. His rear wheel hit my handlebars and even made my Garmin computer rotate. I somehow managed to finesse my way out of that moment of danger, only to end up coming off twice on the descent of the Mont du Chat, caught up in situations I simply couldn't avoid.

'Bad luck.' That was what I heard from everyone at the finish, but I consoled myself by reflecting on the fact that:

1. I had come out of the crash in one piece, unlike Richie, who had been diagnosed with a broken collarbone and pelvis.
2. The crash had happened on the stage before a rest day.
3. I'd dropped two places in the overall classification, but I was still in a very competitive position, sixth, one minute and forty-four seconds behind Chris Froome.

As it always tended to do, fate had treated me relatively well.

The worst moment came when I got off the bike. As soon as I dismounted beyond the finish line in Chambéry, I started to limp. I was bent over like an old man. The team doctor treated the road rash on my elbow. We didn't have time to go to a hospital for X-rays because the pain wasn't that bad. And anyway, a plane was waiting to transfer the riders to Périgueux in the Dordogne and I didn't really want a five-and-a-half-hour journey by car. I boarded the plane. We decided that if the back pain persisted the next day, there would be plenty of time to have some tests done. Besides, since the incident at the Tour de Romandie, I knew that X-rays done right away don't necessarily reveal anything. I put my trust in my own feelings: the pain was 'acceptable'. I didn't feel as bad as I had done when I sustained road rash and concussion in the 2013 Tour of Spain, or the two broken ribs from the 2015 Tour de Romandie.

The next day I couldn't face sacrificing my rest day by paying a visit to the hospital. I spent a lot of time in the hands of the team's physios, did some stretching and then rode on a home trainer. At that point, we thought that a muscle might have been damaged during the impact and the back pain was due to a spasm. I took just a single paracetamol tablet in the morning – if the pain became bad enough that I needed something stronger I would stop the Tour. Likewise I never took sleeping pills, and this time was no different. When the race restarted, I just about managed to hang on in the peloton. I was given time off from working for my friend Marcel Kittel, who won the two bunch sprints that followed. During those two stages, I endeavoured to find a position on my bike in which I could produce power. My back was blocked, the muscles like rocks, the stiffness preventing me from being able to stand on the pedals, so I stayed sitting down, with my back rounded, ready to give all the power that I could while sitting in the saddle.

\*

Four days after the crash, we reached the first stage in the Pyrenees, the ski resort Peyragudes, effectively an extension of the Col de Peyresourde, which sits at an altitude of 1,580 metres. I was excited at the idea of the finish being in the middle of what had once been a James Bond set: the finish line was on the runway of the altiport, where the opening sequence of *Tomorrow Never Dies* had been filmed. In it Pierce Brosnan seems to blow up an illegal arms market in Afghanistan, but the action had actually taken place here in the central Pyrenees. I would have loved to have been in an action movie, but this Tour stage tended towards something more tragic or even epic. I still couldn't really use my upper body and pull on the handlebars, which meant I couldn't stand on the pedals and climb *en danseuse*, which was a serious drawback when it came to following any accelerations.

On the penultimate pass, the Port de Balès, which was shrouded by fog, I was afraid I might lose twenty minutes. Every effort I made demanded three times as much of me. But I held on. On the descent, I replenished my resources. I didn't give a thought to the possibility of crashing. I knew the terrain. I'd only needed to make one reconnaissance trip in May to lodge these roads in my memory, every bend, every acceleration. Twenty kilometres later, at the summit of Peyragudes, I conceded thirteen seconds to Romain Bardet and finished nine ahead of Chris Froome.

Far from breaking my resolve, the accident on Mont du Chat had increased it tenfold. Our team's *directeurs sportifs* had both reassured and challenged me when they'd said: 'Dan, we'll fight every day to recover the seconds you lost. You'll do what you do best: attack.' They didn't want any bad feelings to get the better of me. The day after the James Bond stage, I took nine seconds off the favourites by attacking on the Mur de Péguère, further east in the Pyrenees. And not on the climb: on the descent, 14 kilometres from the finish in Foix. The others were watching each other, so I jumped away with Simon Yates. Two days later, in the Massif Central, I once again benefited from riding aggressively when I went on the attack on a false flat 5 kilometres from the finish in Le Puy-en-Velay. I caught three riders who were in the breakaway, the Belgian Thomas De Gendt, the German Simon Geschke and the Ethiopian Tsgabu Grmay. Working together, by the line we had opened up a gap of fourteen seconds on the peloton.

But things didn't go so well on the next stage, which went into the Rhône valley. The mistral forms in this long corridor between the Massif Central and the Alps, and I'd got well acquainted with this powerful wind during my years in Marseille. For once, though, my team wasn't able to protect me in the kind of conditions where it usually thrives. Philippe Gilbert had already abandoned the race, and Marcel Kittel had been dropped on the first climb. Our rivals at Team Sunweb were riding hard in order to torpedo his chances in the race for the green jersey. When echelons started to tear the peloton apart, I was only able to count on the support of Gianluca Brambilla and the ever-faithful Jack Bauer, a buddy who's always been there to bail me out since we met at Garmin. Jack gave everything to keep me at the front, but the peloton split just in front of me and I couldn't go with the leading group.

I was just a metre or two away from making it. It was like seeing an ice floe split, the two sections slowly but inexorably drifting apart. As if that wasn't enough, I lost more time on a small descent into the finish in Romans-sur-Isère. It's always the same with echelons: I lost fifty-one seconds in one stage, double the gains I'd worked hard to establish in the Pyrenees and the Massif Central.

By now I was experimenting with making attacks while staying in the saddle. I still couldn't stand on the pedals. On the first stage in the Alps, I accelerated 7 kilometres from the summit of the Galibier, which we were climbing via the Classic side from Valloire. I was caught by most of the other contenders 2 kilometres later, but the manoeuvre enabled me to gain some ground on Simon Yates. Then we reached the descent, all 28 kilometres of it, down to the finish at Serre Chevalier. I didn't give a thought to what had happened to me with Richie Porte; my brain was completely absorbed by the imperative of not losing time. Unfortunately, Alberto Contador let a gap open in front of him, and as he was in front of me I didn't dare to overtake him; but I should have done. We'd been caught out and were now dependent on each other. We had our rivals in our sights, but the gap steadily expanded. A second's inattention, a moment of bad positioning, cost us thirty seconds at the finish line.

That evening, I started working out a little theory about descending. I believe that to be successful in this aspect of the sport, you have to be crazy. Not brave, but mad – courage is about overcoming fear, while madness stems from the absence of fear. The riders who love descending also love falling. I realise this is a bit of a weird mindset for anyone to admit to. But I got to wondering about the fact that cyclo-cross riders are also excellent descenders on the road: is this simply down to the fact that they've got a heightened awareness of the right line to follow, of when to brake, of balance on the bike? Or are they used to falling in cyclo-cross and are therefore looking for the same danger when descending a pass?

'You guys are crazy,' my moto rider friends once told me. 'You are basically naked when you race. You know all the protection we have in motorcycle racing.' A mental image came to mind; when I was riding a small one-day race in Italy early in my career and I noticed that the guy in front of me was wearing elbow pads. I had a laugh to myself but it did make me think: is he right? Why the hell didn't we wear more protection? A bit of light padding on the parts of the body that regularly take the brunt of any crash, like your hips, could be nicely hidden under clothing. The fact is, though, we didn't crash that often and most riders live in denial that it will ever be their day. This rider was obviously not one of those. Perhaps he was scared. I moved away from him. A nervous rider often makes for a dangerous rider.

I also got to thinking about Matej Mohorič, who was my teammate in 2015. On the day I reached a speed of 112km/h at the Tour of Austria, he was the rider who had passed us all and left us for dead. In doing so, he'd set his own record of 123km/h. Matej enabled me to understand the psychology of a 'descender': it's all about not being conscious of the risks involved. They're like the child who puts both arms in the fire to make sure they get burned, or at least to confirm that they don't like the sensation. But if they do like it, they can't get enough of it. The world junior and under-23 world champion first started working on his art by descending the mountain where his parents live in Slovenia. Every time he came down it, he always went a little faster. He wasn't discouraged when he ended up in the foliage at the side of the road. In fact, he'd just go a little faster the next time. Matej even invented a technique that enabled him to push the limits, one that would be used by Chris Froome, among others, on some of the descents at the 2016 Tour de France before it was ultimately banned by the UCI in the spring of 2021. The 'Mohorič position' consists of moving yourself forwards from the saddle and lying on the bike, while continuing to pedal. The rider sits on the frame and puts their torso on the handlebars. Their fingers don't touch the brakes; they just have to pray that there isn't the slightest hole in the road . . . Matej explained to me that he had no idea of the pain that could result from a crash, even though he'd experienced it occasionally. Many years later, he admitted to me that he'd finally become aware of the danger because he was now a father. Having a child meant that he had to be careful. But then we all saw his descent on the final run-in at Milan–San Remo in 2022, when he was constantly on the verge of going off the road. At that level, it's no longer about technique, or psychology, but a way of being, a real art.

The day after I'd lost time on the descent from the Galibier, we reached the Col d'Izoard, the race's highest finish, the 'roof' of the Tour. I wanted to climb up there and tear off the tiles. We approached this old stone structure through the village of Guillestre. With 4.5 kilometres to go to the summit, I started to do just that. Michał Kwiatkowski, who was defending Chris Froome's yellow jersey, bridged back up to me with most of the other favourites, but Fabio Aru lost contact. We emerged from the pine forest into a very different landscape; the weather-roughened enamel of the rocks suffused the mountain's flanks with a soft and comforting light. At an altitude of 2,360 metres, I should have been struggling for breath. But I felt quite the opposite: a cascade of fresh air filled my lungs, bringing with it relief.

Despite being penalised by my heavy crash on Mont du Chat, being unable to pull on my handlebars when I wanted to attack in the mountains or even in the final time trial in Marseille, being set back further by the wind and the echelons it created and an error in positioning on the descent of the Galibier, I still managed to haul myself up to sixth place in the final general classification of the 2017 Tour de France, four minutes and forty-two seconds behind Chris Froome. It was my best performance in the race. The Quick-Step bus was shaking with the party going on inside as it arrived on the Champs-Élysées.

Two days later I had a check-up on my back at a clinic in Andorra la Vella. Diagnosis: two fractures of the transverse process, the wing part of the L2 and L3 vertebrae, and two weeks of mandatory rest.

From his apartment where he was recuperating from his injuries, Richie Porte sent me a text message: 'I'm sorry. If I hadn't made you fall, you'd have done better.' But what if, on the other hand, this fall had actually been a blessing?

I'd joined the circle of riders capable of finishing in the Tour's top ten, and maybe a little better. It was at that moment that Mauro Gianetti offered me the chance to join Team UAE Emirates for the 2018 and 2019 seasons. Patrick Lefevere didn't try to keep me. He sent me what's a rare message in this business: 'Thank you.' If he'd known the financial sacrifices I would have been ready to make to stay . . . But he told me: 'You're a good rider, you have a good market value and I don't want to devalue it, I've got too much respect for you.' Even after I joined my new team, Patrick continued to send me messages, congratulating me on my results or consoling me when I crashed. Quick-Step *directeur sportif* Brian Holm, other staff members and riders did the same. As far as they were concerned, I was part of the Quick-Step 'family' for life.

Team UAE Emirates wanted to make me an authentic Grand Tour contender, offering the means and showing belief in me that had hitherto been unknown. We had an unlimited budget designed to make us a team that would shake up the Tour de France. I was ready to take on the responsibility and pressure, to participate in the testing of the most high-tech equipment, to help in the recruitment of my teammates. The opportunity wouldn't come again. Before signing my contract, I asked for just one favour: to be released from any commitment to join the team when they did recons of the Pyrenean passes being used in the Tour de France, because I had a very personal approach to these legendary roads and a rather unusual way of preparing for them ...

## Chapter 20

# 10 Pancakes for 5 Euros (The Fear of Fun)

I climbed into the dark clouds, streaked with cold rain. I was optimistic enough to think that I would break through this layer of gloom and emerge into blue skies above, but the clouds were too dense and the soaking, like that from a state-of-the-art shower head, barely relented, deluging me like a waterfall one moment, then sprinkling me more gently until the next dousing began. Eventually, the black veil of rain gave way to the whiteness of fog. I was now in a cotton-wool like tunnel, my perception of space was blurred and sounds were muffled. But then I became aware of something reminding me that I wasn't lost and alone, the welcome sound of a car. It was Jess. She was trying to hug the right-hand side of the road in order to avoid tipping over into the ravine on the left. She waved me onwards as she passed, encouraging me to continue with my training. A few minutes later, I found the car stopped at the side of the road. We both said at the same time: 'You can't see anything, we'll stop here. It'd be crazy to go up another five kilometres.'

The Col de Portet was the latest Tour de France pass to be opened up in the Pyrenees. It was very much in keeping with the event's scale and was due for its inaugural appearance in the great race in July 2018. The road to it was effectively an extension of the ascent to the Plat d'Adet ski station but ran much higher, reaching an altitude of 2,215 metres, a height more often seen in the Alps than the Pyrenees. 'It's a second Tourmalet,' said Christian Prudhomme, the Tour's organiser. Sacrilege: it was a hundred metres higher than the Tourmalet, my old and favourite friend, the climb that whispered in my ear. When I climbed it just a few weeks before the race would tackle it, the Portet was still very much incomplete, one of those where you'd expect a 'Caution, wet paint' sign alongside it. The road surface consisted of packed earth, loose stone and gravel. I loaded the bike into the boot of the car. Jess searched out a clean towel and a thermos of tea

I was the only top-ten contender for the Tour de France who was organising his own training camp and reconnaissance trip with his wife. No teammates, no *directeurs sportifs*, no *soigneurs* . . . Just Jess. Exactly how I liked it.

Our stay in the Pays Basque, the French Basque Country, was exceptional, the highlight of this personal training camp. We were at one of the crucial stages of the 2018 route, nestled in the region's big hills – or small mountains. The 31-kilometre time trial, which was of course quite hilly, was due to be held the day before the final stage on the Champs-Elysées, and I had to become well acquainted with those undulating roads. I was surprised when the owner of the Auberge Basque, the hotel where we were staying, had offered to save us a place for dinner, but had gratefully accepted; it would save us the trouble of finding another restaurant in town, a town that we soon realised was as tiny as it was pretty. On arrival we discovered that there was another good reason for making a reservation: the hotel's restaurant was celebrated for its gastronomic qualities, which were underlined by a Michelin star. The Basque Country as a whole is renowned as one of the finest gastronomic regions in the world. One of the local specialities is Espelette red peppers, which are aromatic, moderately hot, sometimes with a smoky taste. The locals hang them to dry on the outsides of their houses in the town of Espelette, which they're named for and where the time trial was due to finish. At the Auberge Basque the menu was magnificent, from the reduction of asparagus from the garden served as a starter (accompanied by a mousseline of asparagus, dried skipjack tuna and marjoram) to the savoury version of a Basque cake, with ewe's milk cheese replacing the cream. Our training camp ended on a high note.

This trip together was my way of involving Jess in my work. As much as she enjoyed coming to races, and I loved sharing those moments with her, it was something she rarely did. Scouting out the Tour de France, we'd created time for each other.

spouse going into the office while their partner was working. Scouting out the Tour de France, it was different. We'd created time for each other. Jess accompanied me in the car, which was filled with our bags of clothes, bike spares and all the care and gentleness she could provide. Sometimes she would follow a few yards behind me, but more often than not she would drive on ahead and go straight to the finish town. I preferred to fix my punctures with the spares I had in my jersey pocket rather than ask Jess to carry spare wheels in the car behind me, with the possibility that she would end up half-asleep at the wheel as we ground up passes at 20km/h – fast for a cyclist, but a frustrating and tedious speed for a car driver.

In the Alps I could gladly accept being part of a team training camp, but I wanted to do things on my own when we were riding though the Pyrenees. Quick-Step's and Team Israel Start-Up Nation's *directeurs sportifs* were very surprised by that way of preparing for the Tour de France. They'd ask me: 'Are you sure you don't want two or three team members to ride with you? A masseur at least?' The Team UAE Emirates staff asked me the same question. Each time, I answered the same way: 'Thanks a lot, guys, but it's fine like this riding alone. I can really connect with the terrain and memorise the course.'

One single reconnaissance ride was enough for me to burn the route onto the hard drive in my head, like I had in 2017 for the last part of the famous 'James Bond stage' to Peyragudes. I put special focus on the downhill of the narrow and twisting Port de Balès, which came before the ultimate ascent. I was so focused that I was barely upset when I came face to face with a cow that was taking a nap in the middle of the road. It was one of those big mountain beasts with twisted horns and muscular legs, proud, peaceful, not to be rushed. I waited ten minutes before she moved, and I might have waited longer if a car hadn't pulled up. The purr of the engine woke her up and angered her – I would guess that the panel beater in the local village must have got a decent return that month! But I was able to get going again.

I met with Jess that day after my training ride, on the top of the Peyresourde. There was a wooden hut at the summit selling crêpes. The sign said '10 for 5 euros'. How could they be so cheap? We soon realised when they came out; they were barely 10 centimetres in diameter, but were the perfect thing for refuelling all the same.

Two months later, in the Tour, that pancake stall was an important motivational marker for me: the memory of that time with Jess brought a welcome distraction from the effort of the race and the discomfort of my broken vertebrae.*

Sometimes it was better for everyone that my team didn't know all the details of my personal preparation with Jess. This mist was particularly welcome when, in 2019, Team UAE Emirates nearly lost their Tour de France leader – me – in a snow tempest. The scene took place on the Tourmalet, from Luz-Saint-Sauveur, the flank I'd tackled in my adolescence, and reminded me why this pass had such a tough reputation. It was a beautiful day as I started the climb, but about three kilometres before the summit, I glanced down to the valley to admire the view and saw a storm rolling in. The pursuing clouds quickly caught up with me and snow began to fall from the now leaden sky. I was wearing my summer jersey, but fortunately I had packed a rain jacket. On the top of the pass, I put it on as

---

* See Chapter 19.

fast as I could, not an easy task with the wind now blowing hard and my hands beginning to lose feeling, and started the descent, with next to no visibility. After steady progress down through the now blizzard conditions, my front tyre hit a stone and exploded.

What was I to do? I couldn't possibly stop and change it at 2,000 metres in a snowstorm. Fortunately, my experience paid off. I knew the ski resort of La Mongie was four kilometres from the top, so I continued, albeit at close to walking pace. Everywhere was closed, but I found a stairwell to shelter from the conditions. I replaced the inner tube as quickly as I could before getting back on the road. The snow turned to rain, which actually proved to be colder, especially as the long straights after La Mongie are taken at high speed. The temperatures soon improved on reaching the bottom of the climb in Sainte-Marie-de-Campan, and I was even greeted by warm rays of sunshine when I rejoined the route of my stage victory in 2013 down to Bagnères-de-Bigorre. Jess was waiting for me in the guest house close to Lourdes where we were staying, and I had to tell her the story of a cyclist almost lost in a snowstorm.

Jess was the best teammate I could have ever imagined, because she listened to me. She didn't understand all of cycling's intricacies yet, but she understood me. She encouraged me. She helped prevent cycling from getting on top of me. She reminded me that there was life outside sport. Thanks to her, I became richer inside. In exchange, I wanted to be with her for her new start, in spring 2015 after a one-year break. I shared my nutrition techniques with her, such as having an energy gel before warming up – until then, she just used to drink a bottle of water, no sugars.

Then, we thought about the goal that drives all track athletes onwards: the Olympics. We had a dream: to both compete in Rio.

In August 2016 we flew to Brazil, on separate flights. It was my second experience of the Olympics, after London; but it was all new for Jess. She was racing under the British flag, while I was in Irish colours. We missed the opening ceremony on 5 August; Jess was in a holding camp far from Rio, while for me, as was always the case at the Olympics, I was hidden away in my hotel room as the men's road race started early the next morning.

It was muggy right from sunrise on Copacabana beach. We clocked up 4,886 metres of vertical gain over 237 kilometres. The race was a little bit shorter than Liège–Bastogne–Liège, but the hills were longer than the Belgian Classic. It didn't feel hot, but it clearly was; it was simply impossible to drink enough. Likewise we couldn't get enough bottles, especially once the race started in earnest and going back to the car wasn't an option. Team Ireland had made a big effort but we were still disadvantaged,* and one lost bottle on the cobblestones sector on the first circuit left me without water for 25 kilometres, something that proved costly on the last lap. Once you get into debt it's impossible to repay, no matter how much you drink. I

---

* At the Olympics, the number of team staff each nation can bring is decided by how many riders are in the race. Yet we were only two: me and my cousin Nico, who I'd been delighted to be racing with again, who finished 29th after dropping a chain on the foot of the final climb.

finished 13th, two minutes and fifty seconds behind the winner, Greg Van Avermaet. I was on my knees. For the first time in my career, I was wracked by cramp. I even had it in my arms.

Six days later, I was in the stands at the Maracaña Stadium to watch Jess race in the 10,000 metres final. I kept my eyes fixed on her. I kept wondering what she was thinking. Her face was a picture of focus, but we had talked about this race and she'd said that her plan was to soak up the atmosphere and enjoy the experience. In a race that was run a minute faster than world record pace, Jess didn't allow herself to be over-whelmed. It takes a special mental strength to produce your best performance on the biggest stage. She finished 16th in a personal best time of 31:35.92, and was very happy with it; but I felt ten feet tall such was the pride that I felt.

That was it. We'd achieved our joint goal: we were 'Olym-pians'. Although we hadn't participated in the same event, we felt like we'd been competing together.

We would have liked those Games to have gone on for ever. We were in no hurry to get back to Europe. We travelled around Rio, our adventure enhanced by a trick I'd learned not long after arriving. Normally at the Olympics you only have the right to access your own sporting venues, and have to apply for tickets for other events you would like to watch. But I had learned that by boarding the athletes' bus to the venues we could get access to any event we wanted; they were not checking the accreditations as thoroughly as in London 2012. Thanks to this, we went to watch almost every sport at the Games! We made the most of the opportunity. I'll admit that there were moments when I was afraid that I would get a taste for it, afraid that the golden sands and sea might make me forget the smell of rain and mud on the bike. But I felt that this moment was unique, even seminal as far as our lives were concerned. If any athlete doesn't make the most of these opportunities to ease back and relax, there's every chance that their career will blow apart. Rio had arrived at the right time. Among the highlights was our last evening, in a Copacabana hotel, on 20 August, celebrating my thirtieth birthday in the ideal way. We ate cake and drank champagne while watching the sea. The next day we attended the closing ceremony. But for us this wasn't the end of the adventure, but the beginning. We were due to be married at the end of the year.

I returned to Europe like a toy with new batteries. I was a new man, fresh and full of energy. The intangible rules of cycling set out that holidays take place over the winter, not in the middle of the season. The beach is portrayed as a waste of time. Yet that's where I did my best training. Without my bike. Proof, if needed, came when I finished third on the Tour of Britain's second stage two weeks later.

Even before I'd met Jess, I'd always been sceptical about the mountain of sacrifices that riders forced on themselves and the pride with which they spoke about doing so. I'd witnessed it during mealtimes with some of my teammates at the Vélo Club La Pomme Marseille: what they gained in nutritional perfection, I thought, they lost in pleasure. Ultimately, they lost rather than benefited. To me, cycling seemed a hard enough sport already without making it even more so.

Jess and I loved to dine out, especially at the Bambú Oriental Restaurante, a Chinese restaurant near our home. Its name fitted with the 'Panda Racer' perfectly. And two or three times a year, we treated ourselves to a nice gastronomic dinner. I had discovered this pleasure in Girona, first in El Celler de Can Roca, run by the Roca brothers and sometimes regarded as the best place to eat on the planet. Iberian suckling pig with pepper sauce and garlic and quince terrine. Oyster with earthy distillate. Mini octopus with smoked Vera pepper . . . Everything was superb. My only reservation was about a dessert called 'Old Book', which consisted of a page of edible text and a jelly with the essence of a hundred-year-old book . . .

In these prodigious restaurants, the food fills the mind as much as the belly and is surprisingly fresh and healthy. There was, therefore, good reason for me to invest in a restaurant in London, called The Frog, rather than putting money in the bank. The chef at Frog, Adam Handling, was the white jersey of gastronomy, a promising young guy with a keen awareness of small-scale producers and environmental issues, who soon earned a Michelin star and found himself cooking for the G7 heads of state in 2021 at his new restaurant at Carbis Bay in Cornwall.

The rest of the time, I had a healthy, well-regulated lifestyle, without excess. I went to bed before midnight, ate a lot of white meat and raw vegetables. I was never interested in long evenings in bars, even in winter, when many riders opt to catch up on the time they feel they've lost. I've never been a fan of McDonald's. But I didn't forbid myself anything in the name of fear or a certain kind of morality. My body set the rules. Since it knew I was listening to it, it didn't ask me for anything capricious. In fact, I lived in a very 'normal' way. But I wanted to enjoy myself from time to time.

The fear of fun had been passed down since time immemorial in this sport, but it was accelerating before my eyes. Team Sky had made a great show of the fact that they were going to work on 'marginal gains'. You end up seeing reality through a microscope. Within this kind of system, which was developed by several teams, the riders are used as guinea pigs. They accept it, content to hand over responsibility. They're too afraid of reality, too afraid of not doing things perfectly. But the truth is that reality is imperfect . . . The sports scientists were not only giving valuable advice to riders, they were taking control of them. It made you wonder who was working for whom! But the riders felt reassured because they believed that success would come their way. After streamlining their diet, improving hygiene and cleanliness, eliminating dust mites from the rooms, changing the quality of the bedding – all areas where intervention was deemed necessary – teams like Team Sky set about dictating the riders' social life. Time had to be spent in a sealed bubble, either racing or training. The rider didn't just give his body to his team, he entrusted his whole life to them. Some riders were afraid of pleasure. I was afraid of becoming a robot.

The Team Sky riders and I were almost living on different planets. I learned another example of our difference in approach on the penultimate day of the 2018 Tour de France, after the time trial. We'd just burned our last few matches on the roads of the Basque Country, which I had reconned with Jess. I was sitting with Geraint Thomas and Chris Froome in the place where the most talking gets done at the Tour de France: the doping control truck. The three of us were sitting in the waiting room. The problem was that thanks to the effort we'd just made, the heat, the fatigue, none of us could fill a urine flask. The time passed. We drank half-litres of water and a well-deserved bottle of beer. Nothing helped. So we talked. About everything. About nothing. I ribbed Geraint: 'OK, tomorrow you'll win the Tour de France and that's not bad. But who won the Junior Tour of Wales?' He pretended to take the joke seriously: 'Don't start! The Tour of Wales is the most important race in the world! If only I could make the switch!'

Then the conversation turned to what we were going to eat for our post-Tour dinner. I said without hesitation: 'A hamburger with chips. And a nice dollop of tomato ketchup. I am so tired of pasta!' Geraint and Chris said, 'We're going to have a good salad. We haven't eaten one for three weeks because of the fibres that lead excess water to be retained in the digestive tract.' They were very excited by the dream of a plate of iceberg lettuce. I did have some admiration for their commitment and sacrifice, but it seemed extreme. Then I thought back to the Auberge Basque where I'd dined with Jess, a few kilometres away, during my reconnaissance of the time trial. If only they knew!

# Chapter 21

# Operation Tour de France (The Fear of Missing a Golden Opportunity)

At 10 p.m., the taxi stopped somewhere on the outskirts of Milan, in front of a high gate that opened quietly. The villa, located near Malpensa airport and opposite the UAE Emirates team service course, our technical and logistical HQ, was impressively big and quiet. The gravel on the driveway had been perfectly graded so that the soles of your shoes barely crunched when you crossed it. Someone opened the front door before you had a chance to knock. In the hallway, impressive lions carved from white marble towered over a sumptuous staircase fashioned from white stone that rose from the floor like a fountain. The toilets at the end of the corridor were decorated with gold plate. A man in his sixties of impeccable elegance approached, his suit a snug but stylish fit. He greeted me with a firm handshake, welcomed my agent, Martijn Berkhout, who was accompanying me, and said in Italian: 'Good evening, gentlemen, and welcome. I will show you to your rooms upstairs. You will meet Mr Saronni tomorrow.'

We spent the night in extraordinary, old-fashioned comfort. The rooms were decorated with gleaming mirrors, gilded with gold leaf, and furnished with antiques. The next morning I met Martijn for breakfast by a swimming pool where a fountain of water sang softly. The buffet was huge, but comprised nothing but doughnuts. 'This is a great start,' said Martijn, laughing.

'This must be their definition of marginal gains! This is where we'll be launching Operation Tour de France!' I shot back. After drinking a coffee and forcing down a doughnut, we crossed the street. Within the team's offices was a man waiting for us, who looked quite similar to the gentleman who had welcomed us the day before at the villa. It was the great Giuseppe (Beppe) Saronni. The former champion. The general manager of Team UAE Emirates. My future boss.

His name had been familiar to me since I was a child, probably because he'd become world road champion on the Goodwood circuit in Great Britain in 1982. I knew that 'Beppe' was still admired in Italy and across the cycling world, and that his presence was significant. Next to him was Mauro Gianetti, a former winner of Liège–Bastogne–Liège, calm, personable and even more chiselled than most of his riders. He wasn't officially part of the team yet, but I'd discussed and agreed the issues arising from my prospective transfer with him in the wake of the 2017 Tour de France. He translated for Saronni, who began by complimenting me: 'Danilo, what I really like about you is your *grinta*,' my grit, he said. 'You never give up. That's an attitude I like. With a rider like you, I really think that the team can raise its ambitions higher, with the aim of winning the Tour de France one day.' I knew this already. It was our joint battle plan. In the season I turned thirty-two, I'd allowed myself to be persuaded into taking on this challenge that had seemed too big and crazy. This former Classics rider was going to go hunting for the yellow jersey – or, more precisely, the podium.

During the conversation, Gianetti repeated what he had already explained to my agent during the negotiations, and he seemed absolutely sincere. 'We believe in you,' he asserted. 'We've analysed the riders who have finished in the Tour's top ten in the last two years and we think you're the one with the most room for improvement. There are seven or eight of you who could reasonably finish on the podium. So far you've been unlucky. There's always been a little hiccup that has prevented you achieving that result. Despite that, you've fought hard. You're among the top three or four in the mountains. And your limits as a time triallist aren't so much of a handicap any more, because time trials are no longer that long. You've got a very high capacity for recovery. You're in the optimal period for a cyclist, between twenty-eight and thirty-two years old. With luck, the right equipment and a dedicated team, you can finish on the Tour de France podium.'

Beppe Saronni nodded his head in agreement. My agent then took out our documents. We initialled the contracts with beautiful pens that felt as heavy as tree trunks.

As he escorted us out, Mauro stated: 'We have to build this team together. If you see something wrong or if you've got an idea to improve things, tell me. OK?' We'd already agreed on this way of working in the summer. Every rider has dreamed of having a free hand, especially when you've been plagued by wayward equipment, demotivated staff or a string of logistical errors. When I left Quick-Step, I didn't have this sense of wanting to do things properly because almost everything there had been organised in the correct fashion, but I'd often imagined what it might be like to be on a team that shared my thinking, from top to bottom. To succeed, you needed a surfeit of human values and an equal quantity of technological tools. Gianetti agreed on this. We had to work with the leading scientists in each field, going right down to the smallest details, always applying the theory of marginal gains, which entails improving each element within an athlete's environment by 1 per cent.

Two months later, I returned to the Team UAE Emirates' state-of-the-art laboratory, which was located in our service course. The riders had come in for a bike-fit session, a fundamental task that often goes hand in hand with wind-tunnel testing. We had to determine the height and layback of the saddle, establish the same data for the handlebars ... Every angle of the body and machine is studied in order to create an ideal competitive marriage. But when I saw the measuring device, I took a step back. It was fitted with a leather saddle from the 1960s, and the drivetrain was fitted with cranks that were two sizes too big.

'Next!' The ergonomics specialist got me to sit down, and took some measurements. He was at least twenty years older than the saddle. When the process had been completed, I tried to ask the staff discreetly: 'Who was that man? And what was that bike all about?' I was told that he was a long-time friend of Beppe Saronni's and that, when it came to equipment, the team had always done things this way.

'Don't you think that there's something wrong with this?' I asked. I turned to Rory Sutherland, a friend and training partner from my days in Girona, who was set to become my teammate the following season. The Australian was four years older than me, and we had a good few things in common. Like me, he'd left his home country at the age of nineteen to start his career in Europe, in the Netherlands. He tried to make light of it: 'The team's only been around for a year. They need a bit of time to adapt. And you also have to look at the positive side of things. The atmosphere's excellent, you can feel the sense of family here.' That was true. Almost all of the riders knew each other from the 2017 season, when Team UAE Emirates had been launched, and some from even before that, when the team raced under the Lampre banner. This 'family' had been led for more than twenty years by Beppe Saronni, a former Giro winner, and under his leadership it had won the Giro d'Italia three times. Beppe had delegated most of his powers on the ground to his son Carlo, a warm and genial man, although not a born leader. Even though I'd been recruited as the leader, I had to adapt to the team's long-established habits.

There was talk that my transfer would also enable me to bring on board a *directeur sportif* of my choice, plus a coach, a technical assistant, a doctor and even a cook. I was initially excited at the idea of bringing on board people of integrity and competence with whom I'd worked in the past. Then the parameters narrowed and I was only free to suggest two to three teammates. Then one. That was Rory. But in the end, I was happy with the situation. I didn't want to create a state within a state. Instead, I wanted to help the whole team progress, from the inside, like an ordinary rider, but with the added responsibility of being a leader.

I had to share top billing with a climber from Sardinia, Fabio Aru, winner of the 2015 Vuelta and twice a podium finisher at the Giro. He was four years younger than me. Fabio seemed like a nice guy, even though we didn't talk much to each other and our paths rarely crossed. I'd been surprised to learn in the press that he was joining the team, because Mauro Gianetti had assured me that I would be the sole leader. But Beppe Saronni had insisted on recruiting this Italian talent. The team's management had explained the division of tasks to me, saying, 'Fabio will do the Giro and the Vuelta, you'll do the Tour and the Vuelta.' I didn't mind sharing responsibilities. At Quick-Step, I'd teamed up with Julian Alaphilippe and Philippe Gilbert, who had the same objectives as me in the Ardennes Classics. Two leaders wouldn't be too many when it came to dealing with internal and external pressure . . . Our Norwegian sprinter Alexander Kristoff would also be carrying some of the team's weight. Diego Ulissi, a former two-time junior world champion, would be another of the squad's key men. On paper, we had a strong and experienced team. I could imagine myself having a July as tranquil, solid and impressive as the villa over the road from our service course.

A few weeks earlier, though, I'd considered going in a very different direction by signing for Team Sky. Dave Brailsford wanted me to be his Plan B, or even Plan C, an alternative for the Tour de France to Chris Froome, who was supposed to race in the Giro first – which he did, winning the *maglia rosa*. I could also be their leader in Paris–Nice, the Tour de Romandie, the Critérium du Dauphiné – events that Froomey loved but which he wasn't supposed to race – as well as being their leader in the Ardennes Classics, of course. The idea of leading Team Sky was like being offered the chance to drive a sports car. It was a very attractive proposition. I would also be responsible for mentoring the young riders who had just been recruited: Colombia's Egan Bernal, the Franco-Russian Pavel Sivakov and my compatriot Eddie Dunbar.

Dave's long-term plans were incredibly precise. The former British Cycling performance director had come a long way over the previous decade. And so had I, to tell the truth. It amused me that our paths had crossed again. During our discussions, we never mentioned the past, but we both remembered that our relationship had been complex, beset by missed opportunities. After the disheartening meeting we'd had following the World Junior Championships in Verona in 2004, I'd gone to try my luck in Marseille. The British federation had called me up sometimes for the national team during the 2005 season, but not for the Worlds in Madrid. I never had any explanation for this non-selection, but I felt that Dave didn't see me as anything more than a stopgap. At the same time, Irish Cycling was keen for me to join them. So I started the process of changing my nationality with the UCI and in September 2006 I rode my first U23 World Championship in the emerald-green jersey. Mark Cavendish, leader of the British team and the race favourite, finished 11th on the Salzburg circuit in Austria. He needed another teammate in the final. It could have been me, if only ... At the finish, I caught Dave Brailsford's eye. Not a word passed between us. From then on, each of us followed our own path on the bike.

Then I witnessed the birth of the Sky empire. The creation of the team in 2010. Chris Froome's first sensational Vuelta in 2011 – the year I won my stage. The first Tour victory in 2012 with Bradley Wiggins, who had gained a new dimension since he'd been my teammate at Garmin. Amidst these episodes, my name kept coming up in the press as a possible recruit. A British magazine even put forward the – totally inconceivable – hypothesis that I could sign for this British team for 2010, provided I reverted to my original nationality! Six years later I'd received a slightly more formal transfer offer. Dave texted me to say that he was 'interested' and wanted to 'talk to me', but the conversations didn't go very far and I signed for Quick-Step.

Team Sky had been more aggressive in their approach on this occasion as they looked ahead to 2018. Clearly, they were looking for a rider to fill the gap between Chris Froome and the next leader who would emerge. I told Dave about my other option with Team UAE Emirates. He wanted me to turn down this rival offer without us making any progress with the discussions on his side. One day he called to reassure me: 'I'm waiting to hear if one of our riders stays or goes. If he leaves, we'll take you for sure.' I was led to believe afterwards that he was talking about the Basque climber Mikel Landa. So I made the decision to target the 2018 Tour de France podium without Team Sky – in fact, against Team Sky.

For 'Operation Tour de France' to succeed, we had to commit the same financial resources, to put the same energy into the work, to have the same conviction as our rivals. I wanted to find out their secrets. I'd never forgotten the carnage of the Pierre-Saint-Martin stage in the Pyrenees during the 2015 Tour de France. On that day, on a single climb, Team Sky had dominated the peloton like never before. Chris Froome had won at the summit and Richie Porte had finished second. Geraint Thomas was sixth. We'd all been reduced to a pulp in their wake. The tenth rider was two and a half minutes behind. I lost more than eleven minutes, with my teammate Andrew Talansky on my wheel. That was a minute and a half lost for each kilometre of climbing. I was stunned.

We'd made the mistake of not drinking sufficiently the day before the stage, which was the rest day. We used 'ice socks', packs of ice cubes placed on the back of the neck that trick the brain into thinking that the body is cold and make the heat more bearable. We also made cuts in our clothes with scissors to let a little air through. What's more, Vaughters had told us: 'The lighter colour of the new kit is perfect for hot weather.' We were beaten before we even started. I swore to myself that this would never happen again, that I would never lose a race because of a deficit in equipment or physical preparation.

Perhaps because of the oil economy in the Gulf, Team UAE Emirates was seen as having an unlimited budget. Mauro Gianetti also wanted us to embrace spectacular innovations – obviously within the limits of the anti-doping regulations. We were going to demand the best in every sector, and it didn't matter what contracts we had with suppliers. If necessary, we would buy what we needed, at full price. And, if the products didn't exist, we would invent them.

However, after our bike-fit experience on a set-up from Jacques Anquetil's era, I kept on waiting for the staff to reveal some new products to us. Mattresses co-developed with NASA engineers that would improve our sleep by 8.4 per cent? Gloves made with a synthetic fake skin that would offer no resistance to the wind and would consequently allow us to gain one second per kilometre in a time trial? As I awaited proposals from the team, I was trying to find answers to some lifestyle questions that I'd long been mulling over.

I was ten years into my pro career and I was getting to know my sport as well as my body. My diet, despite occasional visits to good restaurants with Jess, was balanced and very healthy. I'd gone so far as to eliminate milk and gluten in order to put an end to stomach problems – my old Vélo Club La Pomme teammates would have been proud of me! I'd found the right regime for me and I wasn't going to deviate from it, even if the Team UAE Emirates doctor wanted me to change my diet.

The first thing the *dottore*, Roberto Corsetti, asked me was, 'What's your ideal weight?'

I replied: 'I don't know, I let the body decide.' His eyes widened. He was used to setting a number and the rider sticking to it. As for me, I felt like I was going backwards. Since I'd left my amateur team in France, no one had bothered me about my weight. But Dr Corsetti was setting menus that even Team Sky wouldn't dare to eat all year round. During the first little winter training camp at the end of October, at a time when we could finally celebrate completing a full season, he continued to force pasta and white meat on us. I used to tease him: 'So, Doctor? Don't we even get pizza?' No, as it turned out. And for dessert, it was fruit salad.

I continued to not let anyone, even a doctor, try to take control of my body, especially if it was with a view to changing what was working ... As a matter of principle, I refused to follow old, obsolete rules that no one could honestly explain and that had to be applied to everyone, even though we each have a different body and character. I was waiting for the team to offer me tools, not impose protocols. So, I continued to look for ways to move forwards on my own. For example, I was following at a distance a therapeutic method called 'vegetative training', which had been developed by Inge Jarl Clausen, who had been a member of Team Garmin's paramedical staff. It's an incredibly effective form of meditation that uses breathing exercises to release tension within the body. After hours of intense concentration on the bike, instead of staring at a screen I would lie on my bed, eyes closed and breathing deeply, losing myself in my bodily sensations and entering total relaxation. It felt like I was hitting my body's reset button. It enhanced my sleep quality, as I would let go of all the emotional energy and stress that had built up and wake up genuinely refreshed.

My body was keeping track of my whole career. Every single little scar and burn affected it and, after a few years, some old pains were coming back. My broken finger from my 2008 Flèche Wallonne was giving me some discomfort and I could see its abnormal shape. My wrist, which I had injured after awkwardly hitting a pothole after a stage in the 2009 Volta a Catalunya, would be giving me problems years later. At the time I considered myself incredibly fortunate as I'd escaped with just a slight wrist sprain, but perhaps it would have been better to have fallen more heavily and have to rest; instead I continued to race but ended up sitting differently on the bike, protecting this ever-so-slight injury by overcompensating, which caused an imbalance in strength, what some call 'golfer's elbow', and a weakness in my left shoulder that I was still struggling with. After hours of painful physio and rehab, still nothing seemed to reset my left arm. Perhaps I just needed to stop the treatment and let my body self-fix.

In light of the human body's natural powers of healing and recovery, I had decided to give up a century-old tradition in cycling: massage. Despite the respect and liking I had for our physiotherapists and osteopaths, I no longer wanted someone to manipulate my body for my comfort. At the beginning of my career, I used to ask someone to knead my muscles deeper and deeper, like bread dough, to get rid of the toxins. I believed that by submitting to this my body was being revamped for the following day. Like all riders, I also liked the feeling that

I was being looked after and listened to – masseurs are also great psychologists. Over time, though, my position on the subject evolved. I came to the conclusion that massages were an assault on the body and that, while they corrected some problems, they created others. In fact, by the time we even started massage, often a good two hours after the race or even more, our bodies had largely recovered. The body is fully capable of quickly repairing its own small injuries, of expelling fatigue, of compensating for weaknesses.

Nature knows best, it's often said, and I let it do what it wanted. I never got massaged while training at home and I felt better that way, and it was the same during races. Whether it was just coincidence or not, I let my body regenerate itself during the Tour and I didn't get sick. I went through four Tours de France without having my legs massaged in the evenings. This didn't stop me from attacking in the mountains, battling in time trials, clinging on in echelons or on the cobbles, giving all I had in the battle for the final podium on the Champs-Elysées.

# Chapter 22

# Me as Super Combatif (The Fear of Attacking)

**B**ut why did you attack? I've often been asked this question. Everyone makes their own judgement about a rider's attacks: too early, too late, too far, too short, too hard, or even downright 'useless' ... The question is posed from a tactical viewpoint but is often existential in nature. I often joked when it was put to me. My answer: 'Why not?' I was on a bike to attack. Pedalling wasn't enough. Following other riders was necessary, but deadly boring. Attacks were what brought me to life. I didn't attack in scattergun fashion. The moments I chose were perfectly rational to me. Every attack had complex reasoning behind it.

When I was winning, no one asked me the question. But to win, you have to attack. Or you wait for the sprint. A victory justifies every attack, even the most stupid. During the 2018 Tour de France, journalists kept asking me, 'But why did you attack?', right up until the point when I received the prize as the Super Combatif, the most combative rider, at the end of the race, which was one of the most emblematic trophies of my career. No one asked me about my attacks then, and yet there was plenty of reason to do so. That Tour, which I'd spent years preparing for, had been a total fiasco.

After I joined Team UAE Emirates, our manager, Mauro Gianetti, had instigated 'Operation Tour de France', but from my very first weeks with my new team the plan seemed flawed. The bike-fitting in our headquarters had been a bad omen of what was coming. They were more like the Vélo Club La Pomme Marseille set-up of my early days than a credible opponent for Team Sky. Rather than working on marginal gains, the staff felt they should stick with their old habits. I suggested getting input from researchers, sports scientists, biomechanics and materials engineers. Equipment, tyres, textiles, nutrition: everything needed to be reviewed. But every time I proposed something, the team staff got upset: 'It's fine like this, we've always done it this way, for twenty years.'

That meant we were twenty years behind our rivals. Although he had encouraged me to share ideas in order to bring about continuous improvement, it became apparent that Mauro Gianetti wasn't sharing the team management with Giuseppe Saronni; the latter had a very old-fashioned conception of cycling – and, after all, why not? His approach had worked for decades, and I respected that; but the sport had obviously changed.

We got to March and didn't even have a rain jacket as part of our kit. The final turning point was the drinks. After I blew up at the Tour of Catalonia, where I suffered an inexplicable loss of power on the slopes of La Molina, and when the poor run continued at my beloved Ardennes, I carried out a little investigation into our energy drinks. The composition of sugars and minerals was perfectly in line with the recommendations for competitive sport. So what was going on? I found out that the technical assistants were only using 10 per cent of the amount recommended by the manufacturer. 'You've got to understand, it's too sweet otherwise,' they told me. Instead of 40 grams of carbohydrate per bottle, they were giving us four. The mathematical consequences that arose from this were easy to understand. Having two bottles an hour in the heat meant that we were taking in 8 grams of carbohydrate, when we needed 80 to 100. I finally understood why we were all struggling so much. I proposed some changes to the protocol – and I hit a brick wall. The team refused to give, I stood my ground . . . After only three or four months, I was wondering how I had ended up on this strange adventure.

I went through a major crisis after the Ardennes Classics, when I was still without results. I asked myself what I was doing on this team, what I was doing on the bike. It was the first time in my life that I'd asked myself such a question. There was no longer any point in fighting my own team's staff, or even my teammates, who accepted decisions without flinching even if deep down they shared my point of view – they had respect for, and even feared, the authority of the *directeurs sportifs*, the mechanics and the doctor. They never disputed any instructions. So I decided to stand down. Cycling had already given me a lot of joy. What's more, Jess and I were expecting twins in the autumn. It was the right time to move on. There were several options, including ending my career with immediate effect and pushing on to the Tour de France. I could already see myself calling my agent and asking him to break my two-year contract.

I had a kind of revelation during one of my training rides in the Pyrenees. The date: 7 May 2018. The place: the Collada de la Gallina, on the Sant Julià de Lòria side. My legs were spinning as if by themselves. The pure mountain air filled my lungs. I felt light. At the summit, I stopped for a moment. I took off my glasses to remove the filter that bathes a cyclist's world in yellow or orange. I took in nature through my eyes alone, the valiant and increasingly sparse trees at this height of 1,910 metres, the stone teeth of the massif above me, the impression of being surrounded by a very welcoming landscape. Cycling was still worth it; I loved riding my bike. By the time I reached the bottom of the descent, I had decided to remain a rider.

My new aim was just to enjoy. With Rory Sutherland, who had been supporting me from the start, I gave up fighting against the team but also gave up trying to help the team. We were taking control of our own destiny. We bought our own energy drink powder and put it in our water bottles ourselves. The staff weren't happy but they let us get on with it.

The impact was dramatic. In June I claimed my first success in my new team's colours, at the Critérium du Dauphiné. The finish was in the ski resort of Valmorel in Savoie. I attacked with 3 kilometres to go and had a four-second advantage at the finish line. This stage win was a very encouraging sign and I was hoping that the Tour would go the same way. I wanted to have an impact on the race. I wanted my attacks to lead to victories and planned to make them where they would have the maximum effect. I didn't want to rely on taking advantage of those moments of hesitation, those brief instants when the pace among the favourites would slow down, to try to recoup any losses. I wanted to be more proactive than that. I ignored the team's internal organisational concerns. I felt that I had a real chance of finishing on the podium. I was disappointed when we lost more than a minute and a half to Team Sky in the team time trial, but I still believed I could attain my objective.

The Tour's first 'Mountain' finish took place at the 'summit' of Mûr de Bretagne, dubbed the 'Breton Alpe d'Huez', which stands a full 293 metres above sea level. As had been the case at the Dauphiné, I attacked and won. This stage was full of traps. After 100 kilometres of racing, I ended up in the third group on the road after my former Quick-Step teammates tried to blow the race apart in crosswinds. We managed to bridge back up, but I didn't want to be right at the front. It was incredibly nervy, and I preferred to sit back a bit, save energy and watch what was happening and give myself time to brake. I was rolling the dice and it paid off; with 40 kilometres to go, I managed to avoid a crash. There were dangers on all sides on these country roads that wound through small villages of old stone houses. I almost fell two or three times. I kept breathing deeply to keep calm. I moved up the peloton on the wheel of Richie Porte, who was also planning to sprint on the uphill finish.

I attacked 1,200 metres from the line. I didn't know that I could push so hard on the pedals and I opened up a small gap on the peloton. I prolonged my effort with a short sprint. I'd attacked in order to create as much havoc as possible among my rivals, to upset their plans, and to give my legs something to feed on, because they were hungry for action. There was a good chance that the others would bridge up to me, but I had enough strength to hold on. I repeated my tactic from the Côte d'Ans in Liège–Bastogne–Liège, dividing the distance to the line into morsels. I gave it everything I had until the sign marking the final 500 metres. I told myself that was the end. Reaching it, I caught my breath. Then I forced myself to sprint for another hundred metres. Then another hundred metres. These brief hesitations, each followed by an acceleration, were intended to break the morale of my pursuers. I held on to win by a second, beating Frenchman Pierre Latour, with Julian Alaphilippe and Alejandro Valverde three seconds behind. I had set out my stall for the mountain stages ahead.

I was pulled back into line not by the other riders but by a fall. Two days on from my victory, a violent crash within the peloton 12 kilometres from the finish in Amiens on the plains of Picardy, to the north of Paris. The rider in front of me lost his balance and went right. As he switched in that direction, he took away my front wheel and I flipped over the handlebars. I fell on my back, probably onto some metal part of a bike. I felt something pierce my skin. My bike was in pieces so I needed to wait for a replacement, and the delay proved costly; despite me being well supported by my teammates, we finished one minute and sixteen seconds down. I had slipped from 21st to 31st place overall. At the finish, I screamed in pain when the doctor cut open my jersey with scissors to remove the material stuck in the wound. I had a hole in my back the size of a pound coin and a centimetre deep. Lumbar trauma. Abrasions to the elbow. And the next day was the stage over the cobbles.

My personal Super Combatif award was forged on the terrifying roads of Paris–Roubaix. I was invisible on the TV pictures, lost in the shadows, focused on my own race, but I accomplished a real feat, although I was the only one aware of it. I had to resist the pain and avoid another crash. It wasn't easy: there were three crashes between the neutralised start and the official start, on the section of road where the peloton is supposed to parade away from the ceremonial start line. Some riders were twitching with nervous tension, so worried that they didn't take their hands off the bars to grab anything to eat and drink. I did the opposite, constantly refuelling for the first 60 kilometres. This stage, which was feared by everyone but especially the climbers, would require a lot of energy. Suddenly, I saw riders getting out of the saddle and sprinting, as if we'd just reached the *flamme rouge*. We were approaching the first section of cobbles. I decided to hold back a bit.

It was a maelstrom of crashes, punctures, screams, riders raising broken wheels in the sky. I passed through the middle of this mayhem, in a cloud of brown dust. Then I settled in the middle of the peloton. I rode along the crown of the cobbled roads, where the stones protrude the most and the effort required to cope with them is the most demanding, but where there's also less chance of slipping or having a puncture. In the final kilometres, I overtook some of the sprinters, including Arnaud Démare, who had undoubtedly been affected by not paying attention to nutrition earlier in the day. At the finish, close to the mythical Roubaix Velodrome, I was in the group with the other favourites for the general classification, together with Geraint Thomas. I couldn't believe my eyes. With all the adrenaline-fuelled euphoria, I didn't feel the pain of my injuries. It was only when I had crossed the finish line that I realised that the vibrations from the cobblestones had reopened my wounds and my jersey and shorts were encrusted with bodily fluids.

And then, on the following stages, I attacked wherever I could. I wanted to regain the positions I'd lost one by one, to get back into the top twenty, top fifteen, top ten . . . I was more than three minutes behind after our adventure on the cobbles, thanks to the team time trial and my crash. But the final podium still wasn't out of my reach. In the Alps, my rivals would be thinking that I was a few minutes behind, but I'd come back up to them and attack. I was attacking almost from the moment I arrived at the breakfast buffet in the hotels. It was an obsession. I made one attack per day, at a pre-chosen moment, in order to eliminate two or three opponents at once. I was happy to see that my offensives were paying off. I could see that my rivals were beginning to take me seriously; they would increase their pace when I forged ahead, which meant that the group would split apart. I'd finally become a fully fledged participant in the battle for the overall classification. Coming out of the Alps and heading for the Pyrenees, my deficit on Geraint Thomas, who was in the yellow jersey, had increased to almost seven minutes. But I had moved up to 10th place in the classification and I fully intended to keep on rising.

I took a huge risk on the fifteenth stage, a so-called 'transition stage' where there was nothing at stake for the GC contenders. With 55 kilometres to go, I attacked on the climb of the Pic de Nore. My *directeurs sportifs* were worried. They were telling me through my earpiece: 'Dan, ease off. We're a very long way from the finish. You'll get fatigued, the peloton will catch you and you'll lose time in the last twenty kilometres . . .'

Despite their warnings, I pressed on. I was hoping that Alejandro Valverde might come with me. I got the feeling that he was thinking of making a move. We would have made a great combination. But I ended up alone. Far ahead, a breakaway was riding towards the stage win, beneath the ramparts of Carcassonne's medieval citadel. Meanwhile, a minute behind me, the peloton had increased its pace, but wasn't pushing flat out. Their tempo had been calculated in order to limit my advantage and, at the same time, to wear me out slowly. But I was still hopeful. I told myself that I could take advantage of the fast, winding descent off the Pic de Nore. Four or five riders could escape from the peloton, join me, and then we could open up a gap on Geraint and the whole bunch. But the plan didn't work out and I was caught with 14 kilometres to go.

'But why did you attack? The journalists crowded around me at the finish. 'It's been a long time since we've seen an outsider in the general classification take this kind of risk. Why did you do that?' The answer was in the question. Precisely because I was an outsider. Deep down, I think I wanted to escape from those shackles. Since 2012, Team Sky's opponents seemed to have systematically adopted a strategy of accepting whatever crumbs the British team allowed them. They raced defensively, riding on the wheel of the yellow jersey and never attacking him. They raced to finish second or, worse still, seventh or eighth ... I also had long nurtured the ambition of finishing on the podium, but I wouldn't suppress my attacking instincts to achieve it.

That kind of breakaway actually had something to do with my early years. Sport for me was entertainment. It went back to my time as a motorcycle racing fan, when I was with my dad at Mallory Park or Donington Park, brushing shoulders with the riders. For the very first – and last – time I met athletes who let me dream. At the GP Great Britain 1996 I had lunch at the same table as a very young Valentino Rossi, already a showman and creative entertainer even though he was only seventeen. He always found a new style to win and celebrate. One year later he became world champion, and completed his parade lap with a huge yellow 'Number 1' tag on his back. Moto GP was an entertainment business and, according to our contracts, and our tiny links with the communication departments of our sponsors, cycling was the same type of business – it just seems to forget sometimes. It shouldn't be all about winning but about inspiring people too; brightening people's day

I thought of the spectator I'd once been. I would have hated to see myself with my wings clipped, unable to take flight, clamped to my saddle, offering nothing. Attacking was a sign of the respect that I had for my sport. I responded to reporters with words like 'fun'. 'If I don't attack, what else can I do? Stay in the peloton? The rest day is tomorrow. The race was today.'

This 40-kilometre breakaway carried out away from the mountains made an impression on people. There was no doubt that it lent significant weight to the jury's decision to award me the 2018 Tour de France's prize as the race's Super Combatif. I finished ahead of more renowned and popular attackers, notably my former teammate Julian Alaphilippe and the reigning world champion Peter Sagan. Fans on the internet, whose votes had a certain amount of sway, singled out the American Lawson Craddock, who had ridden just ahead of the broom wagon on several occasions, flirting with elimination.

'There was a debate within the jury between Sagan, Alaphilippe and Martin,' acknowledged Thierry Gouvenou, the number two in the Tour organisation and a member of that jury. 'The former pair had their sights set on the green and polka-dot jerseys. Dan Martin was aiming for the overall classification. His task was, therefore, more complicated. His attacks probably weren't as visible but they always came at key moments of the race.' Gouvenou, who was himself a *baroudeur* when he was a rider, was now in charge of the race route, so was a man you'd either love or curse depending on the day. His influence weighed heavily on me receiving the trophy: 'He was the first real attacker of the Tour with his victory at Mûr de Bretagne, and he then had to deal with a huge crash at Amiens that left him in an unbelievable state for the cobbled stage, where he showed great fighting qualities. At every opportunity, at the race's key moments, when the big guns were fighting each other, he was always there attacking or launching hostilities.' What's more, Gouvenou alluded to my counter-attack behind Nairo Quintana on the Col de Portet, the Pyrenean summit finish that Jess and I hadn't managed to recon in its entirety because of the fog: 'He was fifteen seconds behind Quintana the whole way up the Col de Portet, everybody thought he was going to explode but he never eased off and pushed himself right to his limits. He also made what proved to be fruitless attacks, like the one before the finish in Carcassonne where the peloton was fifteen to twenty minutes behind and he attacked and lit up the race.'

So the 'fruitless attacks' proved useful after all! I was informed of my reward for them at the finish of the time trial in the Basque Country, which Jess and I had managed to reconnoitre in detail. When I met Geraint Thomas and Chris Froome in the doping control truck, before we discussed hamburgers and chips versus green salad, I told them: 'Guys, tomorrow I'll be on the podium with you in Paris.'

The stage was set up on the Champs-Elysées, the famous avenue, long and curvy like a last mountain road. The Arc de Triomphe was lit up behind me. Evening was falling. When I heard my name, I went up and contemplated 'the most beautiful avenue in the world': immense, majestic, serene. Even amidst the Tour's clamour, it maintained its elegance. Part of me was sad because I had certainly missed a rare opportunity to fight for the podium. But another part of me savoured this beautiful consolation prize. 'Super Combatif'. It sounded like a superhero's name. I hadn't come to this Tour for nothing!

Jess was among the crowd in Paris, 200 metres from the

podium, seemingly even happier and prouder than I was. She encouraged me to go to the Tour of Spain at the end of August. I hesitated, but she urged me on: 'Don't worry, the due date is a month after the finish in Madrid! So there's plenty of time to do this race.' I agreed, reminding her of a rule I would never compromise: 'If there is any chance they are going to arrive early, I will quit the Vuelta!'

As it turned out, I quit after nine days, following the La Covatilla stage. I'd been worn down by the tension and disorganisation that was still a feature of the team. At the start of one stage, our doctor, who was usually so calm, pushed me around on the bus, furious that I wasn't using the energy bars they were providing us with. That was the last straw. However, I only remember one thing from that summer: Ella and Daisy were born one beautiful morning in Andorra, on 19 September 2018.

'Operation Tour de France' failed a second time at the 2019 edition. It was a pity because the team really seemed determined to improve. Beppe Saronni's clique had taken a step back. Mauro Gianetti and his right-hand man Joxean Matxin had taken command and were making a real effort, but there was too much ground to make up and mistakes continued to be made. For some reason I can't explain, we all gained 3 kilos during the race. I lost the extra weight as soon as I got home. I felt heavy, fat, without energy. The whole team shared the same discomfort and depression.

I was happier than ever to go home. The family brought me happiness and a new balance. It wasn't a sudden change of lifestyle; Jess had been showing me that there were so many other things in life besides cycling since the spring of 2014, but when the girls arrived it consolidated all those things I'd been starting to learn. When I came back from training and lay down on the sofa, I would have company, cuddles with my girls. To them I was not a cyclist, I was Daddy. The difficult nights had ended just four or five months after their birth, just as I started racing again early in the 2019 season. They even encouraged me to go to bed earlier, to concentrate on the essentials and to do without what was superfluous – TV, social networks, shopping. The house in La Massana became one of real happiness.

I'd been the Tour's Super Combatif but had never finished on the podium. For me, that Tour marked the end of the plan that I'd worked so hard to achieve. When I left the team at the end of 2019, I passed the baton to a miraculous rider whom I'd met in January 2018 during a training camp in Sicily. At the time, Tadej Pogačar was coming out of the junior ranks and was only nineteen years old, but he was already driven by a formidable mix of total composure and complete determination. He was set to join our squad the following season and was there to familiarise himself with the group. I remember our training sortie on 13 January 2018, when we went riding in the cave region around the Grotte Monello near Syracuse. The pace was very gentle; the power meter showed we were only putting out 160–180 watts. To shake things up, I attacked on a flat part of road. When I turned around, I didn't see the team's leaders,

Fabio Aru and Diego Ulissi, but Tadej. He may have been young, but he wasn't afraid to mix it up. However, he respected us. The proof? When I flicked my elbow to let him know that he should come through at a steady speed, he actually attacked me with everything he had. I struggled to get back up him. I could see from his eyes that Tadej was enjoying himself. The next generation was ready.

# Chapter 23

# The End of the Panda

I realised that my days as a professional rider were numbered when the organisers of Liège–Bastogne–Liège decided to bury the Côte d'Ans and, with it, the 'Panda Zone'.

The rumour started to spread at the beginning of the 2018 season. I'd just changed teams, signing for Team UAE Emirates and expanding my ambitions beyond the Classics. There was talk that the organisers didn't want the finish line up on a hill any longer, but down in the centre of Liège. While awaiting clarification of these stories, we had one final ascent of the Côte d'Ans to attempt, on 22 April 2018. Unfortunately for me, my bad luck resurfaced. There had been a bad omen four days earlier, when I was delayed by a crash on the penultimate ascent of the Mur de Huy and eventually rolled in nearly ten minutes down at the finish of Flèche Wallonne. As it turned out, I would also be prevented from seeing what I was capable of in Liège.

When Bob Jungels escaped on the Roche-aux-Faucons, with 19 kilometres to go, I knew right away that it was over. My former teammate was certainly the strongest, and when he left us the pursuit didn't get organised. Nobody took the initiative to ride behind him. I attacked several times over the top of that climb and tried again on the next false flat, accompanied by the Belgian Tim Wellens. The group caught up with us. There were about fifteen of us. With 10 kilometres to go, we were thirty-seven seconds behind Bob. Our only chance to close the gap was to climb the Côte de Saint-Nicolas flat out: leaving it to the Côte d'Ans would be too late. We'd still be locked together, still waiting, our fate sealed.

Eight kilometres from the finish: my front tyre burst on a bridge near the Standard de Liège stadium after getting caught in a metal groove perpendicular to the road. The neutral recovery car was quick to intervene, but I was doomed. Suffering a mechanical incident so close to the finish is disastrous. I held my head in my hands. I climbed the Côte d'Ans alone: the closest riders were either 500 metres ahead of me or 300 behind. I finished 18th, two minutes and forty-one seconds behind Bob Jungels.

The decision to move the finish line was subsequently confirmed. La Doyenne said goodbye to the long false flat in Ans. Lots of fans seemed satisfied. They felt that the race was blocked by this climb that produced a sprint at the top more often than an attack by a *puncheur*. As if to belie such a reputation, the 2018 edition had been settled by a long-distance breakaway. I was dismayed at the lack of respect given to this climb and the great tactical plans it demanded of us. The new course wiped Ans off the map, as well as the Saint-Nicolas. Automatically, the centre of gravity became La Roche-aux-Faucons, a climb I'd never liked. The last 10 kilometres consisted of a long downhill, some flat and a 900-metre straight.

The irony is that the finish line was now almost where it had once been in the past; it had been abandoned in 1992 because the organisers were tired of seeing a sprint finish. Cycling is in a state of perpetual renewal . . .

The new finish was located on Boulevard d'Avroy, where a stage of the Tour de France ended in 2012. A few hundred metres further on was the old finish line, on Boulevard de la Sauvenière. This was where my uncle found the 'springboard' for his 1987 season: busy watching his breakaway companion in the finale of La Doyenne, the Belgian Claudy Criquielion, Stephen didn't realise that the Italian Moreno Argentin was closing in on them and was about to burn them off in the sprint. But after this failure, my uncle would go on to win the Giro, the Tour and the World Championship.

My last two appearances in Liège left me feeling disillusioned, as if I were no longer in my natural element. In 2019, I abandoned halfway through the race, weakened by a virus that I hadn't been able to get rid of since the Tour of the Basque Country earlier in April. In 2020, when the race was rescheduled to October in a racing calendar that was completely overhauled as a result of the COVID-19 pandemic, I finished 11th. The following year, I skipped La Doyenne in order to prepare for the Giro d'Italia. It was the first time I'd missed it in my career, after fourteen seasons. I watched the race on TV. Two of my former teammates disputed the victory, with Tadej Pogačar finishing ahead of Julian Alaphilippe. Frenchman David Gaudu completed the podium. My nemesis Alejandro Valverde took fourth place on his forty-first birthday. Mike Woods, my then teammate at Israel Start-Up Nation, our solid Canadian, was fifth.

Something occurred to me about My untraceable Panda: the possibility that my clandestine breakaway companion was hiding out of shame. Philippe Gilbert, who knows the city of Liège like the back of his hand, gave me a tip that only the locals, not passing cyclists, would know: there's a district in the city centre called 'Le Carré', the Square, because it's bounded by four streets in a square shape. It's an area that sleeps by day and lives by night. On Saturday nights, students would do a stage race from bar to bar. I wondered if the Panda had perhaps been drinking too much lemonade the night before Liège. Maybe he and his friends had decided to join the race in their own way, by parading in costumes; maybe, rather than being one of the overly cheerful football fans I'd come across, the Panda was one of these party people from 'Le Carré'.

A few years on from their 2013 feat, the Panda and his friends may have become quiet office workers, honourable shopkeepers or craftsmen, enjoying a comfortable family life and regretting the little follies of their younger days. Perhaps the acolytes who'd been running with their faces uncovered had asked the Panda to remain in the shadows, in order to avoid compromising any member of the commando. They wanted to be forgotten for a while, or maybe for ever.

The funny thing is that Liège–Bastogne–Liège's new finish line is located just a few minutes' walk from 'Le Carré', the place where the Panda may have been born.

# Chapter 24

# One More Team (The Fear of Surprises)

I t felt like I'd gone back to being a junior rider, one who was fresh in the mind and legs, even though I was almost thirty-four years old. The management at Team Israel Start-Up Nation had employed me for the 2020 and 2021 seasons, believing that my career could take a new turn. Paulo Saldanha, the performance director, was convinced of this after analysing some of my training plans. 'I can see that you focus a lot on endurance, which is good for sustaining a big effort over a long period. But you don't have the burst of acceleration that a *puncheur-grimpeur* like you should have. If you want, we'll work on intensity. In any case, your potential is clearly under-exploited.'

So, after signing a two-year contract with this Israeli team that was about to line up in its first Tour de France, I eagerly awaited my training plan, waking each morning like a kid at Christmas. When my present finally arrived, I opened it with great excitement, not knowing what would be inside. My first reaction was to laugh: 'Is he kidding?' I could see that Paulo Saldanha had a lot of monstrous efforts in store for me. 'I'll take you to the limit, to the point where your body breaks down, like it would in a race. You'll be going as far as you can,' he said. As I prepared for the Ardennes Classics, I re-experienced the brutality and joy of those rides with my father. I felt the taste of blood in my mouth again. The body that I thought I knew surprised me every day. They say that 90 per cent of the human brain's potential is unused. It's undoubtedly the same for the human body.

I came out of these sessions proud, light, serene, sharp, full of desire to go through them again or to head to the next race. Over the two years, I never followed the same plan twice. Saldanha was very creative in maintaining my zest. Before I set out, I would study the 'zones' he was asking me to work on. I might, for instance, have to follow an irregular tempo on a climb and sprint every three minutes. Or I might have to ride up a hill for thirty minutes, alternating between a one-and-a-half-minute tempo effort at 4.5 watts per kilo and another at 6W/kg. I tried to exceed his instructions every time, to provoke him. Sometimes I wasn't able to finish half of an effort because I didn't have a joule of energy left inside me. But when I managed to complete the whole plan, Paulo would say: 'Honestly, I sent you this just to see, because I thought it wasn't possible to do it.' He was having fun, and so was I.

Team Israel Start-Up Nation wanted me to be involved in the choice of riders and equipment and the race schedule. In the long run, it would be possible to recruit a core group of friends, not because they were my friends but because they were very solid and honest racers who should have the chance to try their luck at the highest level. To begin with, we were going to ride at Pro Continental level, in the second division, and venture to what would be new events for us in Spain, Italy, North America, and perhaps even Africa or Asia. We would also get occasional invitations to major events. What's more, there was no question of me wasting my time on July's big race, the Tour de France, which was something of a relief. Instead, the plan was for me to line up at the Giro. Even though the team ended up buying the World Tour licence relinquished by the Russian team Katusha–Alpecin, which propelled us into the cycling world's first division, we still maintained the sense of freedom and tranquillity of a Pro Continental outfit.

The architect of the project was a businessman, Sylvan Adams, who had financed some prestigious football matches in Israel and even an appearance by Madonna at the Eurovision Song Contest. He was a good amateur cyclist and initially hired Paulo Saldanha as his personal coach. A few years later, the two compatriots had pieced together a cycling project with another entrepreneur named Ron Baron. The aim was to host the start of the Giro in Jerusalem (which was achieved in 2018), to launch a team that would take part in the Tour and, incidentally, to build a velodrome in Tel Aviv. Sylvan wanted to bring together his two passions in life: his country, and cycling. The sport allowed him to present an image of Israel other than warfare, and the Israeli companies that sponsored us allowed him to pursue his long-held dream of an Israeli rider lining up at the Tour de France for the first time in history.

In December 2019, we rode together in the Negev Desert in

southern Israel. At the beginning of the ride, Sylvan, in spite of being sixty-one years old, drew on his natural ability as a *rouleur* to do some relays at the front of our pace line, and then sat in the wheels of his riders. Within this small peloton, I was riding with two former holders of the hour record, Britain's Alex Dowsett and Austria's Matthias Brändle, as well as the German sprinter André Greipel, the winner of eleven Tour stages, and riders of all nationalities, plus the feeder team of young riders that was composed of motivated Israelis. My friend Rory Sutherland, who had followed me to this new team, was absent because he had broken his femur a few days earlier. We passed by a Bedouin camp, near the Gaza Strip; Sylvan wanted us to experience his country in all of its dimensions. We even encountered a sandstorm that threw up an orange wall in front of us. But it was all just part of this new adventure and we pressed on.

A storm of a different, much more devastating kind hit the world a few weeks later. The COVID-19 pandemic struck country after country. Bike races were cancelled. I managed to take part in the Tour of Valencia and the Tour of Algarve in February, but then my season was interrupted. Positive cases of the new virus spread through the peloton. Soon it was no longer possible to race anywhere. Travel was restricted. After six weeks of total lockdown where we couldn't ride outside, the government in Andorra allowed us to ride on the Col d'Ordino, but as we had to drive there I continued the habit of riding on the home trainer in my living room instead. The idea of loading my bike into the car to drive two kilometres, to then get out and ride back and forth on a single stretch of road, was less appealing even than riding indoors. I didn't find this lockdown onerous, nor did it reveal any aspects of reality that weren't already apparent; some of my cycling buddies told me that they were discovering the joys of family life, or even of life in general, but, thanks to Jess being part of my life since 2014, and thanks also to Daisy and Ella being around since 2018, I already knew all about this. It did give me a chance, though, to spend some quality time with them, to pretend for a while that I wasn't really a racer. I was philosophical about this change of routine. I was simply living my life.

When we were finally able to pin on a race number again, in the summer, the calendar had been turned upside down. The Tour was set to take place in September, followed by the Giro and the Vuelta. The Ardennes Classics would also take place in the autumn. I prepared for the Tour at the end of August by riding the Critérium du Dauphiné, but on the third stage I crashed – an experience I'd not missed ... I fractured my sacrum, the bone that connects the pelvis to the spine. It wasn't too serious, though, and even though I abandoned the race, I was back in training on the bike three days later. Ten days after that, I started the 2020 Tour de France.

I had the necessary motivation, my health was just about intact, but I never got to grips with the race. I passed through the Tour like a ghost, albeit one with a surgical blue mask rather than a white sheet and chains. We had to wear masks at the start and finish, on the podium, on the bus ... These restrictions, introduced to prevent the spread of the Covid virus, were even in force on the mountain stages. Some climbs were silent, totally empty, closed to the public, guarded by gendarmes; the atmosphere on others was rousing, lively, noisy like a normal Tour de France, and we could feel ourselves being lifted once again by the spectators' passion. This semi-locked-down Tour de France was won by Tadej Pogačar, who turned the overall classification upside down on the race's penultimate day, in the time trial to La Planche des Belles Filles. In a way, I was happy for him. Tadej had completed the 'Operation Tour de France' mission that I'd started three years earlier. The kid I had met at our Sicilian training camp was now the winner of the yellow jersey, but to me he was still just Tadej, someone I would regularly joke around with and poke fun at.

The Tour had sharpened my legs for the Vuelta. Under this new calendar, the race started on 20 October, at a time in the season when we usually started our holidays. It ended on 8 November, just before winter began. The average temperature was 15°C, half as hot as any standard edition of the Vuelta. It was almost dark when the stage winners went up onto the podium. On the day my compatriot Sam Bennett won the sprint, we raced into the final at 60km/h, unable to see the road ahead because the setting sun was blazing on the horizon in front of us. But cyclists are warm-blooded animals, and quickly adapt to their environment. Thanks to Paulo's training plans, which surprised me every day, I'd already got used to my routine being disrupted, even before the pandemic. I regarded each stage as one of his challenges. The first two stages provided reason for satisfaction: I twice finished third, racing through the small passes of the Basque Country and Navarra.

The Vuelta enabled me to experience something that had always eluded me at the Tour – a race where I was focused on finishing on the podium. This required a large-scale plan, designed for three weeks and to ensure you don't lose an inch of ground. I made a quick calculation of who could beat me. Slovenia's Primož Roglič, the former ski jumper, was the favourite. Half a dozen riders were vying for a runner-up spot, including me. I was ready. Only the 33.7-kilometre time trial on stage thirteen worried me a little.

My confidence in my prospects was boosted on the third stage, which I won. We finished at an altitude of 1,753 metres in the Urbión mountains in the central province of Castilla y León, at a place called Laguna Negra – the Black Lake. It was a magical body of water, surrounded by cliffs and granite outcrops, bordered by a dense pine forest. These natural elements blocked out the light and gave the water its dark glow. It felt more like we were in a remote valley in Scandinavia or Canada than in Spain, especially as autumn's tawny colours predominated in this landscape.

Legend has it that the Laguna Negra was a bottomless lake, connected to the Atlantic Ocean by a succession of underground cavities, but in reality it's no more than 10 metres deep. It is also said that a monster haunts its waters, like the one in Loch Ness, but fiercer – apparently it devours bathers. Approaching it, I was paddling along with a dozen or so riders. At the *flamme rouge*, I was in eighth position, about 10 metres behind the rider at the front of our group. I had quite some distance to make up if I wanted to make an attack. But I didn't panic. Each time the group slowed, at each bend, I move up a bit. I was fifth with 500 metres to go. Third at 400 metres. First at 200, which was when I launched my sprint, going from a long way out but with all I had. I could hear the group splitting behind me. No one could overtake me in what seemed an endless sprint. Crossing the line, I didn't throw my arms up to celebrate because I was sure that a breakaway group had finished before us.

There was a huge emotional release when I realized that I'd won. This was the first time that I had crossed the line first since my girls had been born. I wanted to win for my three girls, but also to thank the team for the confidence they'd put in me. I was thinking that we, despite being the smallest squad in the World Tour, were on the way to creating a real stir at the Vuelta. We still had almost three weeks to go but my seven team mates were up for the challenge and performed like Team Sky – now known as Team Ineos – in its pomp, leading me up at the right moment, sheltering me from the wind and supplying me with food and water. They stayed close together, none of them getting lost in their thoughts and hanging around at the back. My bodyguards were two Swiss, Matteo Badilatti and Reto Hollenstein, a Canadian, James Piccoli, an Estonian, Mihkel Räim, a French new pro, Alexis Renard, an Israeli, Omer Goldstein, and, completing the line-up, my friend and road captain, the indispensable Rory Sutherland. I felt that I had to give everything I had for them. On the eighth stage, which climbed to the Alto de Moncalvillo, I sprinted from a long way out to take third place and, once I'd crossed the finish line, collapsed onto the road with exhaustion. For a few seconds, I was comforted by the tarmac. The image quickly went viral across the world, an image that encapsulated my ability to push beyond my limits. It wasn't the lactic acid build-up stinging my legs – having fun on the bike delays the onset of this response. It was simply that I was in oxygen debt and couldn't breathe any more.

I lost my third place in the general classification on the twelfth stage, on the slopes of the Alto de l'Angliru, which sits at an altitude of 1,570 metres. This Asturian goat track is one of the most mythical climbs in the cycling world, with an average of 9.98 per cent for 12.5 kilometres. You literally stand still on the climb, like a knife stuck in butter. It was near impossible to turn the pedals and move forward one metre. Once again, due to COVID-19 no spectators were allowed on this stairway to hell. We were accompanied instead by the sounds of our own suffocation as we climbed, and of our tyres grating across the crocodile-skin-like road surface. Because there were no spectators, we could use its full width, so we zigzagged to try to cope with the gradient, which peaks at 23 per cent at one section. I used 36x32, a gear normally used on a mountain bike, but lacked the strength needed for a climb like this. Not surprisingly, I lost time to Britain's Hugh Carthy, who won the stage and nudged me off the podium by three seconds. My mind was already on the next stage, the individual time trial, where I could easily lose two minutes . . .

There was a rest day before the time trial, which took place in Galicia between Muros and Mirador de Ézaro. The latter, a promontory that looks across to Cape Finisterre and out over the Atlantic, has been a sacred place since antiquity and maybe even before that. I was delighted with the battle plans we made, the attention to detail, the ideas we came up with to ensure that a small climber wouldn't end up being massacred by the time trial specialists. The main part of the course, all ups and downs, was more suitable for heavier and more powerful riders than me. But I could gain ground on the seriously steep climb to the finish, which rose for 1.8 kilometres at an average of 14 per cent.

The team booked two hotel rooms for me, one in the place where I spent the night with my teammates and the other right next to the start line so that I could rest and concentrate. I really relished the time I spent alone in bed, napping with the shutters closed, a silent oasis within earshot of the start area. Having had this good little break, at the start podium I was an exemplar of relaxed composure, making small talk and joking around, much to the annoyance of an incredibly focused Hugh Carthy, who has a quite different approach to a time trial.

I knew pacing was going to be a challenge. Many riders set out with a prescribed power to ride at, but deep into a stage race this is sometimes unpredictable. I rode on feeling, but did use the power meter to limit my effort so as not to start too hard; adrenaline often masks the effort in the early stages of a time trial. I kept my head down on the long straight roads and pushed as hard as I thought I could sustain. The best GC climbers are always closely matched, and so it proved as I failed to take back a lot of time on the steep final climb; but on the other hand I had held my own on the flat rolling terrain beforehand and limited my time loss, which was something to be proud of. At the end of the day, I held on to fourth place in the overall classification, which was dominated by Primož Roglič, ahead of Richard Carapaz and Hugh Carthy.

I was right up among the contenders and my teammates had a real leader. With a week to go, we were able to move through the peloton like the big teams did. Only one team was challenging our right to be there, Team Movistar, who also hoped to be on the podium. Their leader was none other than my former Quick-Step teammate Enric Mas, a nice guy by the way. I went to ask Imanol Erviti, Movistar's road captain, for an explanation: 'You're crowding my teammates, preventing them from doing their job in the peloton? If you keep elbowing them, I'll start elbowing Mas.' Erviti didn't believe a word of it and started laughing. So I went up to Enric and started forcing him towards the edge of the road. I felt like I was a Quick-Step rider in an echelon again. 'Stop! Stop!' poor Enric shouted. I didn't want to hurt him but I wanted my team to be respected. From that day on, that was the case. When we reached Madrid, we relished the fact that we'd taken fourth place in the Vuelta a España, my best result in a Grand Tour and the first result our young World Tour team had had at that level.

Over the winter that followed, the team rolled out the red carpet for its new recruit, Chris Froome, who had left Team Ineos. It was obviously a big sporting gamble. For a year and a half, Chris had been fighting to get back into the peloton, showing huge courage. I had witnessed his crash and now I would see up close the work he put in to get back to a competitive level of fitness. It seemed like an impossible mission. I know this because I was there, on 12 June 2019, right behind him in our team car, when he was warming up on the Critérium du Dauphiné time trial course around the town of Roanne, and so understood the gravity of his injuries. Never before had a crash made my blood run cold. Chris was riding down a straight descent, holding a water bottle in one of his hands. On the left-hand side of the road there was a gap between two houses. A strong gust of wind blew through this corridor, lifting Chris's front wheel as he passed. He tried to right the bike's trajectory, but 'overcorrected' and hit the wall of a house. In a fraction of a second, his speed went from 60km/h to zero. He hit the wall head-on and slid down it. He was inert.

I looked at Neil Stephens, the Team UAE Emirates manager, who was in the driver's seat next to me. We didn't say a word. We were thinking the same thing: that Chris was dead. Neil leapt out of the car to offer assistance to the Team Ineos staff. I avoided looking at his immobile body. I didn't need to see that. Wout Poels, his teammate, who was riding just in front of Chris, had returned to the scene. Chris spoke to them. He asked them to help him back onto the bike . . . It didn't take long for the ambulance to arrive, as it happened to be parked close by. I texted Geraint Thomas and Richie Porte. I decided not to say anything about this horrible accident to the press until Chris's wife, Michelle, had been told. He'd escaped with his life, but with fractures to his hip, femur, elbow, ribs . . . His ambitions for the 2019 Tour were broken too, and Team Ineos went on to propel Egan Bernal into the yellow jersey instead. Chris, meanwhile, eight months later managed to get back on a bike, pin on a race number and finish a race. He came to Team Israel Start-Up Nation to finish the job.

Chris believed that he could get back to the Tour de France and even win it, for the fifth time. There were only two people who believed in this venture: Chris himself and Sylvan Adams. There were all kinds of theories within the cycling world about their opportunism, some suggesting that the pair didn't believe Chris could return to the top, and were simply out to make money out of it. Yet they were as sincere as could be. Sylvan and Chris were convinced that they would win the Tour together. The more they heard that it was impossible, the more they supported each other in their belief in what would have been one of the greatest comeback stories in our sport's history. Even though Chris had maybe a 0.01 per cent chance of making a return to the top step of the Tour podium, this possibility was enough for him, and he clung to it. I was simply happy to see him so full of vitality after such a horrific fall. I really respected his determination. Willpower can move mountains . . . What's more, Chris's 'Objective Tour de France' finally allowed me to plot out a nice plan of attack for the Giro d'Italia.

# Chapter 25

# A Last Triumph in the Mountains (The Fear of Stopping)

We could almost taste the champagne in our mouths. It would be well deserved. The Giro was gradually reaching its conclusion. It was the eve of the race's final time trial in Milan. My Israel Start-Up Nation teammates had been as conscientious as they had been combative. Given constant concerns about COVID-19, the team's staff had been split into four parts, but it had become clear that even these precautions hadn't been enough. We were told that a member of the back-room staff had tested positive in one of the tests carried out by the race organisers on the whole caravan. The rule in such cases was uncompromising – exclusion of the whole team. We were less than twenty-four hours away from the end and it was as if our three weeks of adventure and suffering had been reduced to nothing. We pleaded our case, highlighting the fact that in a time trial there was zero risk of contaminating the other teams. The organisers agreed that we could finish the race, on the condition that we limit to an absolute minimum contact within the team. No one massaged our legs, handed us a towel or rubbed us down with oil. We didn't celebrate, we weren't even able to see the people who had shared this epic adventure with us, but we were at least able to finish and preserve what we'd built together, like my stage win and my 10th place in the overall classification.

At the Giro d'Italia finishing was the hardest thing of all. In 2021, on what was just my second appearance in the event, I'd had flashes back to my debut in 2010. Nothing had changed. This labyrinthine challenge still pushed the riders to their limits, much further than the Tour de France. While the Tour overwhelms you with its grandeur, the Giro does it with its sheer craziness. Before riders can start thinking about winning in Italy, they have to survive. I could remember how, as a young rider, I was shocked by the extremity of the conditions and amazed to be experiencing moments that I'd thought belonged to another era in cycling.

## Strade Bianche 2010

It was the first Giro of my career and the Tuscany section featured the first *strade bianche* I'd raced on. The rain made a mockery of them. It kneaded the gravel, limestone and clumps of dust together into a thick paste that flew through the air off the riders' wheels. I had mud in my teeth, in my ears, under my fingernails. It got everywhere. To protect my eyes, I tilted my glasses so that the slivers of mud couldn't get in from underneath. I eyed the road through a tiny slit between my helmet and the top of my glasses. The landscape appeared to be shaking as we bumped along. I'd thought that there were only ten more kilometres to go before we achieved deliverance in the medieval town of Montalcino, famous for its wine Brunello, a fine and fruity red that is very full-bodied, rather like the stones on the route that day. I promised myself we'd drink a glass of it when we'd finished the race to revive ourselves. All around there was panic. I lost twenty-four minutes. The team staff were horrified when they saw us at the finish and refused to allow us onto the team bus until we had been doused by the jet wash.

## Strade Bianche 2021

Twelve years later, the chaos had doubled in intensity. It started with 93 kilometres to go, on the first sector we raced over the compacted stones. Our *directeurs sportifs* had told us: 'Don't worry, it's easy, it's not uphill.' But it was worse than riding uphill: a descent at 60km/h on gravel . . . The road shook us to the core. A rider crashed next to me, going down head-first. I was scared. Lots of us were scared. I could hear riders around me muttering, getting angry, praying or cursing under their breath. They were taking irrational and even desperate lines; it was almost as if their brains had stopped working. For a few seconds I lost control of my bike, and it veered to the left. Luckily, I kept my balance. I wanted to leave a decent gap in front of me, in case there was another crash, but every time I did so panicking riders came through and closed it. It was the most confusing 9.6 kilometres of my career. I was a minute behind the lead group. By the finish, I'd lost six minutes – and some of the relish I had for cycling. Was it really necessary to put the riders in danger to give the Giro an epic dimension?

## Zoncolan 2010

During my first Giro, I discovered how absurd the mountains can get. On Monte Zoncolan, the challenge was to stay on your bike. If you slowed down, you were done for. You're afraid of having to pull your foot out of your pedal and put it down because then you'd fall. On the 20 per cent wall, you'd roll backwards like a marble. It was a balancing act. Racing took a back seat. At the halfway point, I said to myself with a good deal of relief, 'Only five kilometres to go!' But then I realised that this meant another half-hour of slog. 'Shit . . .' I pushed my 34x28 gear with all I had left, I had the feeling that it was effectively a vain effort. That day I finished ninth, three minutes and thirty-one seconds behind Ivan Basso.

## Zoncolan 2021

During my second Giro, the 'Monte' had become even more monstrous. The organisers had given it a nickname: 'The Frankenstein Mountain'. It said so on the Giro website – honestly! We were set to ride onto the set of a horror movie, which was an intriguing prospect to say the least. On this occasion, we were to tackle the monster from another and even more horrifying side. The gradient peaked at 27 per cent. That's steeper than the bend on the Mur de Huy in Flèche Wallonne, where you always feel like your bike is going to stall like an old car. I never felt at ease on these extremely acute ramps. I felt the lack of strength in my legs. I pedalled more with my arms than my calves. I pulled on my handlebars in order to keep moving forwards. But I had the feeling that if I pulled too much, I might fall backwards. It was my introduction to mountaineering, and it was almost vertigo-inducing. I finished 12th on the stage and moved up four places in the general classification, to 13th.

## 26 May 2021, Canazei to Sega di Ala

'Today, I'm going to win.' My magical premonitions returned during my second Giro d'Italia, on the seventeenth stage, in the heart of the Dolomites. I knew that 'something' was going to happen. But, to add to the mystery, I'd been sure of this for almost a month. It hadn't just occurred to me on the morning of the race, as had been the case at Liège-Bastogne-Liège and other races in the past. The moment I saw the finale, the image of a very beautiful day flooded my mind. There were no spectators, no riders, the road was empty, the mountain silent. I'd come to this climb, Sega di Ala, having competed in the Tour of the Alps at the end of April. I chose to inspect the stage of Sega di Ala, in Trentino. This road is 11.2 kilometres long and averages 9.8 per cent. The gradient gets more brutal the higher you climb, the road winding upwards in dizzying fashion, passing through short tunnels. After four pedal strokes, I was captivated by this mountain. I liked everything about it but couldn't figure out exactly why.

I had a very strong premonition. At the summit, I said to Claudio Cozzi, the *directeur sportif* who had accompanied me in the car: 'You'll see, something's going to happen here.' I immediately texted Jess to tell her about this very exciting and calming feeling: 'I've just found a beautiful place. It's for me. On the Giro, something's going happen to me.' A stage victory, a leap up the classification or even the pink jersey. We would have to see. I only knew that this 'something' would be a happy event.

I had been lucky since the beginning of the year, especially when COVID-19, which had been in the world for over twelve months, finally got me. The day of my positive test, in March, I had just completed my final threshold climbing effort ahead of Tirreno–Adriatico without much issue. I was slightly worried about how it would progress, with my history of allergy-induced asthma, but I got off incredibly lightly, the main symptoms being extreme fatigue and muscle soreness. Jess fared much worse than me and was still feeling the effects weeks later. I was back on the bike within a week and, remarkably, raced to fifth on a stage of Volta a Catalunya two weeks later, although the cold mountain air did hurt my compromised airways.

Racing so soon after having the virus was perhaps risky, but the Volta a Catalunya was a crucial step on the path to my ultimate goal of 2021: the Giro.

The day of my Giro stage victory, I was perfectly relaxed. I was detached and focused at the same time. I was going to play cat and mouse with my opponents. But, on this occasion, the mouse would eat the cat ... Everything was meticulously prepared to ensure that my pre-imagined destiny prevailed. I'd decided on the equipment – for the beginning of the stage, I'd use an aerodynamic bike ideal for flat roads, fitted with wheels with 80mm aerodynamic rims. I'd decided to change bikes 5 kilometres from the first climb and use a super-light frame equipped with wheels for the mountains. The first 120 kilometres were downhill or flat.

I joined the breakaway after 50 kilometres. There were around twenty of us at the front. I set quite a strong pace on the first long climb, the Passo San Valentino, but not flat out, because I didn't want my breakaway companions, my allies, to explode. But the BikeExchange team started to increase the pace in the peloton behind us. I had to accelerate; I knew that in order to stand any chance of winning the stage I needed at least two minutes thirty at the summit. We began to lose men from our group. In the end, just three of them remained alongside me – the Frenchman Geoffrey Bouchard, the Spaniard Antonio Pedrero and the Italian Gianni Moscon, a teammate of the pink jersey Egan Bernal and that stage's local rider.

Last climb. We were only a minute and ten seconds ahead going onto it. This was the moment ... I increased the power, but without putting myself in the red. With 10.5 kilometres to go, I was alone in the lead. I knew the calculations my rivals would be making. They'd be thinking that I was tired, that they could reel me in. But I was controlling them. I gave them a reason to hope. I expected them to catch me at any moment, but I was also prepared to hit the gas very hard and very quickly. If they got within ten seconds of me, I'd stop them in their tracks by increasing the gap by five seconds. I would drive them to their wits' end. From that moment on, I didn't want to hear any encouragement or motivational cries. All I needed now was information: time gaps and a detailed breakdown of the road that lay ahead; the gradients, so that I could properly manage my effort. The only thing that mattered to me was the 17 per cent section at Malga Riondera, which we would reach after 7 kilometres of climbing. I'd built my strategy around that precise spot and adjusted my effort according to this landmark.

Instinctively, I knew that the favourites would accelerate on these ramps. If, afterwards, they were still grouped together, they would slow down because they'd be watching each other. If a rider had managed to get away, he would pay for his efforts there and inevitably need to recover from the attack. Whatever the scenario, there would be a timeout. My strategy, on the other hand, was to ride through the steep sections without pushing myself to my limit and then pick up the pace. When the best climbers realised that I wasn't losing any ground, they would think that I'd ridden through this tough section at a high speed. They'd think that I was too strong, and that's when their heads would go.

Everything unfolded just as I'd imagined it would. The favourites overextended themselves at Malga Riondera, while I actually extended my lead on the easier gradients that followed. I got extra motivation by playing a little game with myself. I started to hate the Giro, telling myself: 'You've got to win here so you never have to come back. This will be your first Giro victory and your last. You know that this race is totally ridiculous, but magnificently so. On the previous stage you raced in the snow. Yes, the snow. The organisers removed two passes but you still rode in between banks of snow. Go and win this bloody stage and let that be the end of it.' I had to hate the race to win it.

I didn't know that I had a thirty-second lead going into the final kilometre. That was cut to thirteen seconds when João Almeida attacked in that last 1,000 metres. My family and friends feared for me as they watched on television because they could see the Portuguese climber closing the gap. In any case, my premonition had once again been fulfilled. I had done 'something' on that stage. But was it completely by chance? Perhaps not: unlikely as it may seem, 'he' had returned.

I found out from social media. 'Look! That's funny!' ... 'Unbelievable!' ... 'Did you see that coincidence?' ... It turned out that the Panda had invited itself back. Or, more exactly, a cousin of the Panda, with a less pointed snout and different eyes. He was wearing a blue surgical mask and waving the flag of Sardinia. I was just 2 minutes away from him on the final climb, with, according to the TV footage, still 7.8 kilometres to go. He was standing on the right-hand side of the road, half-hidden behind his flag. As was the case at Liège–Bastogne–Liège, I didn't notice it at the time, I was too focused on the race. A mixture of bemusement and amusement hit me when I saw the images. With the exception of the Tour of Beijing, I hadn't come across my lucky animal in any race since Liège in 2013. I had seen all sorts of other costumed characters in the crowd, but no panda. Was it just by chance that 'he' had come out to encourage me on the day I won the best mountain stage of my career?

After stage wins at the Vuelta and the Tour, the Giro was the missing piece in my collection. I'd now won a stage in all three Grand Tours and by finishing 10th overall in Milan, I would also complete my trilogy of top ten general classification placings. It was also my first victory as a climber-*baroudeur* rather than as a climber-sprinter, searching out the breakaway as the springboard for my victory rather than depending on my finishing speed from the group of favourites. I'd always dreamed of winning a stage in this manner and I'd finally achieved it.

## After the Giro ...

Satisfied with my performance at the Giro, the management at Israel Start-Up wanted to discuss a contract extension. They wanted me to stay for another two seasons, until the end of 2023. But I would have preferred to continue for just one more year. It would have been an opportunity to try some new things, maybe go for the polka-dot jersey at the Tour de France and, above all, to mentor a young rider, to guide him, to hand on some of my motivation and know-how.

The Giro left a strange taste in my mouth. I just didn't get the satisfaction and enjoyment from the race that I would have expected. I spoke to Rory Sutherland. He had retired the winter before and was now part of the staff, a 'rider liaison', but I approached him as a friend to explain my feelings of confusion about why such a big win didn't bring me any real pleasure. Rory was always a good listener and gave valuable advice, just as he'd often done when we'd shared a room at races. He asked me a few questions, including, 'Do you think that the riders around you are taking crazy risks?'

'Yes, I do. The *strade bianche* stage was crazy, with guys always filling the gaps that I left for safety reasons. On the climbs, it was the other way around, with some riders making a game out of leaving big gaps. At the Giro, Quick-Step attacked on stage nineteen, with the whole team on a tricky downhill. Team DSM did the same on stage twenty. Strategically, it was a clever move, but it increased the risks massively.'

'You're getting old, I think!' he laughingly exclaimed.

'You know all too well that I never liked taking crazy risks. It's often said that you get more cautious when you become a father, but I was already very cautious before.'

'Yeah, mate, I know. I'm messing with you. Cycling has changed, the guys are more stressed, they need results right away and are willing to take more risks. You've definitely still got the legs, but the question is, do you still enjoy it?'

I then discussed it with André Greipel, who was four years older than me and doyen of the team. He told me, 'It's normal, I've had that feeling too. Ultimately, you're no longer winning for yourself, you're no longer racing for yourself, you're doing it all for others. You don't derive pleasure directly from racing. You just want to provide it for the people who are close to you and those who've been with you from the beginning. '

There is nothing like discussing these matters with a German sprinter. Fortunately, the contacts list on my phone was full of them ...

Under 'K' was Kittel. Following Marcel's retirement eighteen months previously, I had kept in close contact with him. He immediately recognised the position I was in, having retired when he potentially still had many years left in the peloton; at the same time, he confirmed my impression that I was nearing the end of my career. But he did add that I could still achieve some special things on the bike in the meantime. He explained his thought process when he decided to retire and that if I was starting to lack motivation it was because I had acheived an incredible amount during my career. Whether or not this would be my last Tour, he suggested I go and enjoy every moment.

On 26 June 2021, I started what I thought would be my penultimate Tour de France. We were hunting for a stage win. On the first day, in Brittany, I managed to avoid the crash when a spectator brandishing an 'Opi-Omi' sign sent my 'cousin' Tony Martin tumbling to the ground. A large part of the peloton went down. An even more horrific incident followed when, at high speed just 7 kilometres from the finish, the majority of the peloton crashed. Chris Froome was one of those injured. The most surprising thing was that he got back on his bike and, in the following days, refused to abandon. The fans cheered on the four-time Tour winner, who was swathed in bandages, was coming back from injury and was, as a consequence, dropped every day. His mental strength was really impressive. Chris was unable to challenge for a top ten finish or even to win a stage, but he remained upbeat. Every day he would say: 'Tomorrow will be better.'

I got into the break on the fifteenth stage on home roads to Andorra la Vella, via Beixalis. My legs felt heavy with fatigue. Since September 2020, I'd ridden the Tour, the Vuelta, the Giro and the Tour, in other words almost eighty Grand Tour stages over eleven months. But I really wanted to enjoy myself and take some pleasure from racing on those roads. Our breakaway of about twenty riders split apart on the Beixalis, firstly on the climb and again on the descent. I ended up riding in a group battling for eighth place, while Sepp Kuss, one of my Andorran neighbours who was also familiar with the roads, rode away to victory. Racing in not far behind him, I put everything into the sprint, as if I was going for the stage win. And I finished first. COVID-19 continued to require strict social distancing measures, which meant that Jess, Daisy and Ella weren't at the finish, nor at the hotel on the rest day that followed, and not on the day after either, when the start was located at Pas de la Casa, right on the border between Andorra and France.

I was in the break again on the eighteenth stage, which passed over my other 'home', the Col du Tourmalet, and finished at the tiny ski station of Luz-Ardiden, another climb I knew from my teenage years. I had less weight to carry than my rivals. Amidst a group filled with climbers, I was the only one who was no longer focused on securing a good place in the overall classification. I could see that my opponents were very nervous, that they were concerned when the smallest gap opened up, and were always talking with their teammates and *directeurs sportifs* through their earpieces. In the meantime, I was able to savour the most relaxed ascent of the Tourmalet of my racing career. The pass whispered in my ear: 'Take the time to look around. Did you see that huge waterfall on the left, just before reaching the steep ramps leading into La Mongie? And those rocks on the right, did you notice them?' I snapped out of my sweet dream at the beginning of the descent, when I nearly missed the first corner, the road surface so bumpy under braking that I almost lost control; but I had a little smile on my face. The Tourmalet, so formidable for many, had always treated me very well. I relished every metre of road. On the final climb of Luz-Ardiden, I couldn't follow Tadej Pogačar's attack with 3 kilometres to go, but I made an attack of my own with 1.7 kilometres remaining to take fifth place on the stage.

I'd had better finishes in the Tour, but on this occasion I felt liberated, able to control my body, my thoughts, my goals, at one with the terrain, the public and my teammates. I had imagined that I would return in 2022 to prolong that feeling of pleasure, but I'd actually reached the end of my relationship with this race. I already considered the 2021 edition a nice bonus. I remembered a little bit of advice that Rory Sutherland had given me: 'Take stock after the Tour. You might not want to do another season. You've got nothing to prove any more. You might not be feeling any pleasure any more. Thanks to

Jess, thanks to your daughters, you know that there are other things in life besides cycling.'

I still had a twenty-second stage of the Tour de France to ride before returning home to my family: the Olympic Games in Tokyo. The day after the Champs-Elysées, I boarded a flight in Paris along with the Irish team staff and my two teammates, my cousin Nico and Eddie Dunbar, a rider who has the potential needed to pick up the baton from us. There were ten years between us. He's modest, a hard worker who climbs well. But the Olympic racecourse around Mount Fuji didn't allow either of us to distinguish ourselves. We didn't have the legs. There was no joy in the Olympic experience either because we had to make the journeys between the airport and our hotel and from our hotel to the race start without coming into contact with anyone because of COVID-19.

Meanwhile, there was no progress in my contract negotiations. I was losing some of my motivation; and, on the other side, my team manager was trying to gamble. Israel Start-Up Nation was about to cut my contract in half, just to see my reaction.

When I got home from Japan, after more than a month on the road, I had a sense of accomplishment. Daisy and Ella were in their bedroom playing with the box of stuffed animals that I'd brought back from races over the fifteen preceding years. There was the Red Dragon (which I had kept from the Junior Tour of Wales and was still in perfect condition) and the Green Dragon (a souvenir from the Tour of Poland). The Lion (a traditional gift from the Tour de France *maillot jaune* that a fan gave me) was having a tea party with the Cow (the team classification trophy at the Tour de France, which Quick-Step had dominated on a few days). The guest at this party was none other than the Green Giant (the mascot of the green jersey, which had been a present from Marcel Kittel). In the middle of this throng, the Panda was majestically enthroned. I'd won it at the Tour of Beijing. The girls seemed to understand that this animal had a special place within the family. I'd been wondering if there was another stuffed animal I could get for them on the bike. But then I realised that Ella and Daisy had almost the whole collection and that they were happy with it.

## Chapter 26

# 'Mr Martin, You've Got Something in Your Brain . . .'

I had slipped into a breakaway of eight riders with Bradley Wiggins. The fifth stage of the 2010 Tour of Britain ran from Tavistock to Glastonbury, the capital of summer festivals (music, theatre, circus . . .). With 10 kilometres to go, I got away with Marco Frapporti on a rising false flat, but the Italian went away to win. I had nothing left in the tank. I finished seventh. Things would be better the next day.

The day's nervy action had put me in a good mood. That's why I made a phone call to the Harley Street Medical Centre in London. I'd had a sinus scan there six days earlier, on Friday, 10 September 2010. The appointment had taken place two days before the start of the Tour of Britain. Since my appointment, the clinic had been leaving lots of messages on my voicemail. The secretary at the clinic was saying, 'Mr Martin, you need to come back as soon as possible for a follow-up scan'. I listened to the messages with some annoyance. Had they lost the results or made a mistake? I left it for a few days but on the Thursday, as the team bus was driving towards our hotel after the stage had finished, I decided to call the clinic.

The consultant who had supervised the examination was very firm in his tone. He requested that I return to London immediately for further examinations, something that simply wasn't feasible while competing in a stage race. I explained that I could come the following week but his tone intensified. His insistence was spine-chilling and made me question what on earth could be wrong, as he booked me in for an emergency appointment the following afternoon, which meant I had to withdraw from the Tour of Britain.

I thought I was being lined up for an operation on my nasal septum, in order to solve my allergy problems once and for all. Apparently, though, there was something else, the consultant said; they'd found something serious. But what? The consultant didn't want to say too much, but I insisted. My heart was starting to pound as fast as it had in the attacks I'd made during the stage. Finally, the consultant blurted out, 'Mr Martin, you have something in your brain. We think we have detected a suspicious mass, and we would like to check that it's not a tumour.'

A second passed that seemed like an hour. I didn't know you could cram so many thoughts into one second. Your career is over/it's a misdiagnosis, everything is fine/it's very serious . . . I was saying 'you' to myself. I was addressing myself, to reassure myself. 'I' was paralysed by fear. I had to talk to him, distract him, lie to him. Medicine has made great progress/you're lucky that it's been detected/the hospital's machine is not working properly . . . The word ricocheted like an echo around my head. 'Tumour', 'Tumour', 'Tumour', 'Tumour' . . .

Then the team bus parked up in front of the hotel. I didn't want to make eye contact with any of the riders or staff. The story that was unfolding was an extremely personal one, for me alone. I went to my room, locked the door and sat on my bed. My mind ran riot again. Strange, unrealistic thoughts came to me: 'Maybe you'll be lucky, because the tumour can affect certain areas and make you insensitive to pain.' When I was thirteen, I saw the James Bond movie *The World Is Not Enough*. The villain, Victor Zokas, aka 'The Fox', had a bullet lodged in his brain and got superhuman strength from it, because nothing could hurt him.

I started to get annoyed. My career couldn't fall completely apart on this Tour of Britain, after I'd been active in the break-away and gone close to winning the stage. I couldn't just drop out of the race and leave my friends behind, especially for a medical problem that didn't exist. The clinic had made a mistake. That was for certain.

The only thought that didn't go through my head was, 'You're going to die.' Other people would think that way about me. But I was in denial.

I was sharing my hotel room with Christian Meier, a close friend from my early pro years. He could see that my world had been turned upside down and asked me what was wrong, and I finally told him my secret. He paused. I could see that he was trying very hard to hide his fear, shock, disbelief, and to remain composed. I looked into his eyes and he didn't look away, and tried to transmit a feeling of calmness with his expression. There was little that he could say except, 'Don't worry,' although obviously we both spoke without knowing the full reality of the problem. He listened to me, then we turned the light off. What more could we say?

The next morning, I ripped off the two numbers stuck to the back of my jersey and returned to London, pretending that I'd caught a cold in order to justify my withdrawal. The peloton was due to arrive in the capital three days later, so I had a head start. I took the train and then a taxi. I texted a few relatives. Andy Birley, my faithful friend since the days we went training around Birmingham, was one of the few in the know. He offered to let me stay at his place after the examination. I wasn't going to stay in a hotel room for the night. There was no question of me being completely on my own. I arrived at the Harley Street Medical Centre and got out of the taxi with my cycling suitcase.

I was in the waiting room for no more than two minutes. I lay down in a cold white cylinder and was bathed in a surreal light; the doctors had wanted me to undergo an MRI scan, which was much more detailed and would help them to make a better diagnosis. After this, the consultant received me in his office. The images scrolled through on his computer. He enlarged them, adjusted the contrast, looked for another angle. He wasn't sure of the result. A doctor will never say, 'I am sure.' But he went as far as he felt he could, telling me, 'If it's a tumour, it's probably a benign tumour.'

You don't know whether to be relieved. Through racing, your body has already got used to the fact that you don't submit to adversity any more. You accept things as they are. You know that, whatever happens, you'll adapt your life to the evolution of this strange shadow in your brain.

I was twenty-four years old. I'd been a professional cyclist for three seasons. The previous month I had won the general classification of the Tour of Poland, my first Pro Tour victory, and the Tre Valli Varesine, a beautiful Classic in the Italian lake district. Suddenly, though, I'd just been reminded how fragile things can be. I'd always had some intuition of this, and riders generally, even though we are sometimes depicted as naive, joyful and light-hearted, are well aware of this over-arching sense of gravity. We know that death does sometimes claim us when we're young. We internalise it, not so much as 'death' as an 'accident'. We all know riders who have never recovered from a serious fall, whose career or life has never been the same again.

However, despite this 'incident', I refused to stop making plans. I kept on thinking about 2011, 2012, 2013, almost as if nothing had happened.

I resumed racing in October. At the Giro dell Emilia, I finished second behind Robert Gesink. At the Gran Premio Bruno Beghelli, in Bologna, I finished in the middle of the pack. At the Giro di Lombardia, I was forced to abandon after a crash. At the Japan Cup, I found the key to victory, finishing alone with a one-minute lead on my pursuers. I was back doing what I liked doing. Not only was this thing in my brain not penalising me, it was becoming less and less likely to be dangerous. I had consulted several doctors, and it seemed that the 'benign tumour' might simply be a 'birthmark'. I just had to get it checked out regularly, to ensure it wasn't growing. But if it wasn't that? The doctors didn't know, so . . .

I hesitated between hiding this story, which came under the description of medical confidentiality and had no direct effect on my career, and speaking out about the moment of huge anxiety that had gripped me during the Tour of Britain and in the days afterwards. I hesitated about revealing this possible time bomb within me, which the latest medical advice said was defused – although this wasn't 100 per cent certain. Jonathan Vaughters was keen for me to say something about it in the media. My employer was aware of the problem, as was our team doctor, Prentice Steffen, as I had cut short my participation in the Tour of Britain. I am grateful to him for ensuring that it was all kept under wraps at the time.

'What doesn't kill you makes you stronger': I could certainly tell a story based on this maxim. It was obvious that September 2010 would have an impact on my outlook on life. But if I spoke out, I would run into two pitfalls that I wanted to avoid above all else. Firstly, I would become 'the rider with the tumour' and would be reminded of it again and again throughout my career. Secondly, I was afraid of being seen as an impostor by people with illnesses more serious and more obvious than mine. What did I really have to say? Nothing that was precise, nothing that was sure, nothing that was intelligent. I didn't feel like I had the legitimacy to get involved in the cause of brain tumour treatment, especially as there was still some doubt about my diagnosis.

After my Tour of Britain, I locked this chapter of my life up in a canvas bag and threw it into the sea with a large stone so that it wouldn't come back to the surface. Of course, I had follow-up MRI scans for four or five years after the shadow was discovered – the exact dates have faded from my memory. Then I stopped having the tests. I 'forgot' them. My brain decided that nothing had happened. I'd received this information without me looking for it and hadn't known what to do with it. What exactly was the nature of this shadow? How could it be treated, if at all? Thousands of people probably have a more or less identical spot in their brain, but almost all of them are unaware of it. Basically, I don't think we should know. If there were a watch that told the day and time of our death, I'd be the last person to buy it.

This story has certainly influenced my career in one way or another and given additional meaning to my life, although I can't put my finger on what precisely it has done for me. It probably reinforced my view of destiny and my belief in the existence of a lucky star. I repudiated the risk associated with this 'shadow' in the same way as I rebuffed the danger of falling. If a rider thinks about crashing, they'll think about the pain that it inflicts and will be tempted to race differently; they might perhaps even feel some disgust or fear about their profession. The idea of falling was everywhere and nowhere in my mind. I had absorbed it, digested it. I suppose the same is true of the 'shadow' in my brain. I had assimilated it to an extent that I didn't need to think about it as such. I've tamed the possibility of fate associated with it.

I was often lucky. I only fell off my bike a few times – very few indeed – and if you analyse the falls in detail, every one has been less serious than it could have been. I like to imagine that my destiny will continue to follow the same fortunate path. I still rely on it.

I'm not afraid.

Consciously or not – and perhaps it was related to those dramatic days in 2010 – I went back to the Tour of Britain one last time in the twilight of my career. After the 2020 Olympics in Tokyo, I was sure about my decision. I decided to make my announcement and I was happy about it. So was Jess.

The Tour of Britain set off from Penzance, on the western tip of Cornwall, on 5 September 2021. Two days before, I'd announced my decision to retire from the peloton: 'After fourteen seasons as a professional cyclist, I have decided to call it a day. Though this huge decision has taken much thought, I feel that the time is right to move on as I want to achieve so many other things in life. [. . .] Giving 100 per cent to what I do has always been how I operate. Though I could continue racing for a few years to come, and for many, this would seem like the obvious thing to do, I am at a point where I'm ready to take on some exciting new challenges in life.'

I still had a handful of races left in Italy, including the Giro di Lombardia, the final summit, the race that would mark the ultimate finale, contested over 239 kilometres between Como and Bergamo, on 9 October 2021. But the Tour of Britain was a magnificent farewell tour. Many of my long-standing friends, former teammates and rivals were there. From my junior years there was Mark Cavendish, still ready for the sprints, as well as Matt Brammeier and Ian Stannard, who had become *directeurs sportifs*. But where on earth was Geraint Thomas? The party was set to take place without dear old 'G' . . .

I was racing against three former Quick-Step teammates: Julian Alaphilippe, who was preparing to defend his world road title; Yves Lampaert, the man to shadow in echelons; and my homonym Tony Martin, who had helped me so much when we were up against the wind and was also about to retire. I also had a chance to put the world to rights once again with Richie Porte, to reflect on our battles and our horrible crash on the descent from Mont du Chat. What's more, I was also going to be pedalling alongside Nico. My cousin and I were bound together by a huge amount of emotion: he'd also decided to retire but was waiting a few more days to announce it.

Within the team, I was surrounded by friends who were set on devoting as much focus to laughing as they would to stomping on the pedals. To announce the six-rider line-up on social media, Israel Start-Up Nation used a picture of us all crammed into a red telephone box. I was with Swiss Reto Hollenstein, Canadian Mike Woods, who shared my hotel rooms, and two Brits, Alex Dowsett, as solid and friendly as ever, and Mason Hollyman, a young trainee from Yorkshire. We would be lining up with André Greipel, 'The Gorilla', a habitué of bunch sprints in the race, having won three stages in 2010, the year I'd dashed away in a hurry. A group of laidback, chortling old men who'd decided to combine business with pleasure. This Tour of Britain would be both a fierce competition and a gourmet getaway.

The event started in Cornwall: we were going to treat ourselves to Cornish pasties. It ended in Aberdeen: haggis for everyone! At the start of the third stage, in Llandeilo, we even got the management involved: 'What? You've never had real fish and chips? You must try it. But we're going to have to skip it.' We riders had a team time trial on our plate, 27 kilometres on Welsh roads. As we warmed up on our home trainers, the smell of the staff's lunch wafted over. Just the scent of fish and chips turned out to be an effective stimulant: we finished fourth, forty-three seconds behind Team Ineos.

The next day, still in Wales, we climbed the Great Orme, a climb that had a special significance for my family. My father had ridden a good time trial there on the 1984 Tour of Britain, which was then called the Milk Race. Thanks largely to that performance, he finished fourth in the overall classification, which was won by Oleg Petrovich Chuzhda of the USSR team. A collector's edition of *Cycling Weekly* has pride of place in our archive at home, the cover showing my father going flat out in the time trial, jaw clenched, woollen jersey and leather hairnet helmet. As for me, I finished sixth on the Great Orme road stage, thirteen seconds behind Wout van Aert, after helping Mike Woods to third place. As a thank you, Woodsy bought the whole team a Mr Whippy ice cream at the finish – with a Cadbury's Flake stuck in the top, 99-style. Better than any recovery drink . . .

At the finish in Scotland, my Canadian teammate was fifth

overall and I was seventh. The race had been dominated by van Aert, who won no fewer than four of the eight stages. The haul up to Scotland helped us to digest our treats: the numerous false flats that peppered the route were gobbled up thanks to record power outputs as riders did their final tests before the World Championships. Although I wasn't due to be competing on the rather 'Flandrian' circuit in Belgium, I watched how the favourites were faring and relished being able to hold their wheels at the critical moments. I was delighted to be part of it, so happy to enjoy the atmosphere, taking in everything going on around me, the little comments, gestures, smiles and nods. Even the members of the race organisation were cheering me on during my last few laps, notably race director Mick Bennett, an eternal enthusiast who'd seen my father racing in the same event forty years earlier.

I was surprised by the number of signs with my name on them. My eyes took in the messages of congratulations and thanks. My ears soaked up the shouts of support. For 1,320 kilometres, I was pushed on by fans in the country where I was born and raised. Even though the race was a long way from my home in the Midlands, the public showed me a lot of gratitude. I'd become Irish, taking my mother's nationality. I had never belonged to the burgeoning British Cycling system and the Team Sky set-up that had dominated the Tour de France. Yet on every stage I sensed the respect fans had for me and that touched me deeply. The words that I kept noticing weren't 'well done' but 'thank you'. I didn't feel any sense of nostalgia or sadness, but simply, and for the first time in my career, a little pride. It had taken me until one of the final races of my career to realise that you don't just ride for yourself, but for others as well, and that through a simple bike race you can transmit a little joy, a little comfort, a little courage. Talking to people before and after stages, I realised that the public appreciated me not so much for my results as for my attempts, successful or not, to shake up the big names I'd rubbed shoulders with and to win monumental races. People saw me as having put on a show and, more importantly, as having given them some hope. They'd seen me get up from my falls and push fate back a few millimetres. To them, I was that cyclist who'd snatched a few moments of light with his fingertips, his face battered by pain, his legs and shoulders jolting, his body straining beyond its physical means, extended by a kind of challenge, by the gentlest and most serious game in the world.

People sometimes tell me that I should have won a second Liège–Bastogne–Liège, or even won the polka-dot jersey, worn the yellow jersey for a few days in the Tour de France, or possibly claimed a world title. Each hypothesis becomes credible with the addition of, 'If you hadn't crashed ...' But I'm at peace. I don't feel that there's anything missing, that there's any incompleteness, any injustice when I look over my *palmarès*. I have just one single regret: that I didn't see the Panda again.

All those years, I waited in vain for a postcard to arrive at home, a small piece of paper fixed to the leg of a carrier pigeon, a message in a bottle ... At the very least, a private message on Instagram or Twitter. It would start like this: 'Hi, I'm the Panda ...'. The rest could vary radically: 'I was coming out of a student party with three friends'; or, on the contrary, 'I was perfectly sober, it was a bet between friends'; or perhaps it wasn't a man but a woman; or there might even be an unexpected scenario: 'We wanted to alert the public to the ravages of deforestation, but the operation went wrong. Sincere and heartfelt apologies'; or 'I wanted to make money out of my panda costume outside Carnival'; or perhaps even, 'We were running away after a failed bank robbery and, unfortunately, we ended up on the route of a bike race' . . .

The Panda could have suggested we meet for a pint of Belgian beer. I would certainly have gone to meet him. Depending on how he wanted to play things, he could have kept his suit and hat on. I don't think I need to know who he is, why he dressed up like that, or why he was in that place on that day. I like the sense of mystery. As we toasted, I would have simply said to the Panda: 'We had a good laugh – thank you.'

La Massana, Andorra, 6 July 2022

# Glossary

Baroudeur
A style of rider who launches a breakaway far from the finish, either solo or in a small group. 'Rouleurs' (riders who like flat terrain) or climbers can be called 'baroudeurs' if their tactics consist of such a long break. I won my mountain stage at the 2021 Giro d'Italia in a 'baroudeur' style.

Broom wagon
The vehicle in a race that 'sweeps' the course and picks up injured, sick or tired riders who can't continue. Getting off the bike and sitting inside this wagon means you withdraw from the race. Its first appearance was in the 1910 Tour de France to 'sweep' not the weakened riders but the cheaters who used to quit the route, travel by train and then cross the finish line back on their bikes.

Commissaire
A race official sent by the International Cycling Union (UCI) to apply the regulations and thus ensure the integrity of the race. Commissaires follow the riders in cars, broom wagons, on motorbikes and more rarely in helicopters. They are also in charge of the time-keeping.

### Directeur sportif

Race directors operate in every team in a position between the team management, the riders and the coaches. They are in charge of the tactics before and during the race, setting the team meetings and then driving the team car which follows the peloton.

### Domestique

Another word for 'team mate', and used with a lot of respect. The best of them are labelled "deluxe domestiques". Their mission includes leading out the team leader at the right moment, sheltering him from the wind and supplying him with food (musettes) and bottles of water (bidons). The last task explains why they used to be called 'water carriers' in the past, when the regulations prohibited riders from picking up water at any point of the route.

### Echelon

A tricky race situation when a strong crosswind hits the peloton. The slipstream or draft from the rider in front is offset from directly behind him when the wind is from the side. This means each cyclist rides slightly to one side of the guy in front, attempting to gain shelter from the elements, forming these diagonal lines of groups of cyclists called echelons. Once the width of the road is full of riders riding almost side by side, there is no space for another rider to shelter so a split appears as a new 'echelon' or diagonal group of riders forms, seeking to work as a unit to shelter each other from the wind.

## Flamme rouge

The archway at the start of the final kilometer. It used to be a red pennant hanging from a cable, or a red kite (*flamme rouge* in French).

## Grand Tour

A stage race with a three-week duration. There are only three 'grand tours' in the calendar: the Tour de France, the Giro d'Italia and the Vuelta a Espana (respectively founded in 1903, 1909 and 1935).

## Gruppetto

Italian word for the 'small group' of riders who ride together on the mountain stages, aiming to finish within the stage's time limit to allow them to start the next day.

## Monument

One of the five most prestigious classics on the cycling calendar: Milan-Sanremo, the Tour of Flanders, Paris-Roubaix, Liège-Bastogne-Liège and the Tour of Lombardy. I am humbled and privileged to have captured two of them, in Liège and Lombardy.

## Musette

A feed bag containing food and beverage, filled by the *soigneurs* prior to the race and delivered by them to the riders in the 'feed zones' during the race. The lunchbox was the same from the 1920s to the 1980s, comprising various sandwiches, rice cake, chicken wings, banana and peaches. The bag now includes energetic bars and gels, plus sweet and salty cakes.

## Puncheur

From onomatopoeic French, a category of riders who can produce powerful attacks on shorts ascents (up to three kilometers) and strong gradients. Liège-Bastogne-Liège and the Tour of Lombardy are the two 'monuments' that suit the 'puncheurs' alongside some hill finishes in the grand tours. Although I have never been keen on categorizing pro riders, I was mostly considered as a 'puncheur' throughout my career.

## Stagiaire

A rider doing an internship within a professional team. Slipstream hired me as a 'stagiaire' in 2007 but I never raced for them that season, waiting for my pro debut the following year.

## World Tour

The world's first division of cycling, formerly known as Pro Tour until 2010.

# Acknowledgements

Writing this book has been a true voyage down memory lane and encouraged me to relive the moments that formed me as a person. There are too many people to list who played a part in my life, but thank you to you all.

A special thank you to my rock, my wife Jess who was by my side and ever supportive through the highs and lows of my career, and of course during the writing of this book as I spent hours and even days piecing together all the details.

Thank you too to:

My parents for their support throughout my career and in unearthing so many photos to embarrass me;

Pierre Carrey who became a close friend during my time at VC La Pomme Marseille, who followed me through much of what you read here and who pieced together my story in a way that I never could have imagined alone;

Peter Cossins for working with us in creating the English version and bringing an additional Pyrenean flavour to the story as he is now living in the same mountains as me;

David Luxton, for his patience as he saw the potential in my story well over a decade ago, and who helped us through much of this process;

Richard Milner and all at Quercus for their help in turning our words into a hard copy publication.